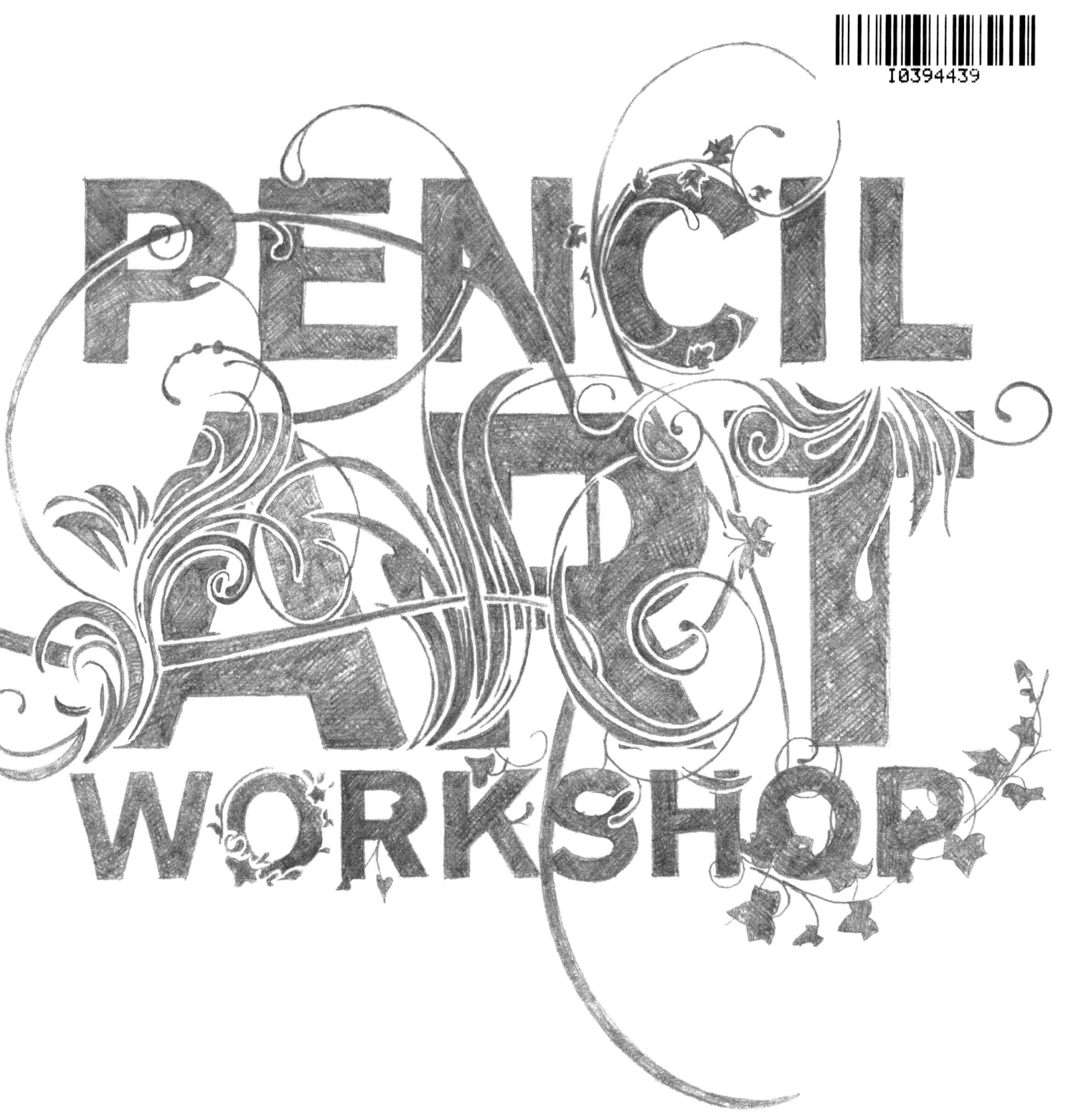

Quarto.com

© 2017 Quarto Publishing Group USA Inc.
Original Artwork and Project Designs © 2017
Matt Rota

First Published in 2017 by Rockport
Publishers, an imprint of The Quarto Group,
100 Cummings Center, Suite 265-D, Beverly,
Massachusetts 01915-6101, USA.
T (978) 282-9590 F (978) 283-2742

Rockport Publishers titles are also available
at discount for retail, wholesale, promotional,
and bulk purchase. For details, contact
the Special Sales Manager by email at
specialsales@quarto.com or by mail at The
Quarto Group, Attn: Special Sales Manager,
100 Cummings Center, Suite 265-D,
Beverly, MA 01915, USA.

ISBN: 978-1-63159-269-0

Library of Congress Cataloging-in-Publication
Data

Names: Rota, Matt, author.
Title: Pencil art workshop : techniques, ideas,
and inspiration for drawing
   and designing with pencil / Matt Rota.
Description: Beverly, Massachusetts :
Rockport Publishers, 2017.
Identifiers: LCCN 2016049138 | ISBN
9781631592690 (paperback)
Subjects: LCSH: Pencil drawing--Technique. |
BISAC: ART / Techniques / Pencil
   Drawing. | ART / Techniques / Drawing. |
ART / Techniques / General.
Classification: LCC NC890 .R68 2017 | DDC
741.2/4--dc23
LC record available at https://lccn.loc.
gov/2016049138

Design: Burge Agency
Cover Image: Burge Agency
Page Layout: Paul Burgess and Archie Strong
   at Burge Agency
Photography: Matt Rota, except pages 95–97,
   courtesy of Shutterstock; and as indicated
Illustrations: Matt Rota, except as indicated

PENCIL ART WORKSHOP

MATT ROTA

WORKSHOP

TECHNIQUES, IDEAS, AND
INSPIRATION FOR DRAWING
AND DESIGNING WITH PENCIL

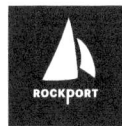

ROCKPORT

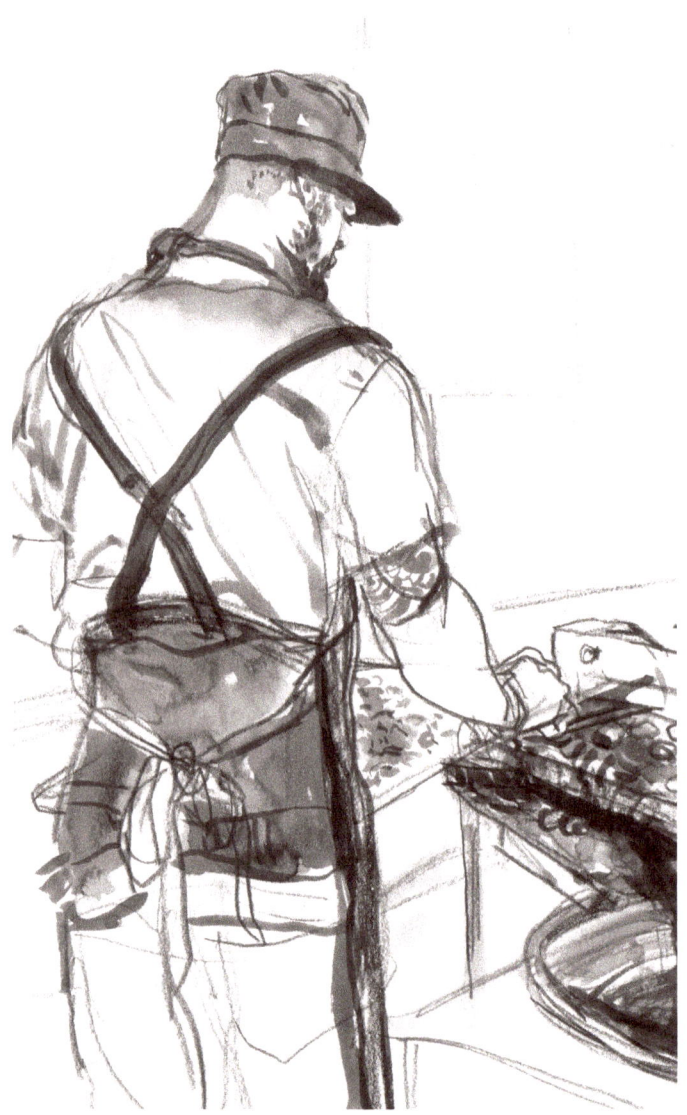

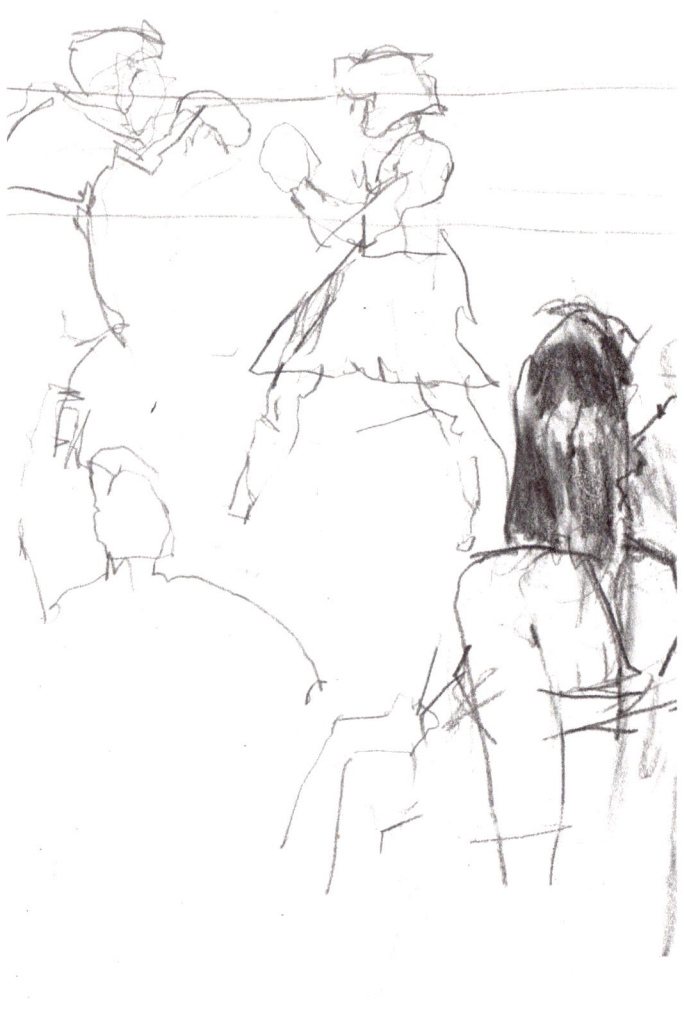

Carol Fabricatore, *Lilac Factory Worker*,
pencil, watercolor graphite, and brush pen on paper

Warren Linn, *Boxing*, pencil on paper

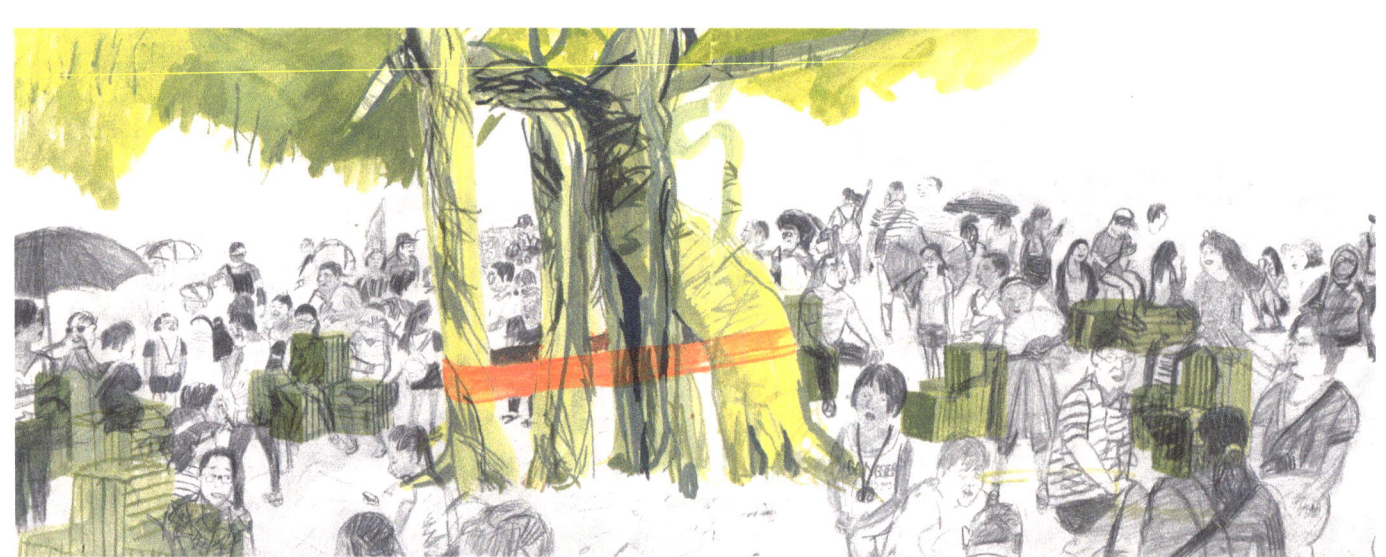

Benoit Guillaume, *Tourist in Kaohsiung*,
acrylic and pencil on paper

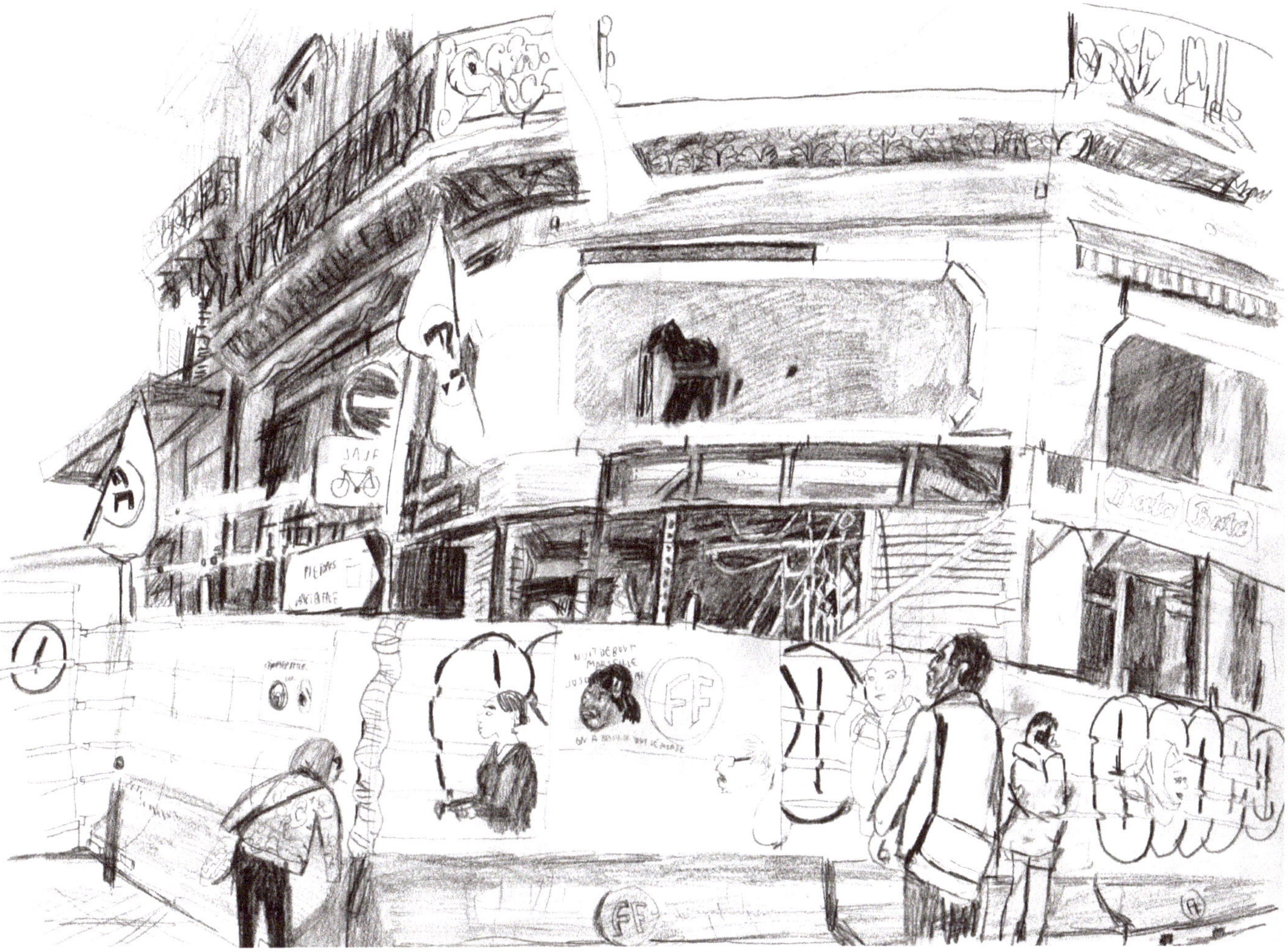

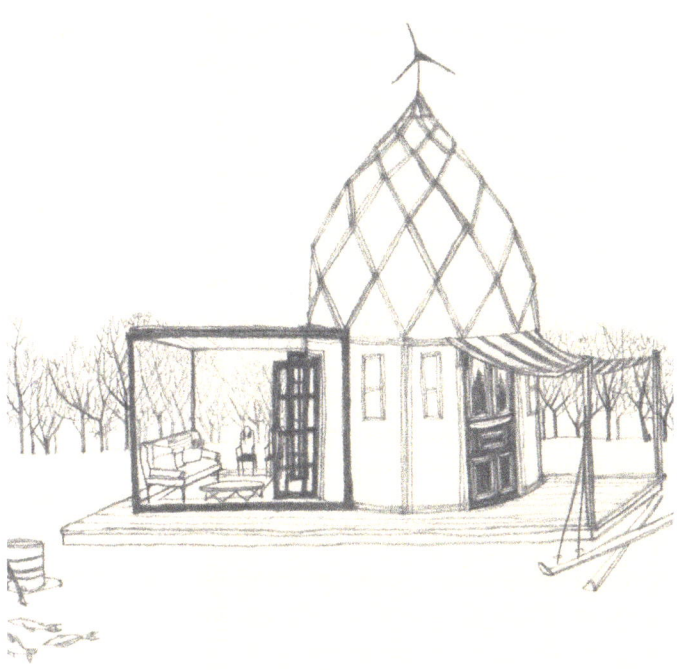

Benoit Guillaume, *Marseille*, pencil on paper

Deanna Staffo, *My Winter Hibernation*, pencil on paper

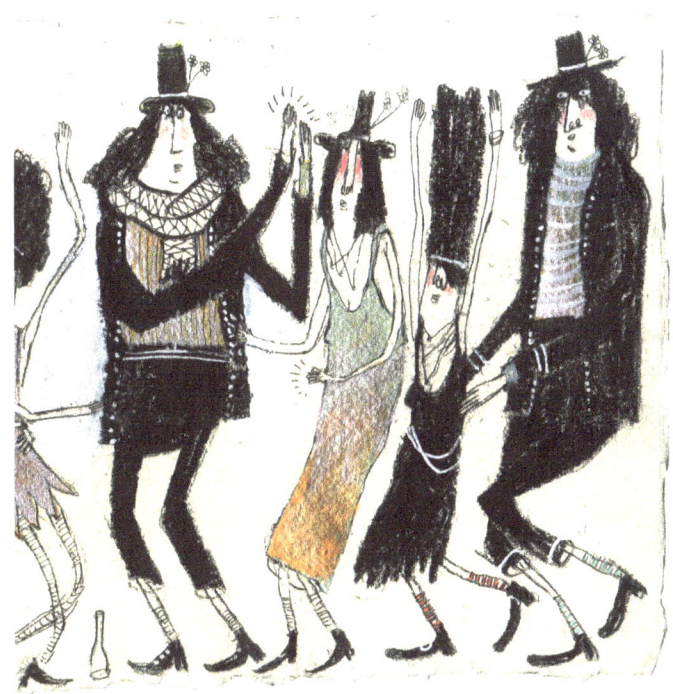

Ryan Peltier, *Transients 7*, pencil, colored pencil, gouache, and acrylic

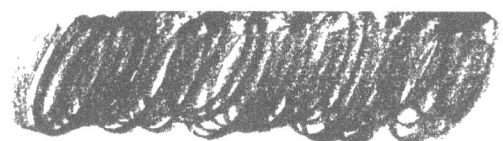

CONTENTS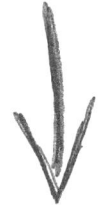

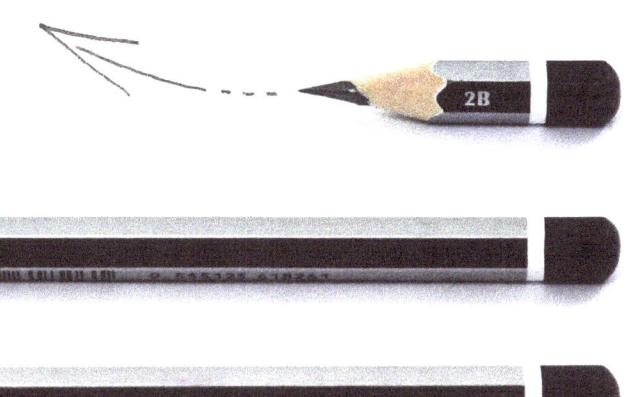

INTRODUCTION

The pencil is perhaps the most flexible and forgiving utensil for writing, drawing, scribbling, and scrawling in the history of human creativity. In fact, the pencil is the most common of all writing and drawing tools, and it's impossible to imagine a world without it.

What makes this tool so unique and useful? In a word, graphite, a soft claylike mineral. Graphite's malleability allows it to be sharpened to a fine point. It also makes it possible for a pencil's tip to be formed with both a sharp edge and a wide shape. This flexibility allows for a great range of markmaking. Due to graphite's softness, the mark the pencil makes is significantly darker than that of the drawing tools that preceded it. Before graphite pencils came into use, artists used metal styluses with copper, silver, or lead tips that made much lighter marks.

The pencil's phenomenal mark-making range is the subject of this book. We'll explore its full range of possibilities and discuss its refined precision and bold, expressive capabilities. We'll look at the myriad ways that contemporary artists are making use of it today. We'll also look at how the simple pencil became responsible for some of the greatest artistic achievements from the sixteenth century onward.

All these things point out the most remarkable thing of all about the pencil: that the humblest and least expensive of art tools can be carried in your pocket with a sketchpad, taken anywhere, and is always ready to help you create works of the highest potential genius.

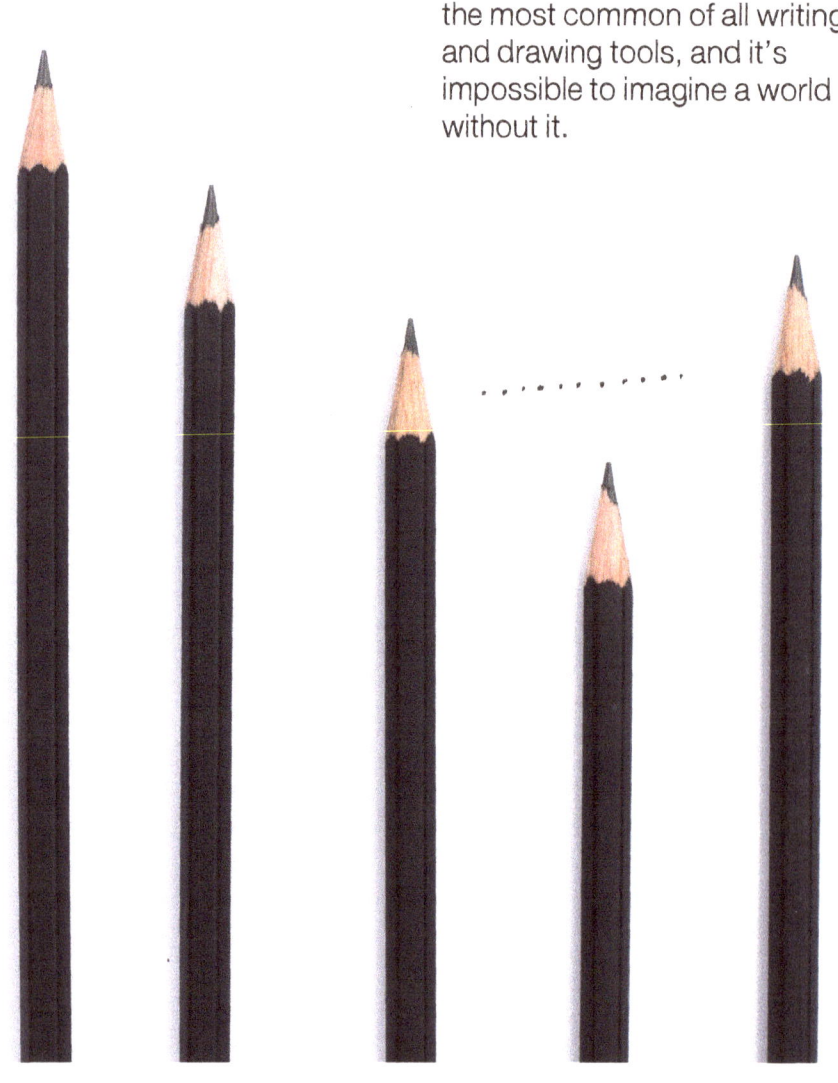

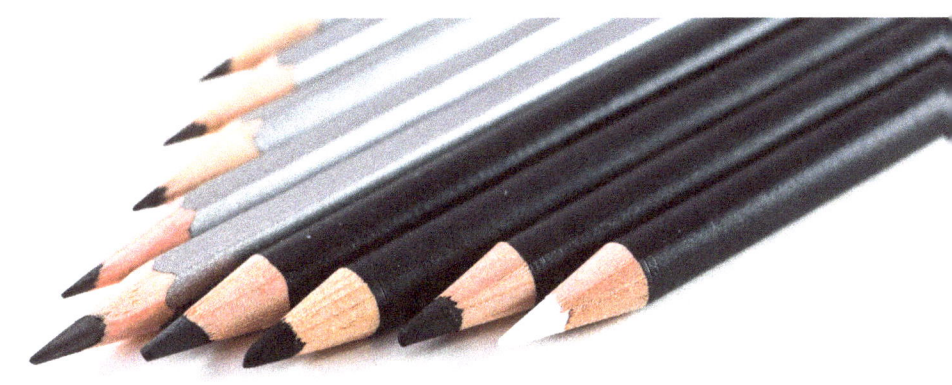

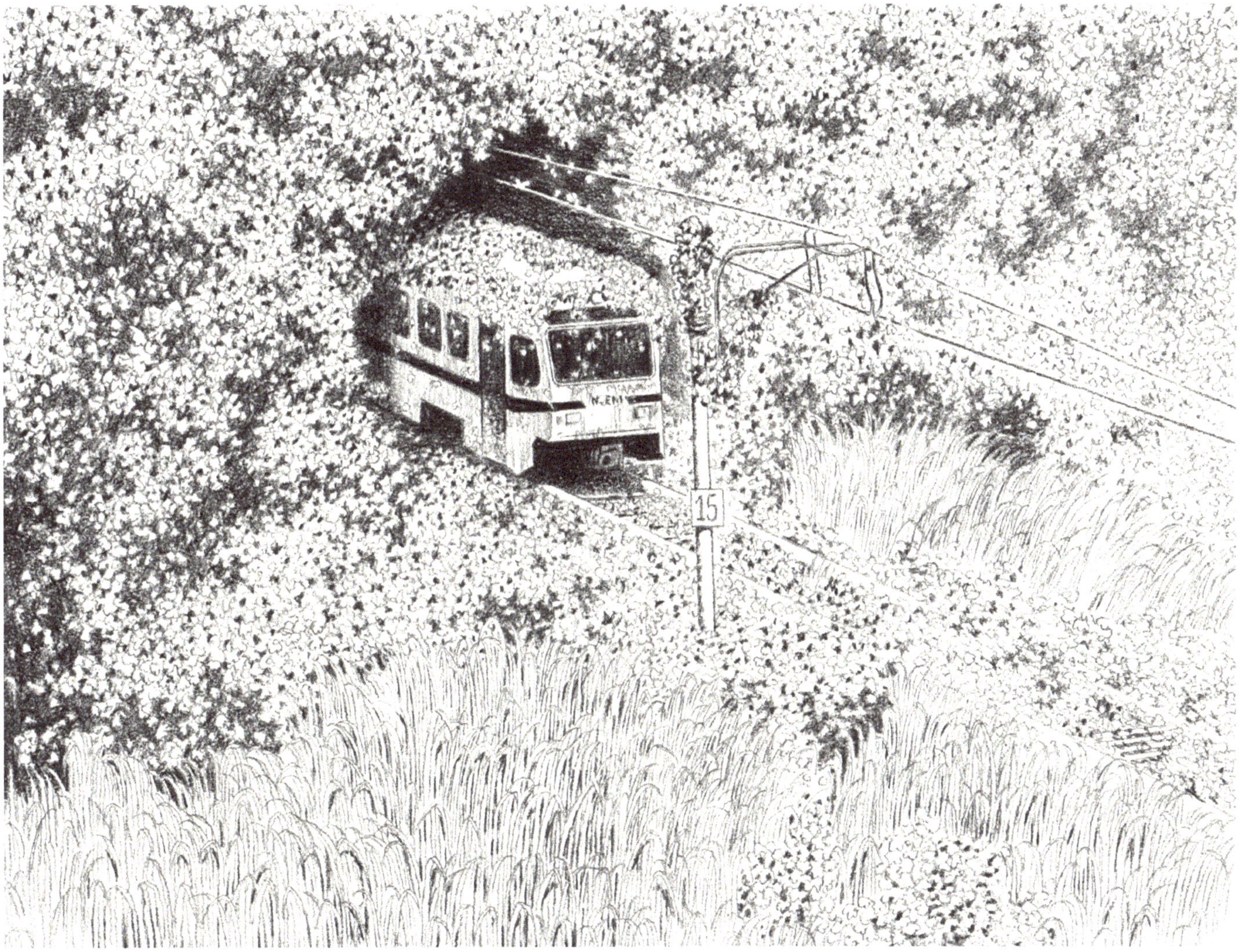

Jun Cen, *Mutual Tunnels 11*,
pencil on paper

A PENCIL TIMELINE

1564	**1565**	**LATE 1500s to 1600s**	**1600s to 1700s**	**1790**
The largest graphite deposit ever discovered was unearthed in Cumbria, England. At first, the mineral was thought to be a soft type of lead, and the association stuck: We still refer to pencil "lead," even though there is no lead in pencils.	Conrad Gesner, a Swiss naturalist, is the first person to study and describe graphite.	Graphite is used as a lubricant for cannons and other armaments. It was also sawed into sticks and used as a tool for marking sheep, which led to the discovery of its possibilities for drawing. Its artistic uses soon became apparent.	The first drawings in graphite were called Plumbago drawings. They were done primarily on vellum, as preparatory drawings for engravings. Early Dutch and British pencil artists included Simon van de Passe, Nicholas Hilliard, Isaac and Peter Oliver, and Abraham Blooteling. Later, Thomas Forster is thought to be one of the first artists to make drawings in graphite purely for their own sake.	Joseph Hardtmuth in Vienna mixes clay and graphite powder, making the pencil more widely available. His company, Koh-i-Noor, was the first company to copyright the mass-produced pencil. (Earlier pencil-manufacturing companies, such as Faber-Castell, existed in Germany, but were using pure graphite imported from England.)

Evolution of the modern pencil

Since graphite is relatively soft, it must be encased in something in order to be used as a drawing tool. Early pencils were wrapped with string or sheepskin, but inventors also began experimenting with wood casings for pencils from the 1560s onward.

The wood used to make the first pencils was juniper. After a slot was cut into the wood, a flat graphite stick was inserted from the side. Later, a strip of wood with a groove carved down the center was used and the graphite was glued into the groove and covered by a second strip of wood.

Next came the round pencil. Two halves of a round shaft were carved with a groove down the center, the graphite was glued in the groove, and then the two shafts were joined and glued, sealing the graphite in the core. This is how pencils are still made today.

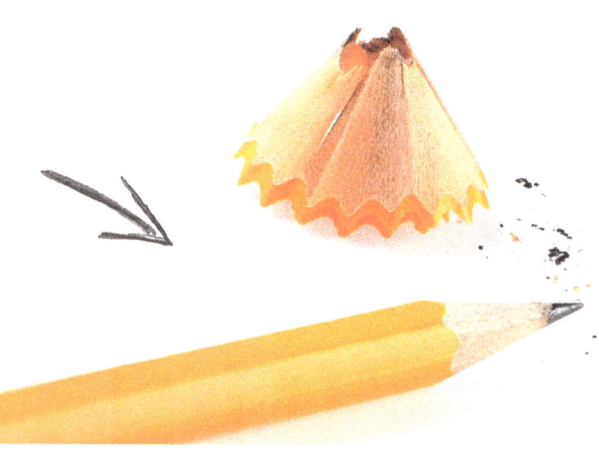

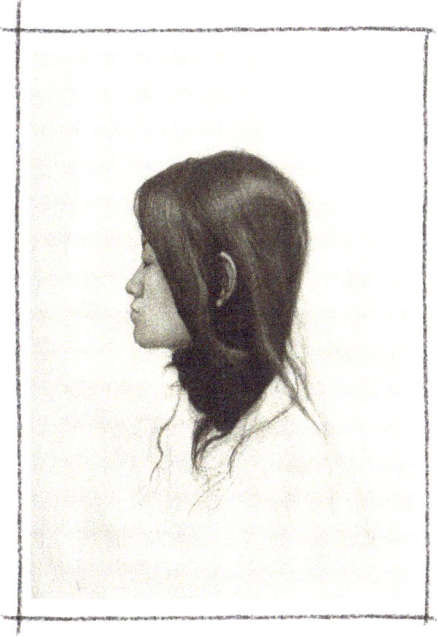

Isaac Pelepko,
Mako in Profile,
pencil on paper

1795   1812   1827   1858

Naval blockades during the Napoleonic Wars prevented France from importing pencils from England or Germany. Nicolas-Jacques Conté discovered a technique similar to Hardtmuth's, mixing clay and graphite. By varying the ratios of clay and graphite, he developed the tonal gradations of pencils that are still used today. This innovation corresponded with the rise of the Romantic and Neoclassical movements in France, when some of the first masterpieces in pencil drawing were created by artists such as Jean-Auguste-Dominique Ingres and Eugène Delacroix.

Trade embargoes during the War of 1812, led to a recession and a shortage of imported goods in the United States, including a shortage of pencils. A cabinetmaker from Massachusetts, William Munroe, tried to capitalize on this, devising his own graphite-paste formula (inferior to that of the Europeans) and began manufacturing the first American pencils.

Joseph Dixon, whose family owned a graphite mine in Massachusetts, manufactured many graphite products including crucibles, bearings, polishes, lubricants, and noncorrosive paint. In 1827, he introduced his own graphite pencil, and his interest in new industrial technology led to innovations in mass production, making the Dixon pencil the most widely produced pencil of its time.

The eraser, an innovation created by Hymen Lipman of Philadelphia, is attached to pencils. The first rubber erasers had been around since the 1770s. They were not commonly used until Charles Goodyear discovered the process of vulcanization in 1839, making the rubber more durable. To this day, pencil erasers are mainly an American phenomenon.

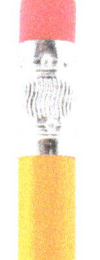

TOOLS AND MATERIALS

The list of materials required for the exercises in this book is a short one: a pencil, paper, and an eraser are all you really need. But having a few other items on hand, including chamois cloth or paper towel and a utility knife, will allow you to fine tune and add subtleties to your work.

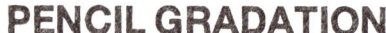

PENCIL GRADATION

In France, around 1795, the painter and inventor Nicolas-Jacques Conté began experimenting with mixing graphite with clay to create a less fragile drawing material. By adding different amounts of clay to achieve a harder or softer consistency, Conté discovered that the ratio also affected graphite's drawing quality. The softer the graphite, the darker the mark. Conté's experiments had led him to develop a pencil-gradation system that is still in use today. American manufacturers use the system with a 1–4 rating, but outside the United States, the rating is H–B.

The H–B system came first and actually consists of three letters (H, F, B), with numeric grading within those numbers. H represents hardness. The hardest pencil in the system is a 9H, which produces the lightest line. The numbers descend—8, 7, 6, and so on, down to 2H and then simply H, with each getting progressively darker. B represents blackness, and 9B is the blackest. The graphite color grows lighter as the numbers descend to 2B and, lastly, B. A pencil labeled HB is both hard and black. A pencil labeled F (fine) is mid-range between H and B and sharpens to a fine point.

The American pencil grading system is significantly more compact, going only from #1 to #4. It's sometimes referred to as the Thoreau System after the family of writer Henry David Thoreau, which had one of the first pencil-manufacturing companies in the United States.

The American numbering system loosely corresponds to equivalents in the European system: #1 equals B, #2 equals HB, #3 equals H, and #4 equals 2H. That said, the darkness or lightness of a graded pencil will vary slightly depending on the manufacturer.

Within the two grading systems, the most flexible pencils for general use are those in the middle grades, #2 and #3 (with #2 as the most common of all), and HB and H. These are neither too light nor too dark. They represent a rich middle tone that can render a wide range of subtlety. Drawing with only the darkest range can make it hard to capture subtle detail. It also forces you to sharpen your pencil often. The lightest range of graphite makes for a slow drawing experience as the graphite does not leave much of a mark on the page and builds up slowly. These pencils are used more for architectural drawing, which demands precision without smudging.

Pencil brands such as Dixon Ticonderoga, Eberhard Faber, and Paper Mate, created for everyday non-art use, rely on the American numeric system. Most pencils created for artistic purposes, including Faber-Castell, Staedtler, and Derwent, use the European method of gradation.

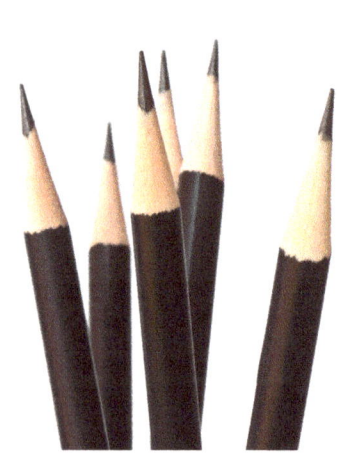

Deanna Staffo,
Man with Glasses Reading,
pencil on paper

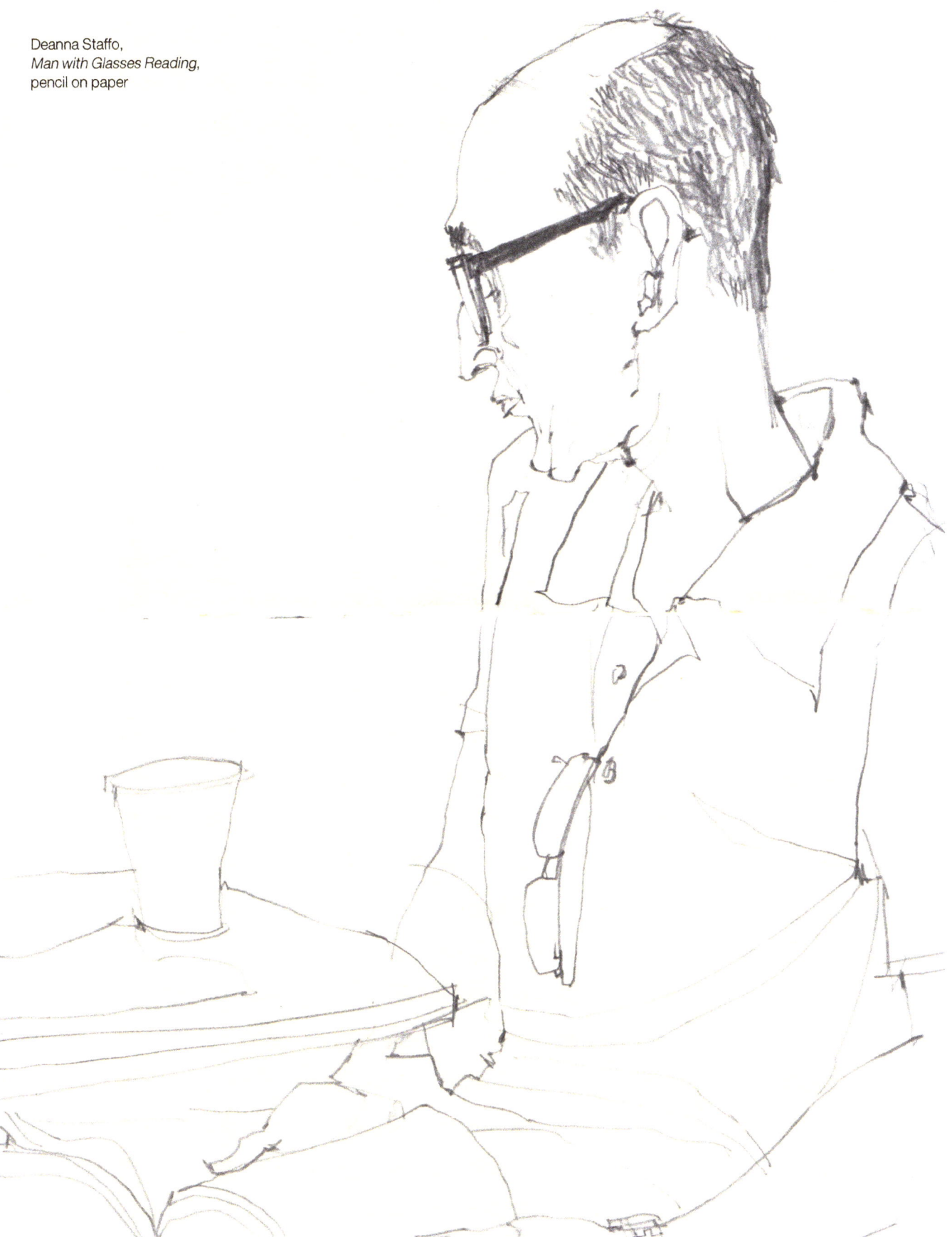

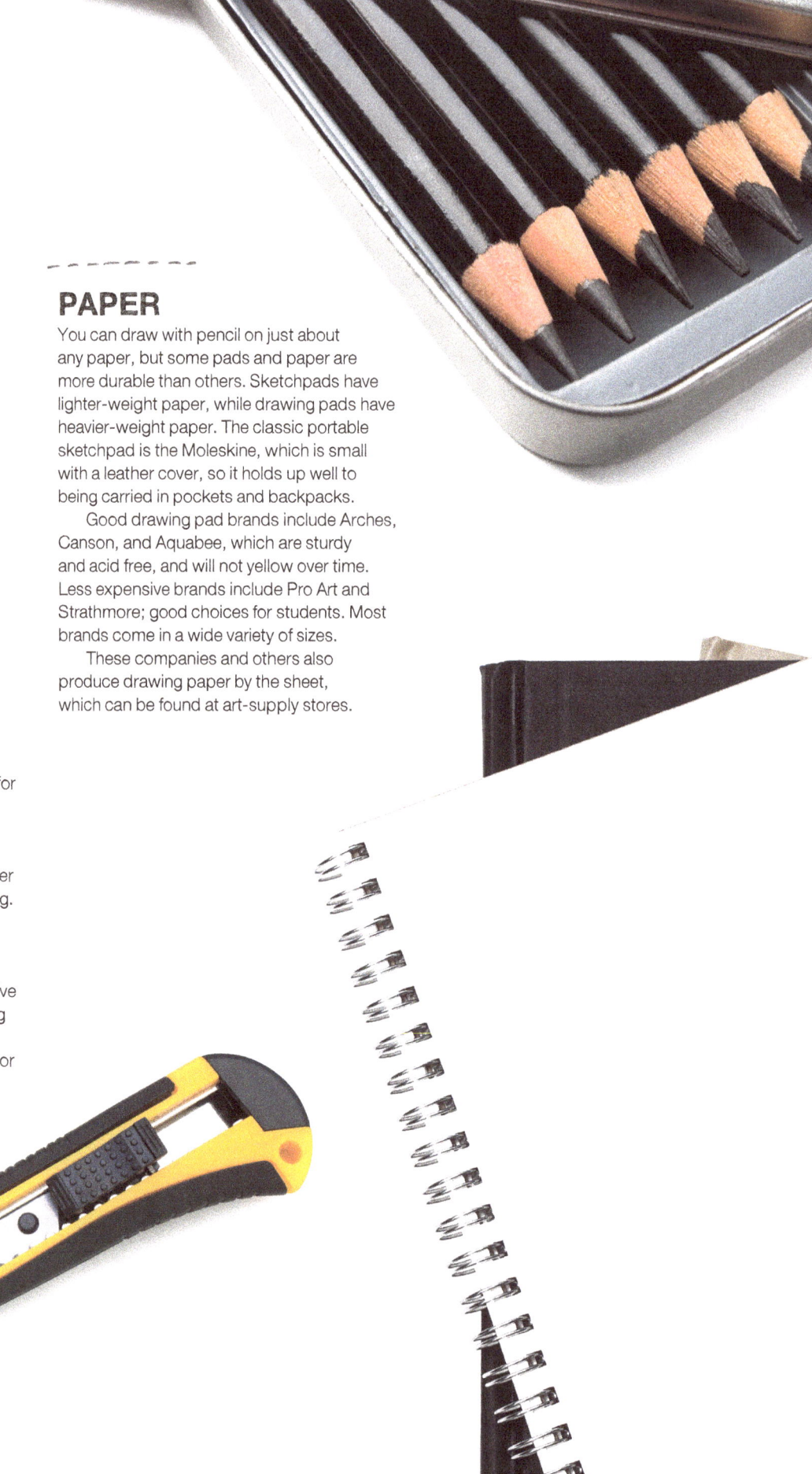

PAPER

You can draw with pencil on just about any paper, but some pads and paper are more durable than others. Sketchpads have lighter-weight paper, while drawing pads have heavier-weight paper. The classic portable sketchpad is the Moleskine, which is small with a leather cover, so it holds up well to being carried in pockets and backpacks.

Good drawing pad brands include Arches, Canson, and Aquabee, which are sturdy and acid free, and will not yellow over time. Less expensive brands include Pro Art and Strathmore; good choices for students. Most brands come in a wide variety of sizes.

These companies and others also produce drawing paper by the sheet, which can be found at art-supply stores.

UTILITY KNIFE

A sharpened pencil has a tight line, good for fine details. It's best when the sharpened tip of the pencil is smooth, so that it does not scratch or indent the drawing paper. Sharpening a pencil with a rotary sharpener may give the tip too fine a point for drawing. You might find that by sharpening your drawing pencils with a utility knife, you'll get the custom tip you're looking for. By controlling the length of the point, you'll give yourself the greatest range in mark making and shading, but those things are also controlled by the gradation (the hardness or softness) of the pencil's graphite.

CHAMOIS CLOTH OR PAPER TOWEL

Chamois is a soft, leather cloth used to smudge and blend graphite for a softening effect. A chamois can be helpful for creating smooth transitions in a drawing, where the marks are hidden, or softened and then drawn over with a pencil. A chamois cloth can spread graphite powder or blend pencil strokes to a similar effect. If you don't have a chamois cloth on hand, a square or two of paper towel can be used instead.

ERASERS

Erasers are as essential to the drawing process as pencils. Use them for correcting mistakes, as well as for creating highlights and softening or lightening areas that are too dark. The two essential types to have on hand are kneaded and plastic erasers, neither of which create erasure crumbs that have to be brushed away.

A kneaded or gum eraser can be sculpted and stretched. It can be pinched into a fine tip or used as a broad, flat surface. If a kneaded or gum eraser is applied with light pressure, it can be used to pick up color and soften a mark or tone, without fully lifting it.

The plastic eraser is much harder than a kneaded eraser and lifts up much more graphite. This makes it the right choice for thoroughly erasing mistakes. A plastic eraser can be carved into a point, allowing it to erase small details.

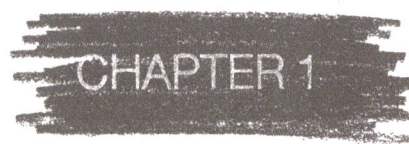

CHAPTER 1

DRAWING WITH LINE

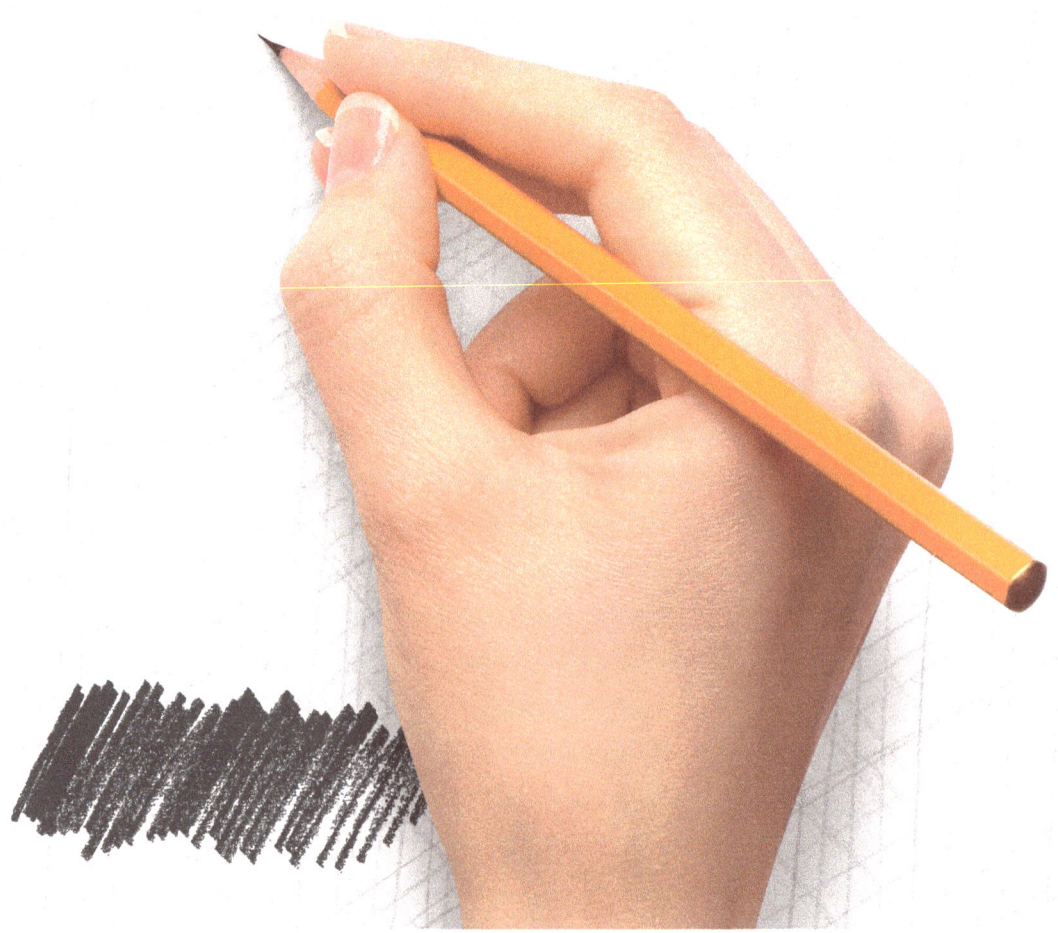

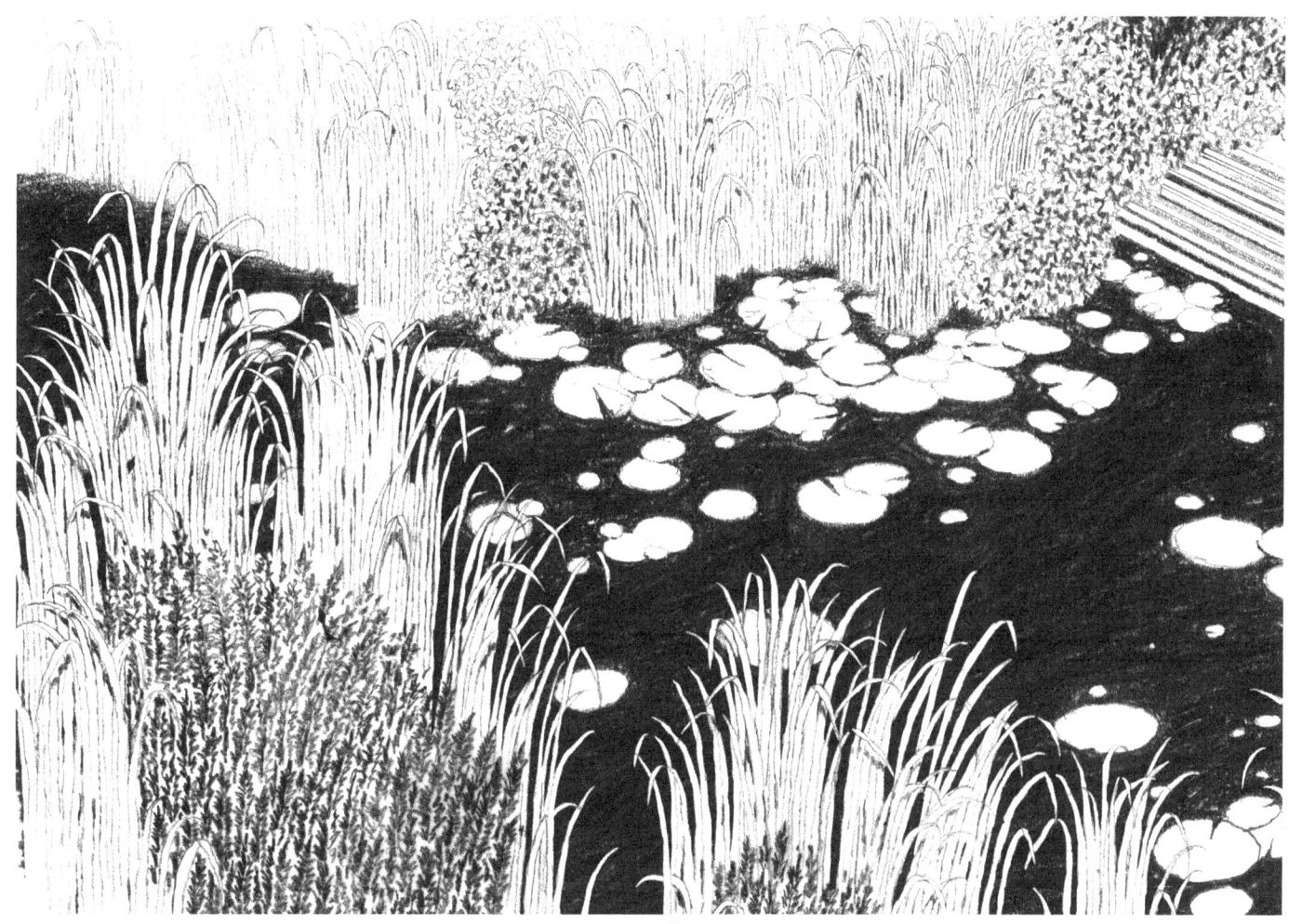

Jun Cen,
Mutual Tunnels 10,
pencil on paper

Drawing with line is the primary instinct when we learn to draw. Ask children to draw a picture of their family, and they'll usually interpret the subject through a series of stick figures.

Ideas come to us as abstractions in the form of line, but line is not how the eye sees the world. A line is an imaginary concept. If you consider that people instead see in light and shadow, then it's logical to conclude that lines do not exist outside of our imagination. In our minds, we use lines to delineate one form from another, such as a cup from the table on which it sits, a leaf from a tree, or a single person from a crowd of people. Lines clarify and distinguish one object from another, but lines as a concept are an abstraction.

The process of drawing an image purely with line is the process of editing and simplifying the subject. The challenge in line drawing is the challenge of clarity—deciding what to include and what to leave out.

TYPE OF LINE AND LINE PERSONALITY

When you're drawing with line, consider how it defines the personality of the work of art. Line quality describes the feeling of a line, whether it's smooth or rough, whether it has a consistent weight or a wide variation in thickness. These considerations will determine the style and mood of the finished drawing.

Line quality is determined by a number of factors: the hardness of the graphite, the pencil's sharpness, how the pencil is held, how the hand moves, and how hard the pencil is pressed into the paper. There are two distinct approaches to line quality—direct line and sculpted line.

A direct line is one in which pressure is applied directly and evenly while the tip of the pencil is pulled across the page. A softer graphite pencil works best to create a bolder line. With a direct line, all the subtleties of the movement in the hand are captured in minute detail. This style reflects the idiosyncrasies and peculiarities in the motion of the arm and wrist.

There should be little hesitation in this approach so that there is a boldness to the line. This can lead to distortion, but the strength of this type of line is not in accuracy, it is in the confidence of the mark, which is the beauty of the line. The feeling in the line can be smooth or rough. Line weight variation is determined by the pressure placed on the pencil. Turning the pencil from the tip to the broad side of the tip during the stroke will also create a shift from a thin line to a thick one. Since the purpose of the line is its directness, the line, once drawn, should not be retraced, or its spontaneity will be lost.

Another approach is to sculpt a line. This involves discovering the line by building it up slowly through a series of shorter strokes. It reveals less of the gesture and does more to disguise the mark of the artist. The resulting line is refined and can be more subtle than a direct line.

Start lightly with a sculpted line, allowing the pencil to softly diagram the subject. A harder graphite is good for this. Make many passes at the line to discover the correct curve and line weight.

Drawing the line lightly at first makes it easy to erase with no smudging. The softer marks build up the harder, darker marks as the precise line is discovered. A softer graphite, or heavier mark, can be used to trace over the softer marks if a darker line is needed. The drawing that results from this style is one where the line serves to reveal the subject while calling as little attention to the process of the drawing as possible.

These approaches represent two extremes in style. A drawing typically uses a full range of lines in between these two types. A single drawing can go from very refined to very loose. The same subject can be drawn several times: If a different kind of line is used each time, the subject will feel very different.

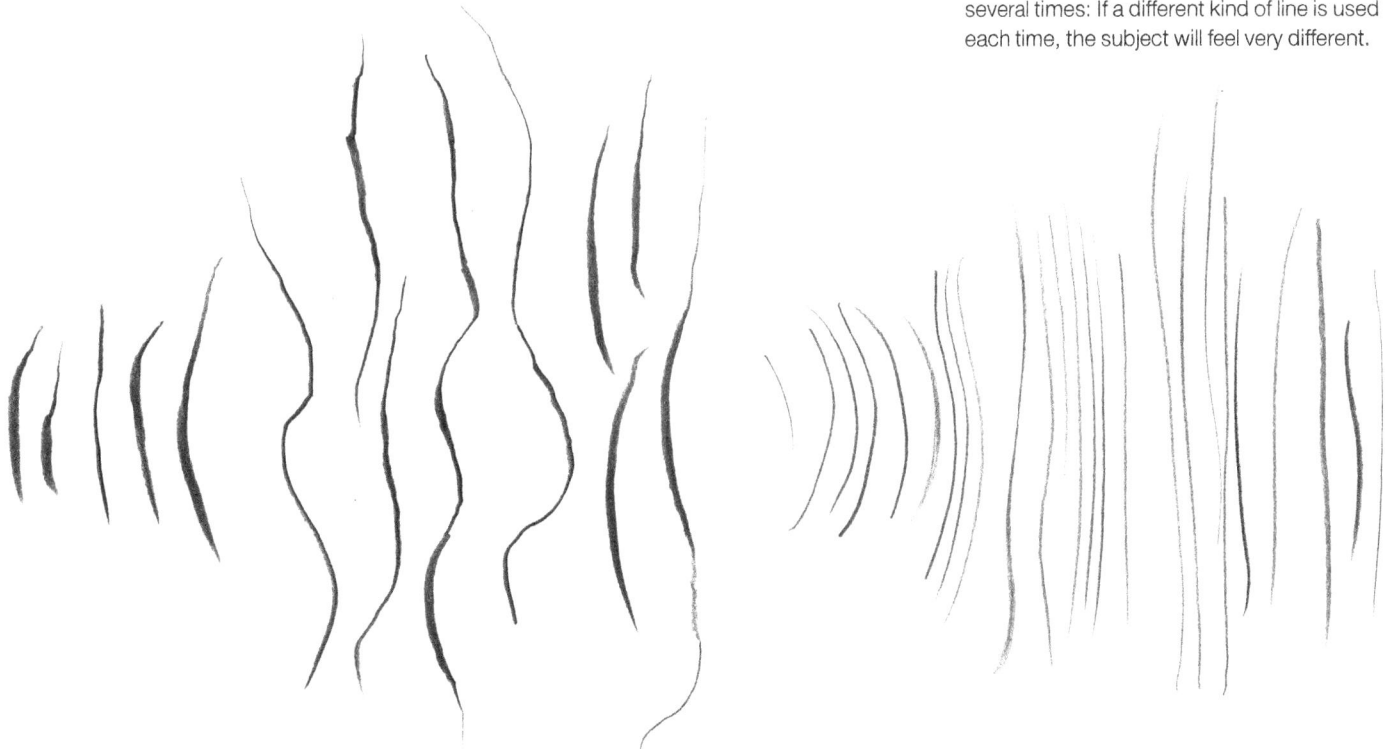

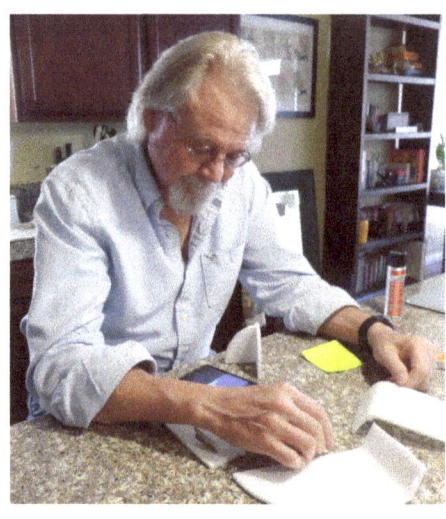

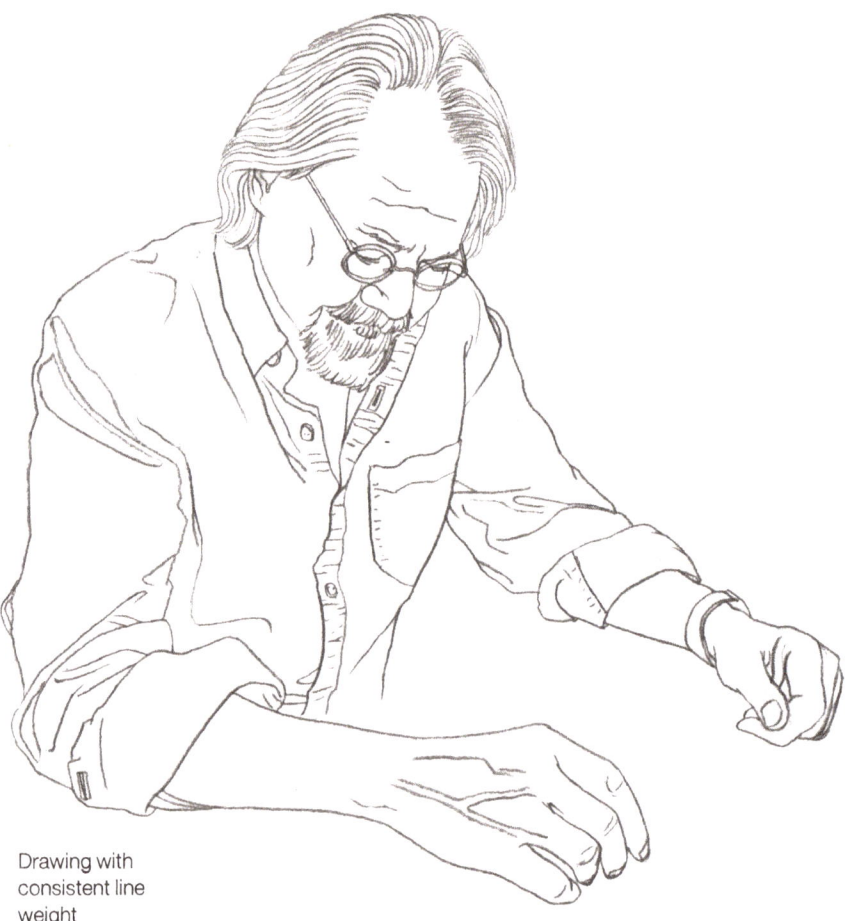

Drawing with
consistent line
weight

LOOKING AT THE SAME SUBJECT USING DIFFERENT LINES

USING A SINGLE LINE WEIGHT

In this drawing, the focus is on using a single line weight, drawing directly without reworking the line to show the least expressive, most basic style of line. The consistent weight flattens the drawing, almost to the point of abstraction. There is no illusion of space, and the drawing feels emotionally empty and clinical. The directness calls attention to the texture of the pencil and paper, bringing the lines to the forefront. This approach makes the lines the subject of the drawing rather than the person being depicted.

USING A DIRECT LINE AND REWORKING IT

This style of line is more expressive. The lines used are direct, similar to the previous drawing, but they're worked beyond the first pass as a way of discovering more depth in the character of the subject. The wider range of line weights helps to define space and distance (heavy lines in the closer hand, lighter in the hand farther away).

In this drawing, lines whose proportions or positions were off are reworked. The corrections are drawn on top of the mistakes, giving the drawing a look of evolution and history. This leads to a messier drawing, but also one with a sense of motion and energy. These help to develop a more personal quality in the subject, as if this drawing was done while watching the person in real life. The subject feels present, he might have moved while the drawing was being done. The artists' drawing process is also documented in this version. When you look at it, you see not only the final state of the drawing, but also the thinking that was involved in reaching the final state. Both the artist and subject feel real in this work.

An important aspect of this drawing is the balance between the areas that are more heavily drawn with multiple passes and the lighter, looser lines that were left from the first pass. If the entire drawing were made up of only the former, the drawing would feel overworked. If the drawing were made solely of the latter, it would feel more like a sketch, and less finished.

The variable line weights in areas such as the closer hand and the face help to give a realistic structure to those areas. The line variation between the fingers becomes very specific, showing the subtle gaps between the knuckles. The line variation in the bridge of the nose creates the illusion that it points outward from the face, revealing the particular bone structure of this specific nose. In the folds of the shirt, the heavier lines emphasize the more dramatic wrinkles, and the lighter lines show the more subtle ones.

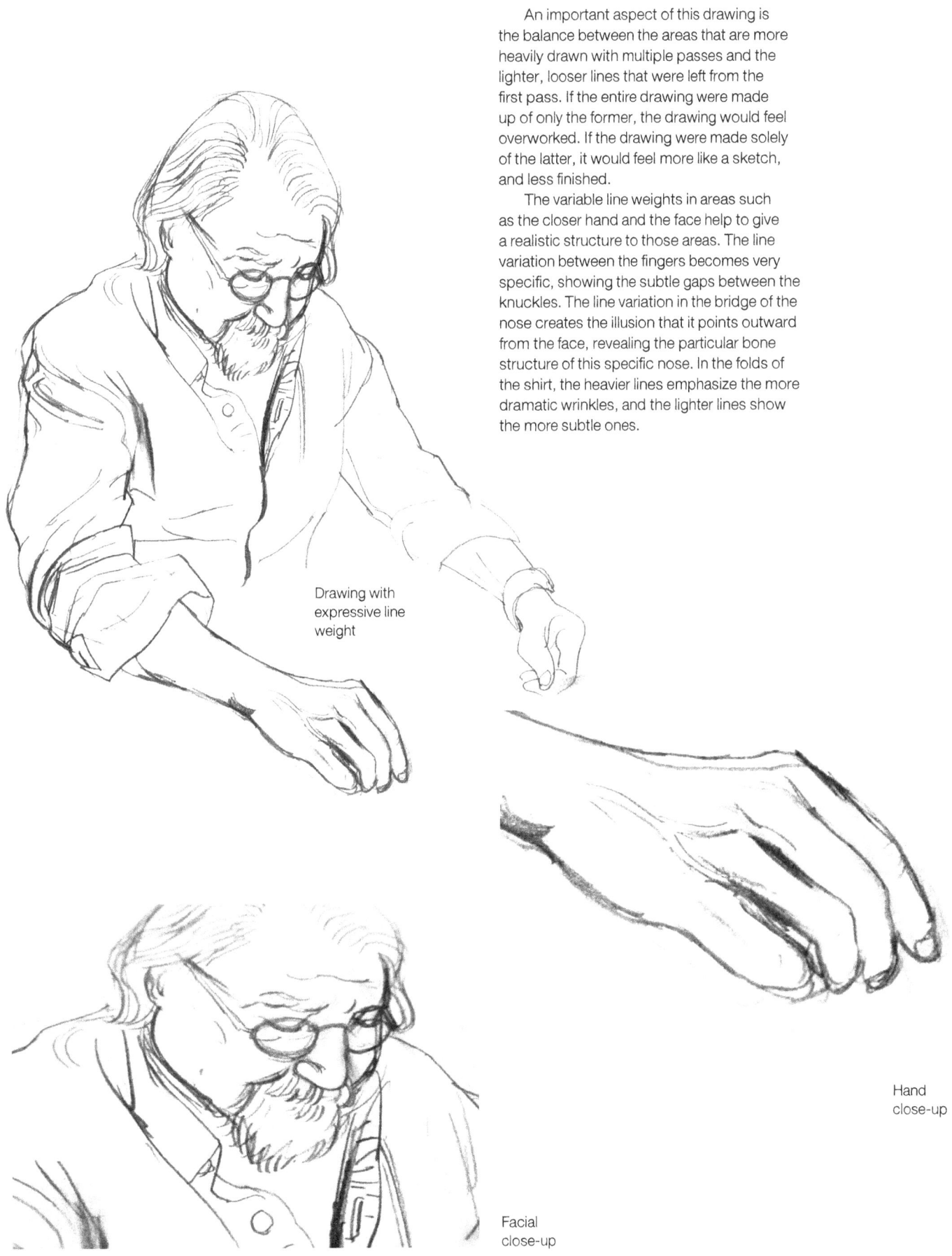

Drawing with expressive line weight

Hand close-up

Facial close-up

USING A REFINED LINE

The lines used in this drawing were built up over softer lines and required many small strokes, several passes, and several revisions. Passes were made lightly with the pencil to find the right curves and shapes, then the initial exploratory marks were erased, and a more confident line was used on top.

The pencil used was kept sharpened to draw the fine lines, and the graphite was harder (2H). This makes the line less expressive and reveals the subject clearly. Each line is precise, specific, and deliberate. Each line has a wider range of weight, transitioning from thin to thick. Multiple techniques are used in a single line to sculpt it, more pressure is used to darken, less pressure to lighten, multiple strokes to thicken, and an eraser to thin the line.

There is a noticeable lack of correction or history in this drawing. It's much cleaner than the previous one, emphasizing the subject rather than the drawing process or the hand of the artist.

Another important quality in this drawing is the ends of the lines. Some fray at the ends, some come to a point, and others fade out. With each, the effect is deliberate.

A line that fades out can show it diminishing in space, a frayed edge or point can display a curve at the tip or a soft edge and soft contrast. A point and a sharp line create a sense of sharp contrast, a distinct edge that is being emphasized.

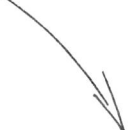

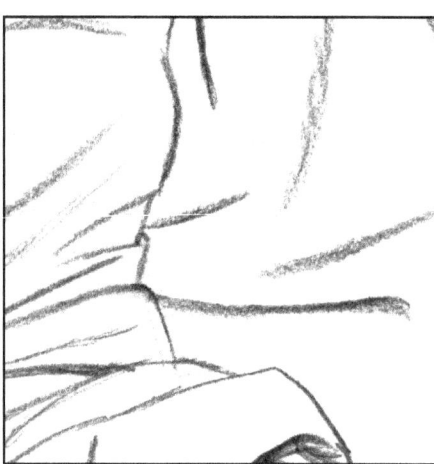

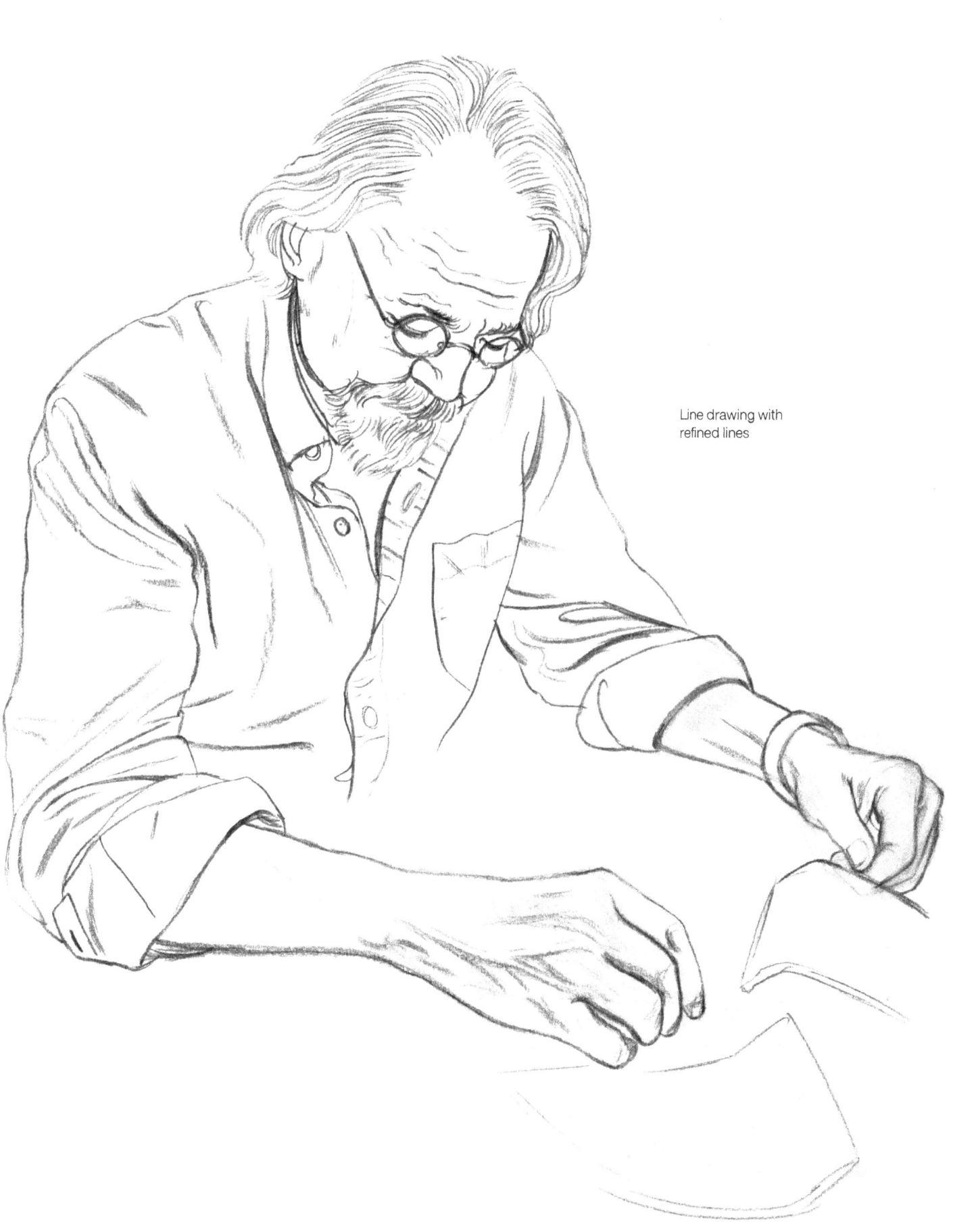

Line drawing with
refined lines

Photo reference for
clean line drawing
(Courtesy of Barry
Carpenter)

EXERCISE 1: LINE AND SPACE

This is an exploration of the specific properties in pencil line that can be used to create depth in a drawing. There are rules that can be relied on to heighten the sense of depth and space with line alone, but you must interpret what is seen in reality through what will actually work to create the illusion. The important points of articulating space with line include how line weight is used, the contrast between both thick and thin lines and dark and light lines, the converging of lines along the closeness of parallel lines, and the presence (or lack) of detail.

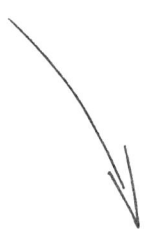

Lines in the foreground tend to have the widest range of thick to thinness and light to darkness. That is to say, these lines have the most contrast: There are heavy lines, but not all of the lines will be heavy. In the foreground, you can employ heavy dark lines next to thin light lines. As the lines recede, they occupy a narrower and lighter range in contrast. Thin lines in the foreground add a greater sense of detail, making objects feel closer in space.

For heavier lines, use a duller pencil and more pressure or use a soft graphite (2B–8B). As the lines move farther back in space, use a sharper pencil and a hard graphite (2H–4H). The lines and details should slowly grow closer together, though individual objects will have fewer and fewer details the farther back in space they sit.

Think about reducing background forms to basic shapes and outline silhouettes. To create thinner, lighter lines, use a kneaded eraser, flatten the tip and tap (don't brush or rub) the line to lighten it. Coupling these practices with, say, one point perspective, will further enhance the illusion of space.

The more general principles of drawing deep space, which are not specific to pencil, are the rules of linear perspective and atmospheric perspective.

In linear perspective, the rule is that all lines converge into a single point as they recede. The rule in atmospheric perspective is that contrast and warmth in light and color diminish as they recede into space. This is because warmer colors on the spectrum have a shorter wavelength, which means they're not visible at farther distances and are the first colors blocked by atmospheric interference like fog, moisture, and rain. When translating that into the simplicity of line, consider what has been mentioned already about line as a simplification of reality.

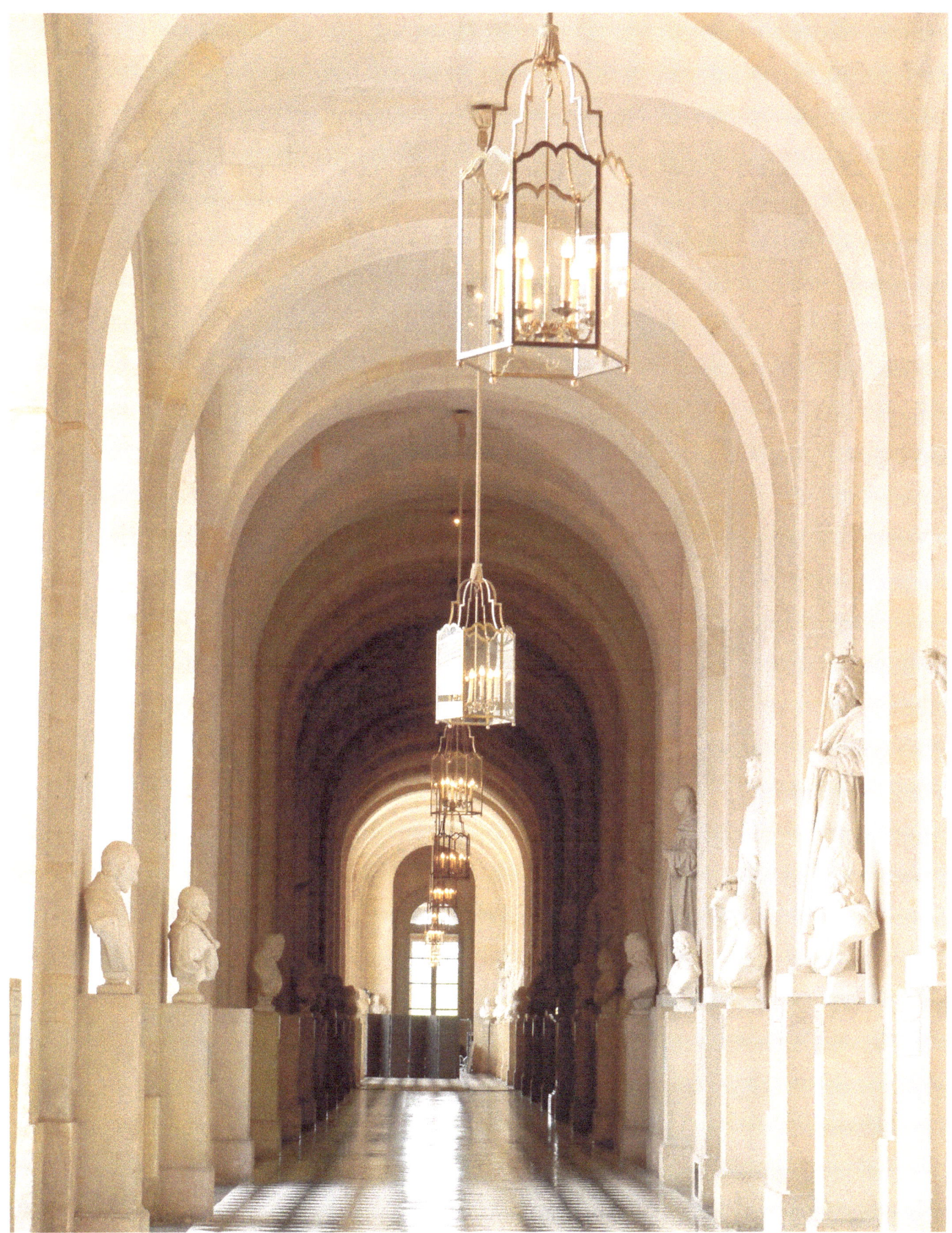

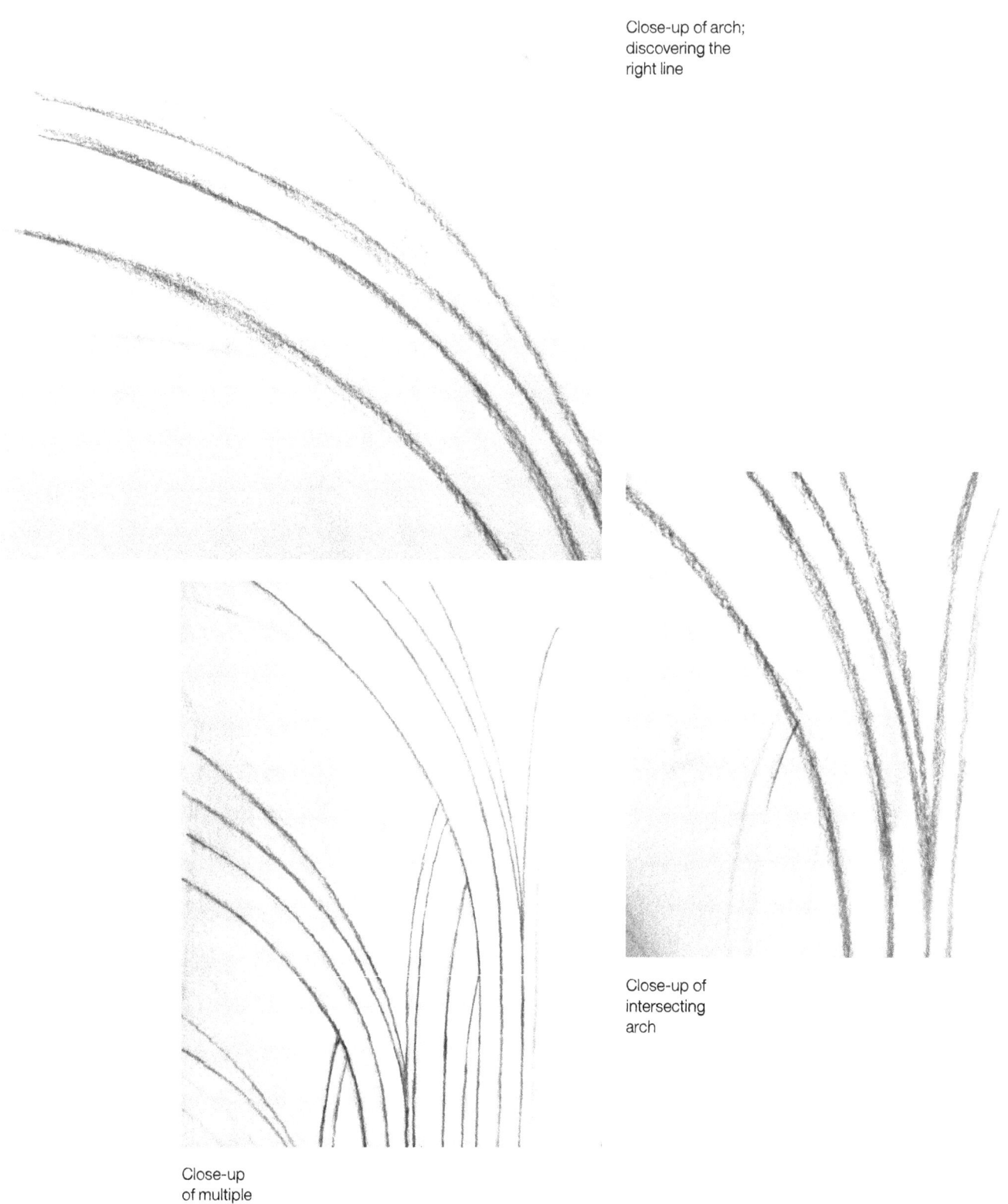

Close-up of arch;
discovering the
right line

Close-up of
intersecting
arch

Close-up
of multiple
arches

Line weight
describing
space

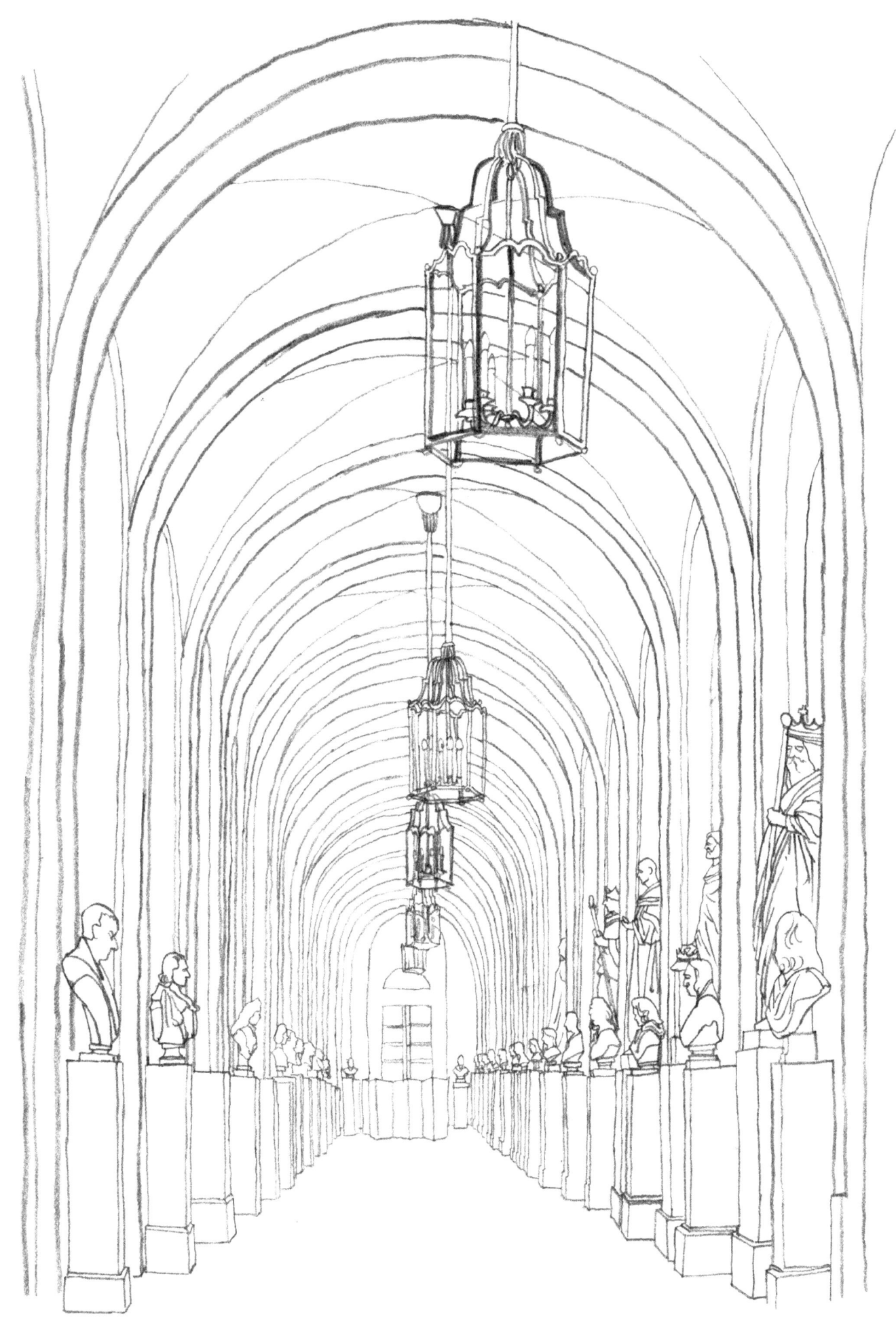

When describing textures such as leaves, grass, hair, fur, or surfaces like water, rock, or wood, in pencil line, start by identifying a mark or combination of marks that resemble the essence of the surface. Is the texture smooth or jagged? Will the texture be curvy or angular? Will the marks be long strokes or short dashes?

Often, the tendency in drawing a texture is to draw every leaf, every strand of hair, or every ripple. Understanding what makes the texture feel a certain way helps simplify the process of reproducing the sensation, rather than repeating the exact look of the surface. Look at the whole object—the tree instead of the leaf, the shape of the haircut instead of the individual strands of hair.

Draw the shape of the whole object very loosely, and then squint at it so the details of the texture are reduced to a blur of light and shadow. Describe the shadows using the simplified texture as a substitute for shading: the V-shaped marks of rippled water, the long, curvy lines for hair, the short dashes for grass. If these textures are drawn evenly across a surface (even pressure, even line weight), it can have the effect of flattening the object. So when rendering the texture, consider which direction the lines of the texture should move: The texture should flow in the same direction that the form of the object flows, to give it a sense of dimension.

Stagger the size of the mark and the weight and lightness of the line to create a sense of space. Use heavier and darker lines (softer graphite) in the shadow areas. When applying the texture to highlights, use a sharper, lighter (harder) graphite.

The entire object does not need to be filled with texture. You may leave the texture out all together in highlights to enhance contrast and create a bolder sense of light and shadow, even if the texture in the actual object is visible over the entire surface. Drawing is an edited process and learning what to leave out is an important part of the creative process.

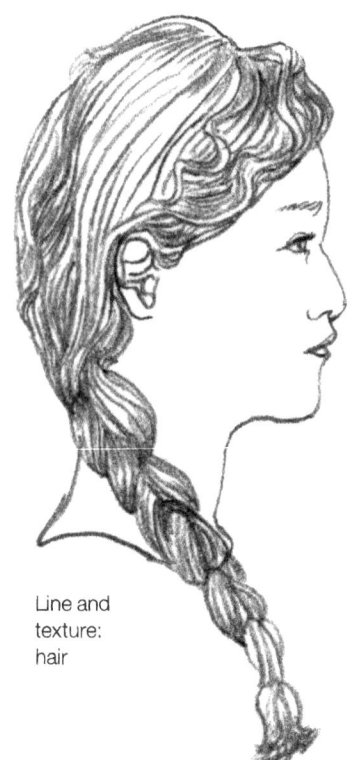

Line and texture: hair

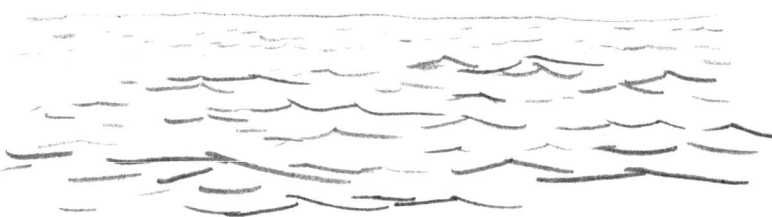

Line and texture: waves

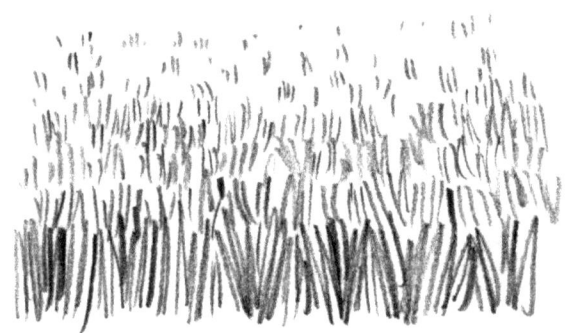

Line and texture: grass

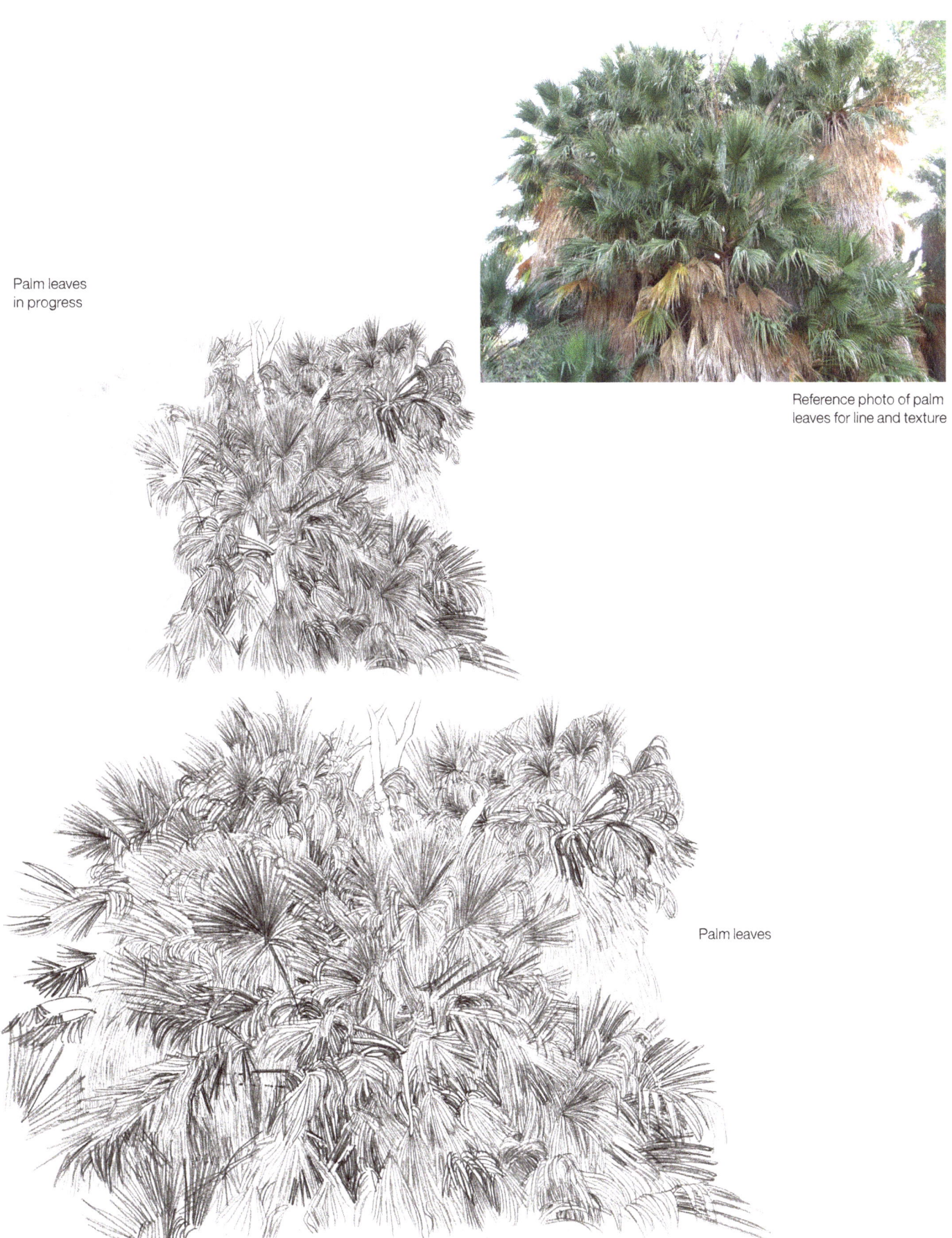

Palm leaves
in progress

Reference photo of palm
leaves for line and texture

Palm leaves

EXERCISE 3: VOLUME

The most important quality to consider when drawing volume with a single line is controlling the shifting weight of the line. A single line must shift in weight smoothly from thin to thick and light to dark (or vice versa).

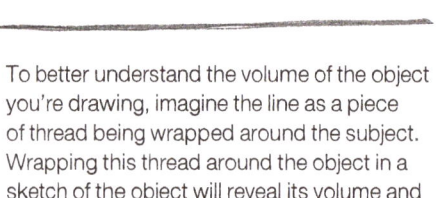

To better understand the volume of the object you're drawing, imagine the line as a piece of thread being wrapped around the subject. Wrapping this thread around the object in a sketch of the object will reveal its volume and help you understand how to use shading and line weight in the final drawing to best describe the volume.

Shifts in line weight can be done using the refined sculpted approach mentioned earlier: carefully modeling the line by lightly layering a series of smaller lines. Line weight can also be varied by using direct line, shifting from the point of the pencil's tip to the broadside of the tip through the motion of the wrist while drawing the line. Be sure to have the pencil sharpened so that a broad portion of the tip's edge is revealed (the amount of the broadside exposed will determine the width of the line).

Drawing a direct line with a smooth shift in weight requires confidence (pausing to think in the middle of drawing a line will create an interruption in the line and can spoil its elegance). Practicing the line as a warm up on a separate sheet of paper will help you figure out the right motion and angle for the pencil before applying the line to the actual drawing.

Make the line in one smooth motion with a lot of control for accuracy. The curve of the line and shift in width indicate light moving over the surface of the volumetric object. The thin line transitioning to a heavy line shows where light hits the object (on the thinnest part of the line), and how the surface transitions away from the light into shadow (as the line gets heavier).

The curving of lines and the gradation of light to shadow on an object are usually the details that reveal volume, but in a line drawing where no shadows are used, the line weight has to illustrate the same point.

Photo reference for line and volume

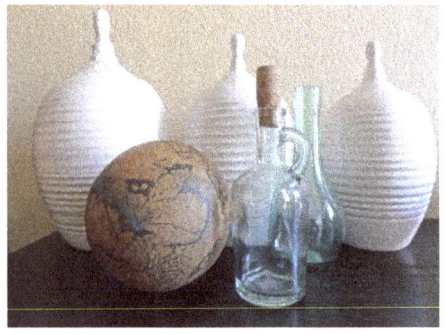

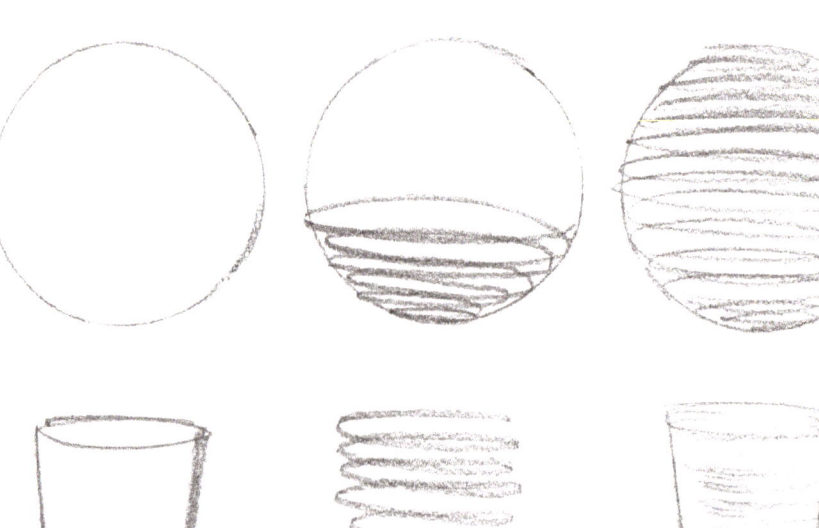

Basic shapes with lines to emphasize volume

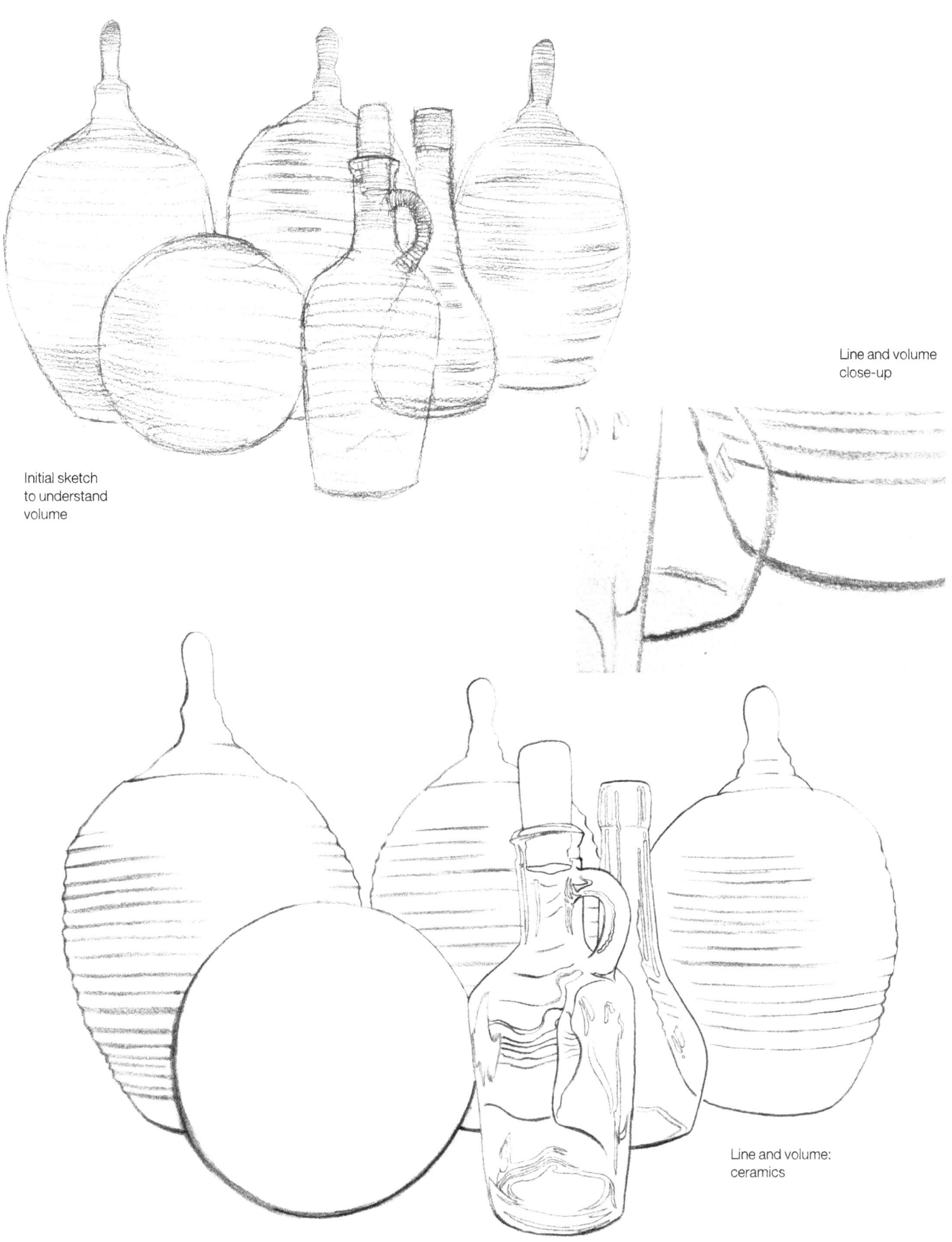

Line and volume
close-up

Initial sketch
to understand
volume

Line and volume:
ceramics

EXERCISE 4: COMPLETING A FULL COMPOSITION IN LINE

Practice the preceding exercises, then, using line to interpret individual topics, combine the challenges of drawing space, texture, and volume in a single composition. Consider line as an edited, or simplified, version of the subject being drawn. Decide which elements need to be included and which should be left out. Don't just re-create the subject with the techniques, use the subject as a starting point to explore the more expressive qualities in line. Bring the raw quality of the line itself forward, making the *process* the subject the drawing.

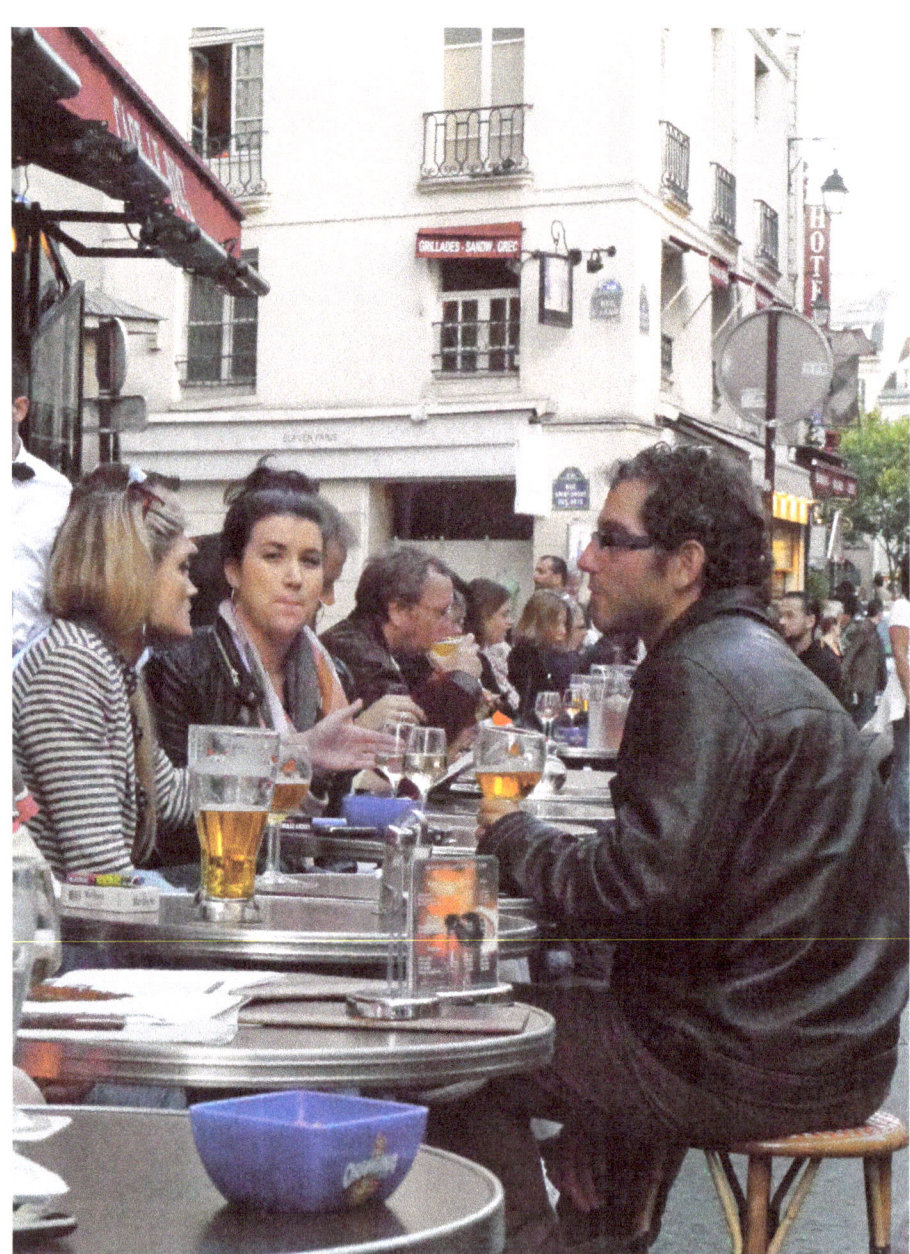

Photo reference for completing a composition (Courtesy of Barry Carpenter)

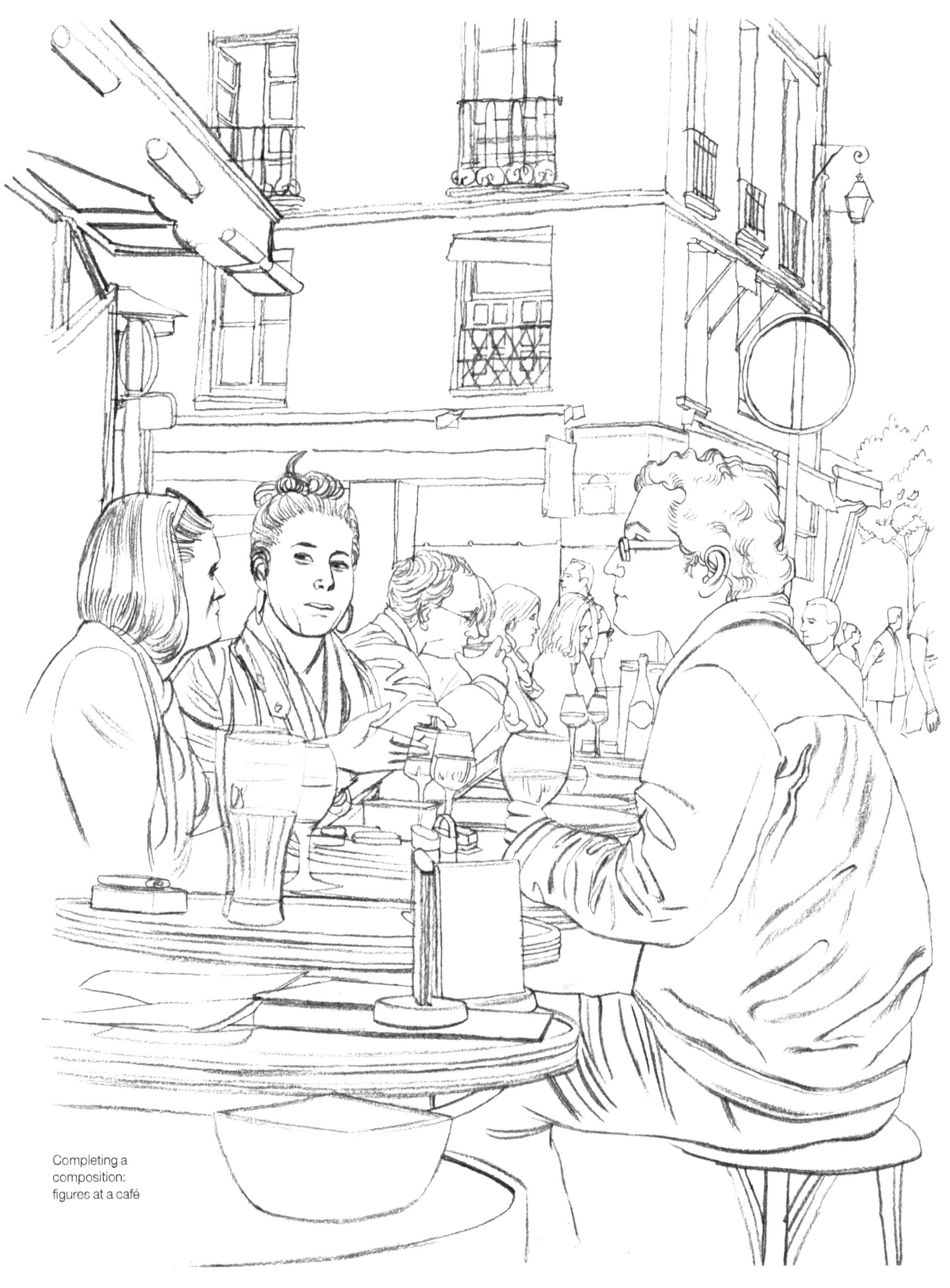

Completing a
composition:
figures at a café

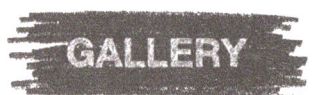

Deanna Staffo,
Girl with Ring,
pencil on paper

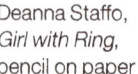

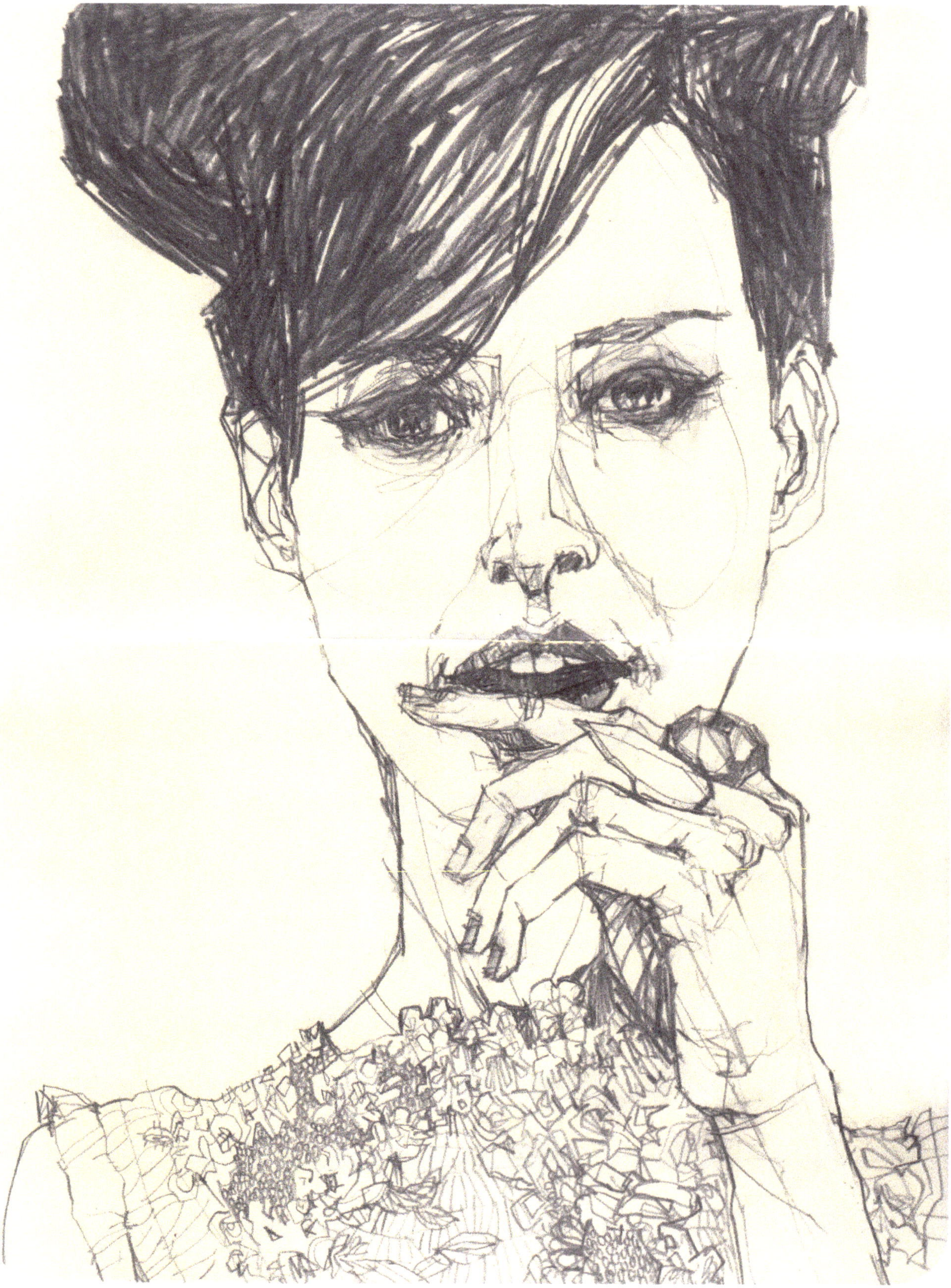

Deanna Staffo,
Antelope Herd,
pencil on paper

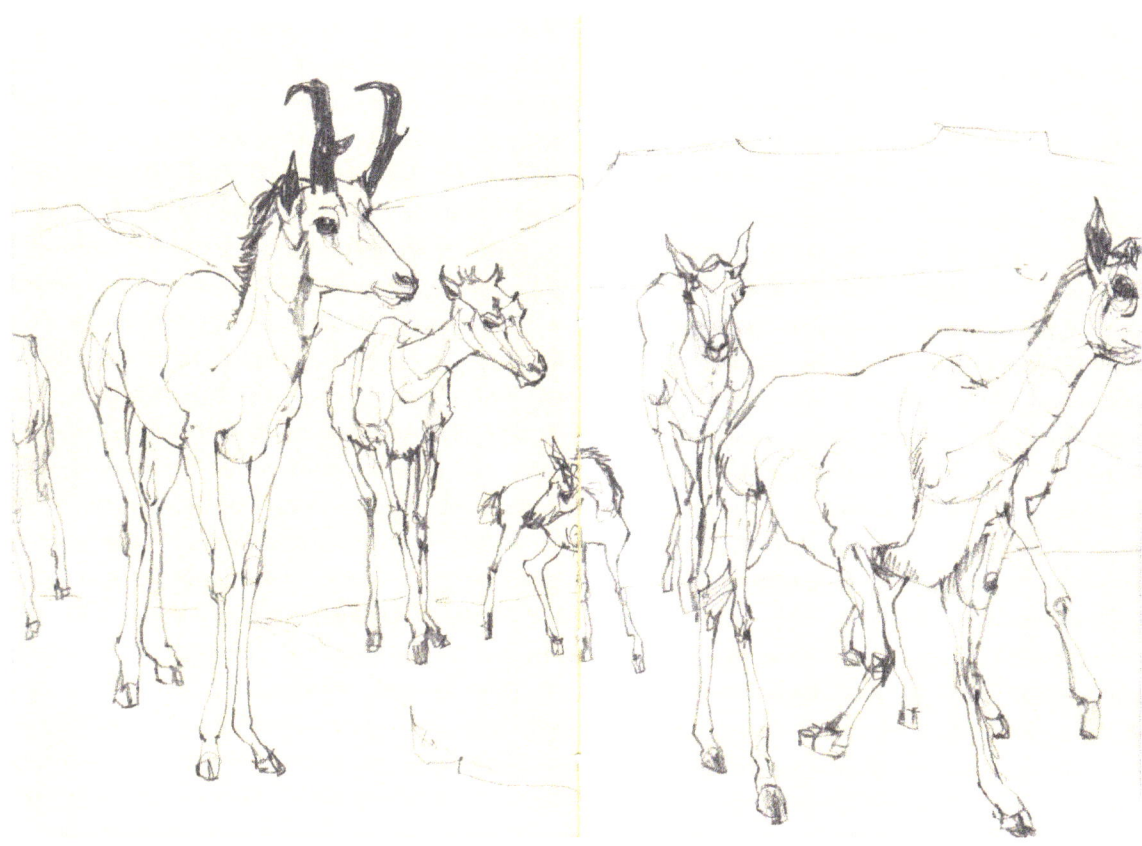

Deanna Staffo,
Sarah in the Cafe,
pencil on paper

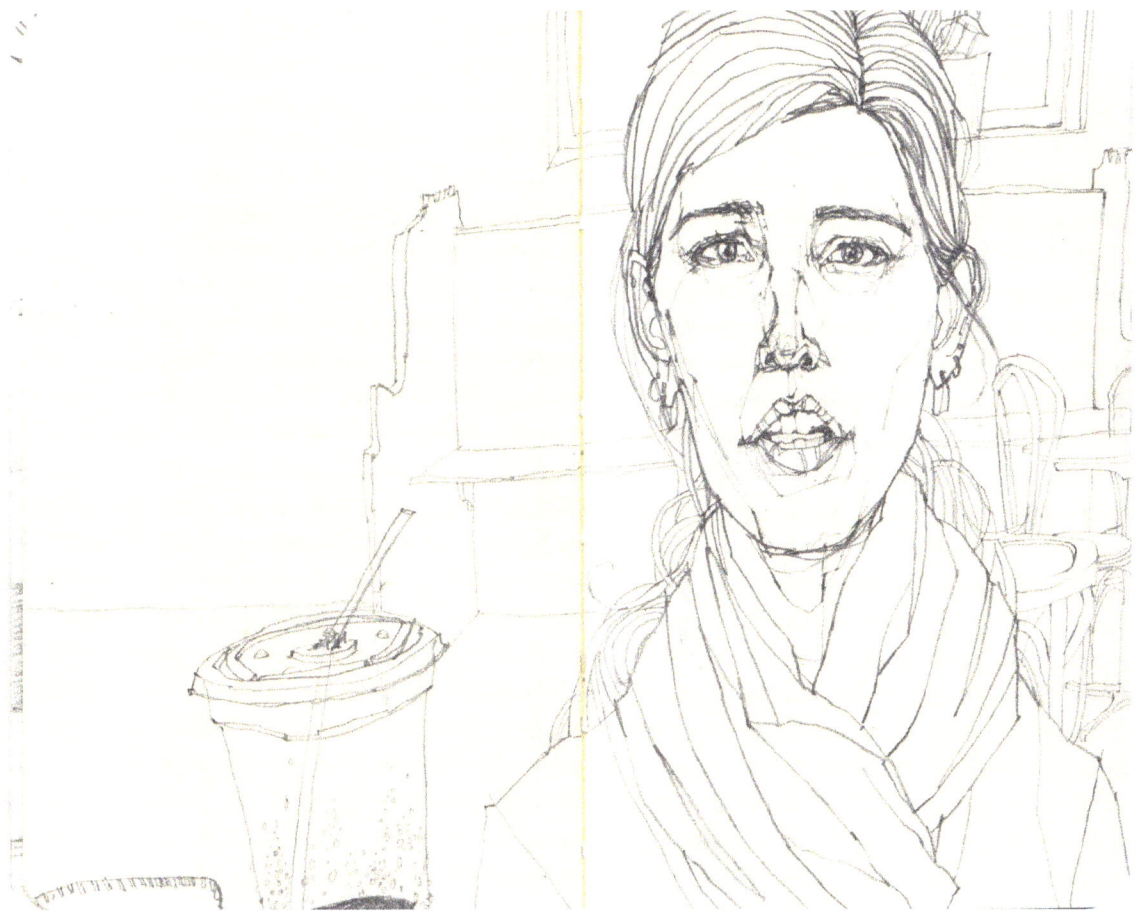

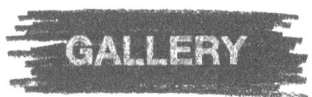
Deanna Staffo,
Danger Ahead,
pencil on paper

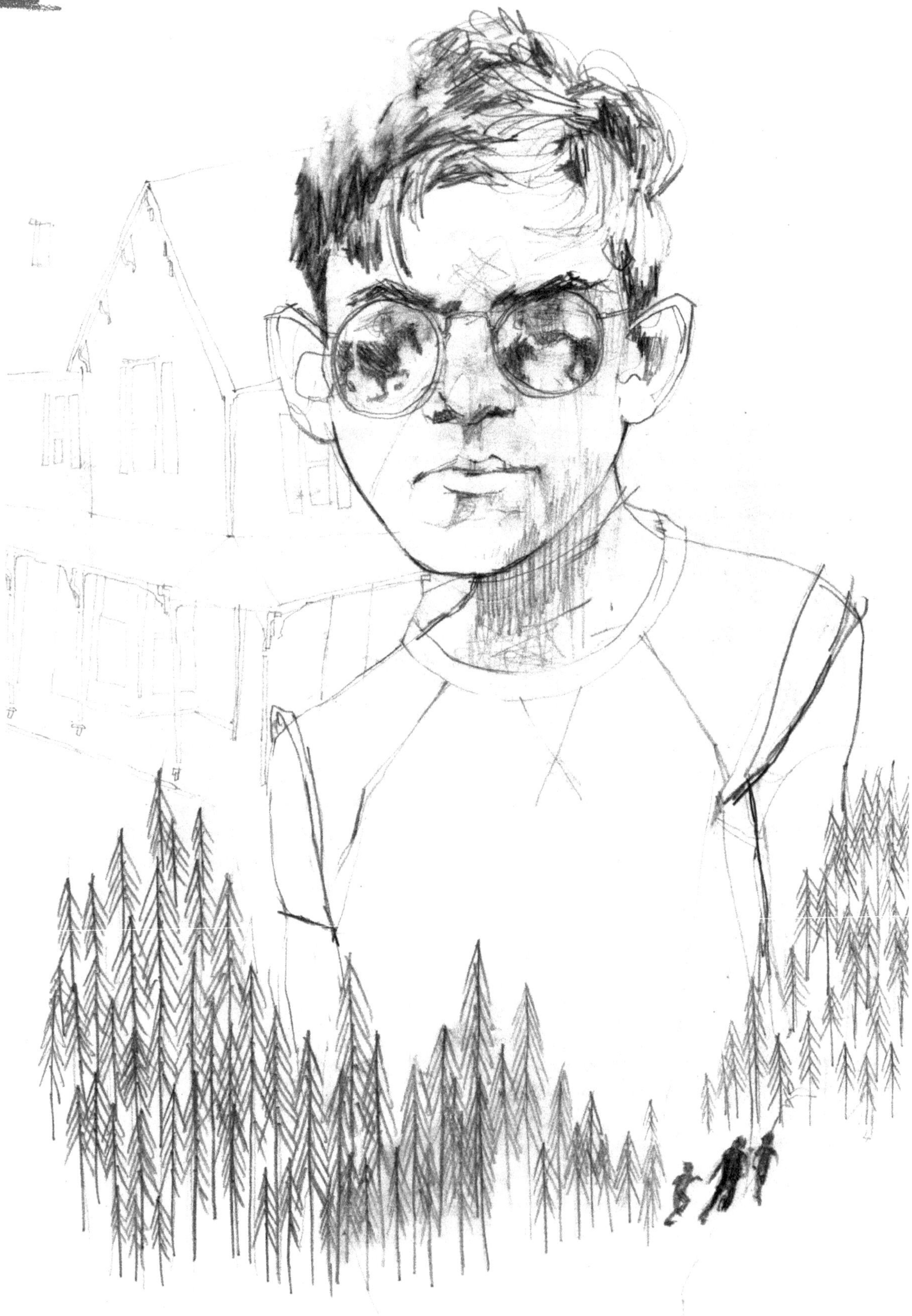

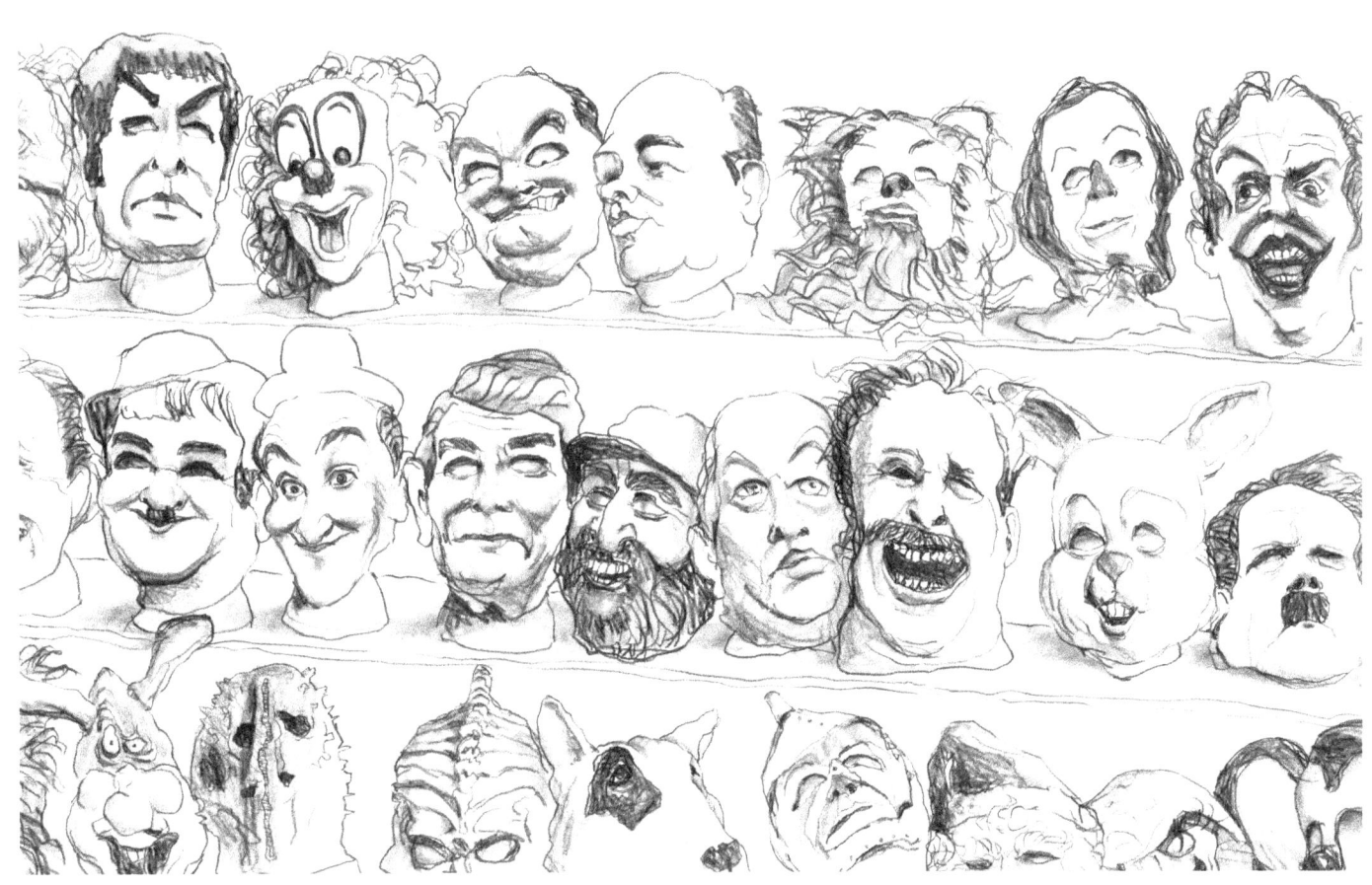

Carol Fabricatore,
The Johns (Masks),
pencil on paper

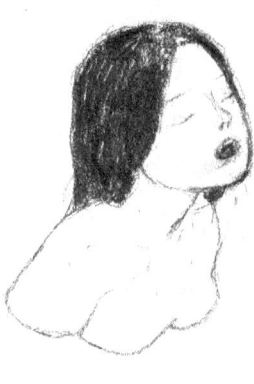

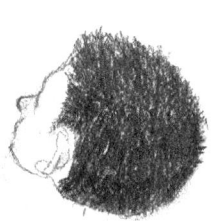

Jun Cen, *Entrance/Exit 3*,
pencil on paper

Jun Cen, *Entrance/Exit 4*,
pencil on paper

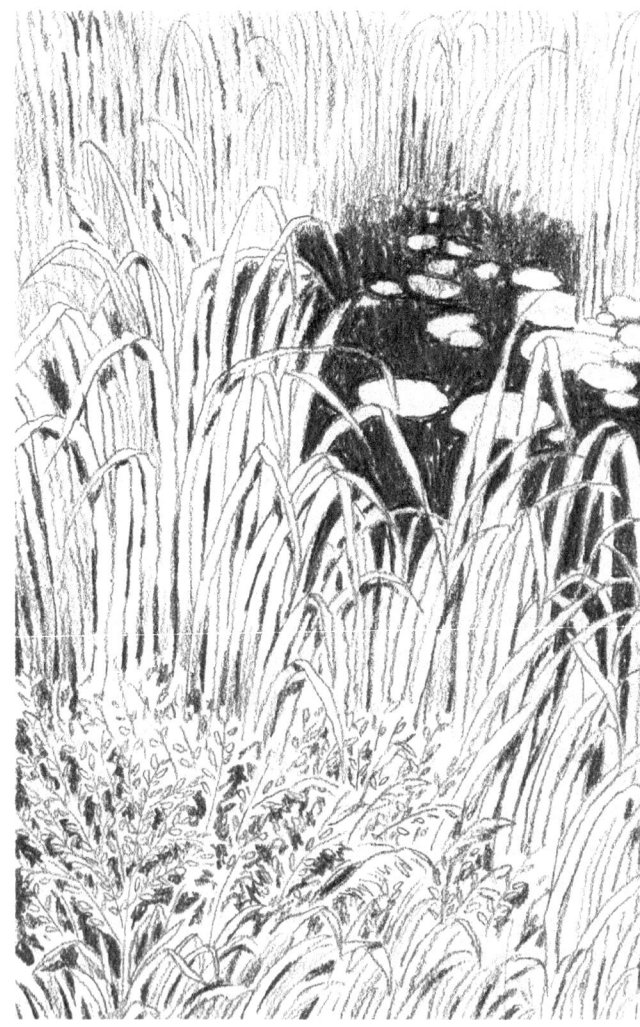

Jun Cen, *Entrance/Exit 3*,
pencil on paper

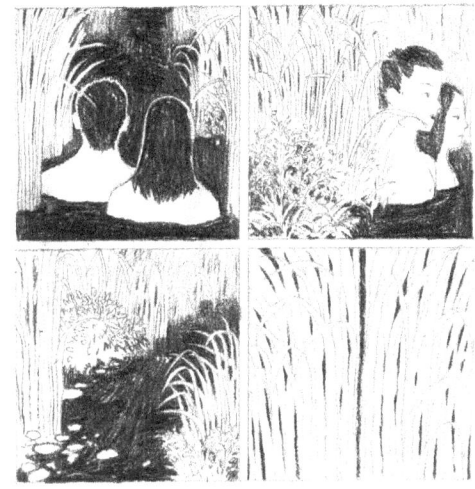

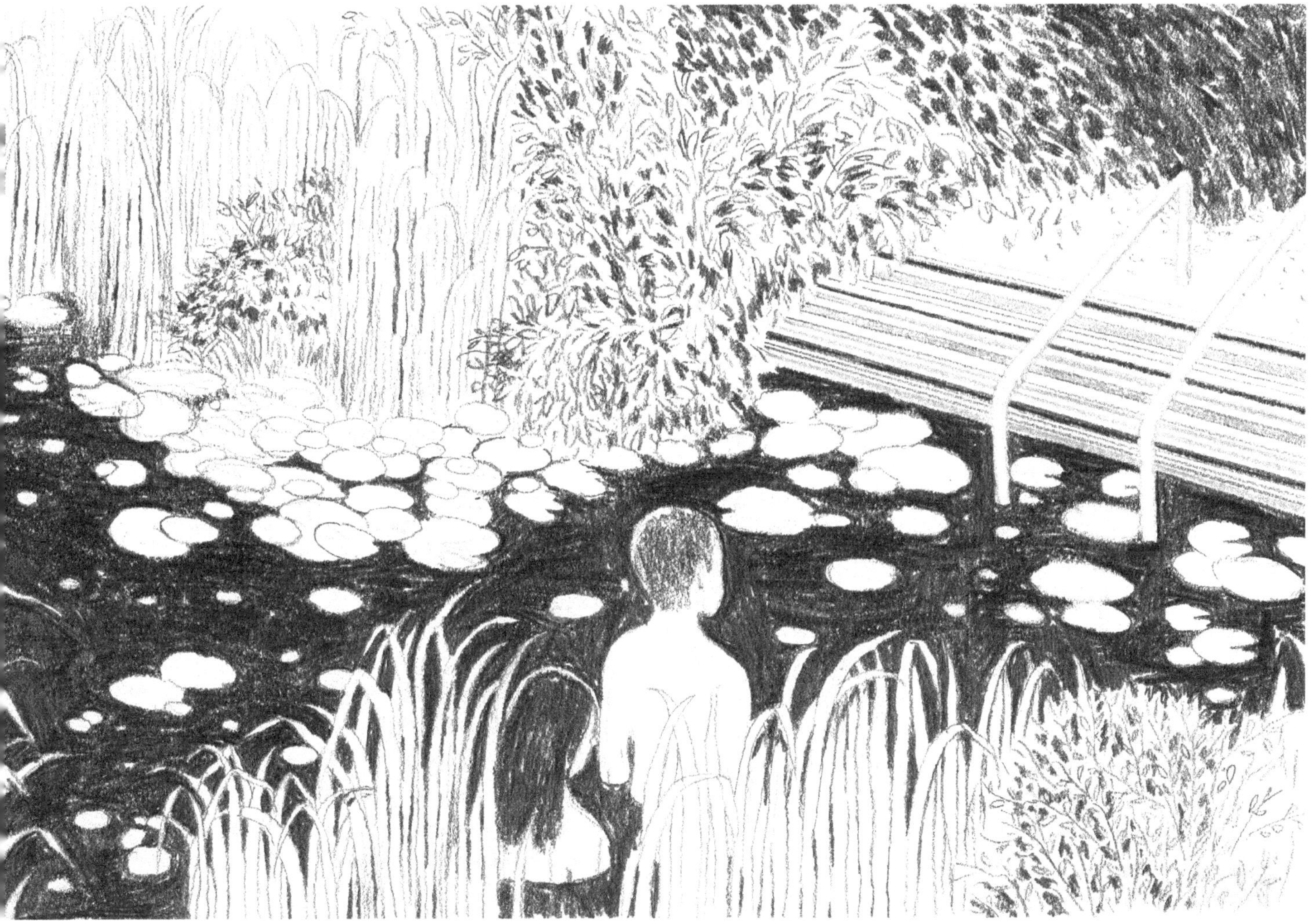

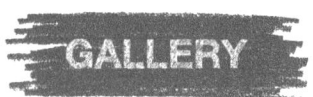

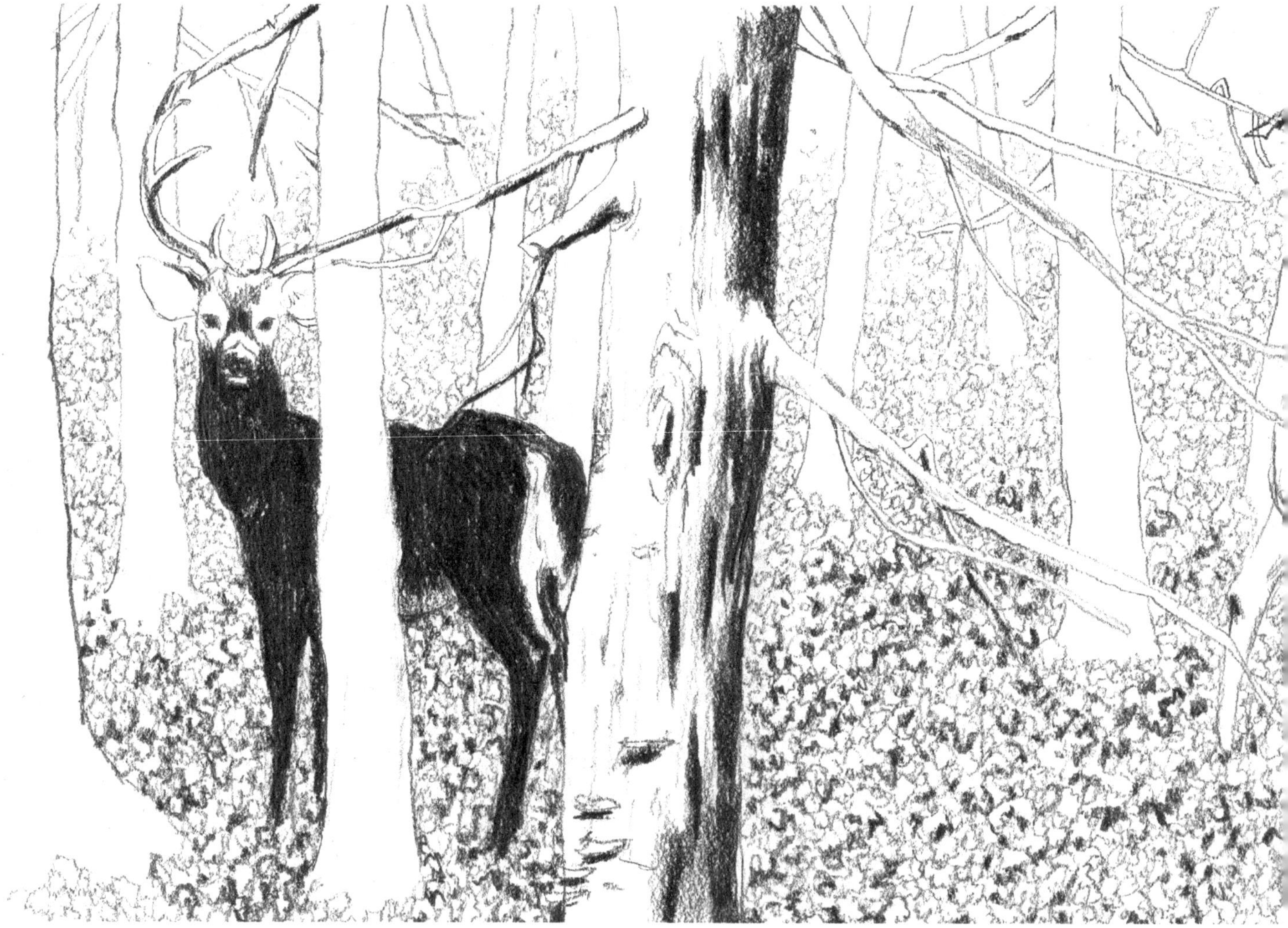

Jun Cen, *Entrance/Exit 6,*
pencil on paper

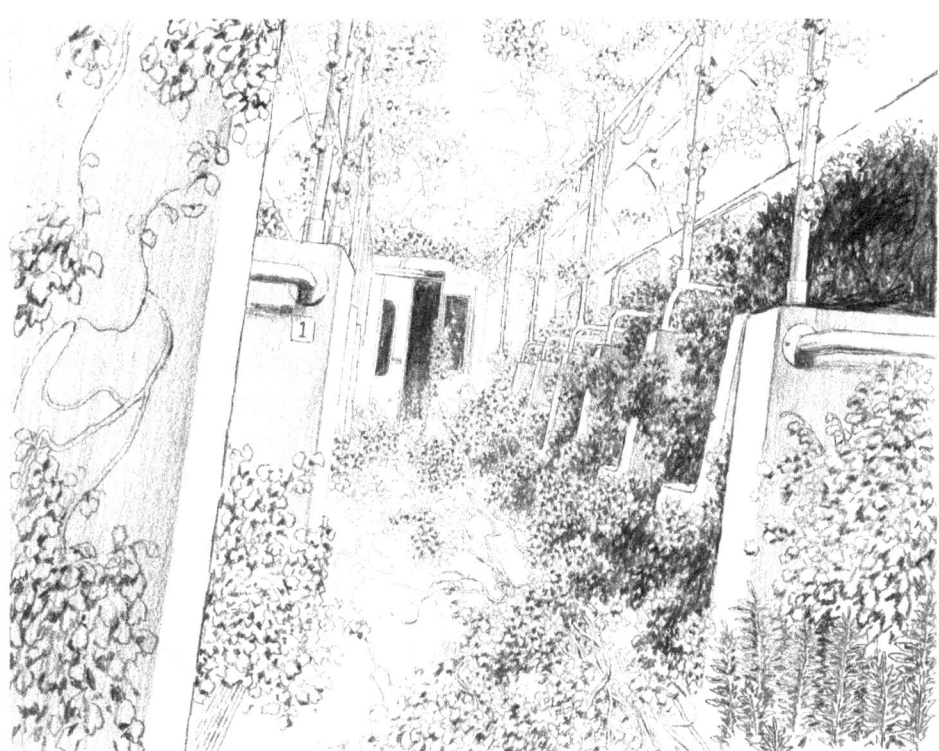

Jun Cen, *Mutual Tunnels 1*, pencil on paper

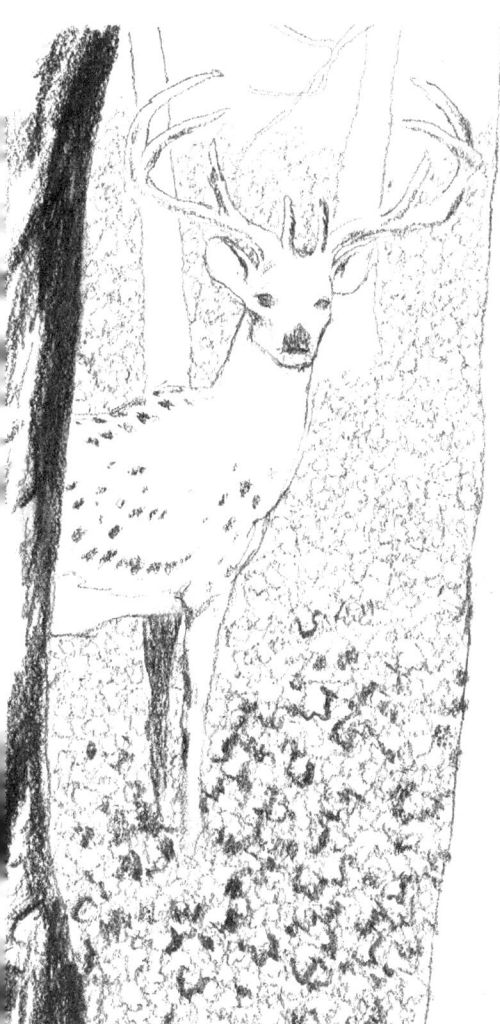

CHAPTER 2

DRAWING WITH TONE

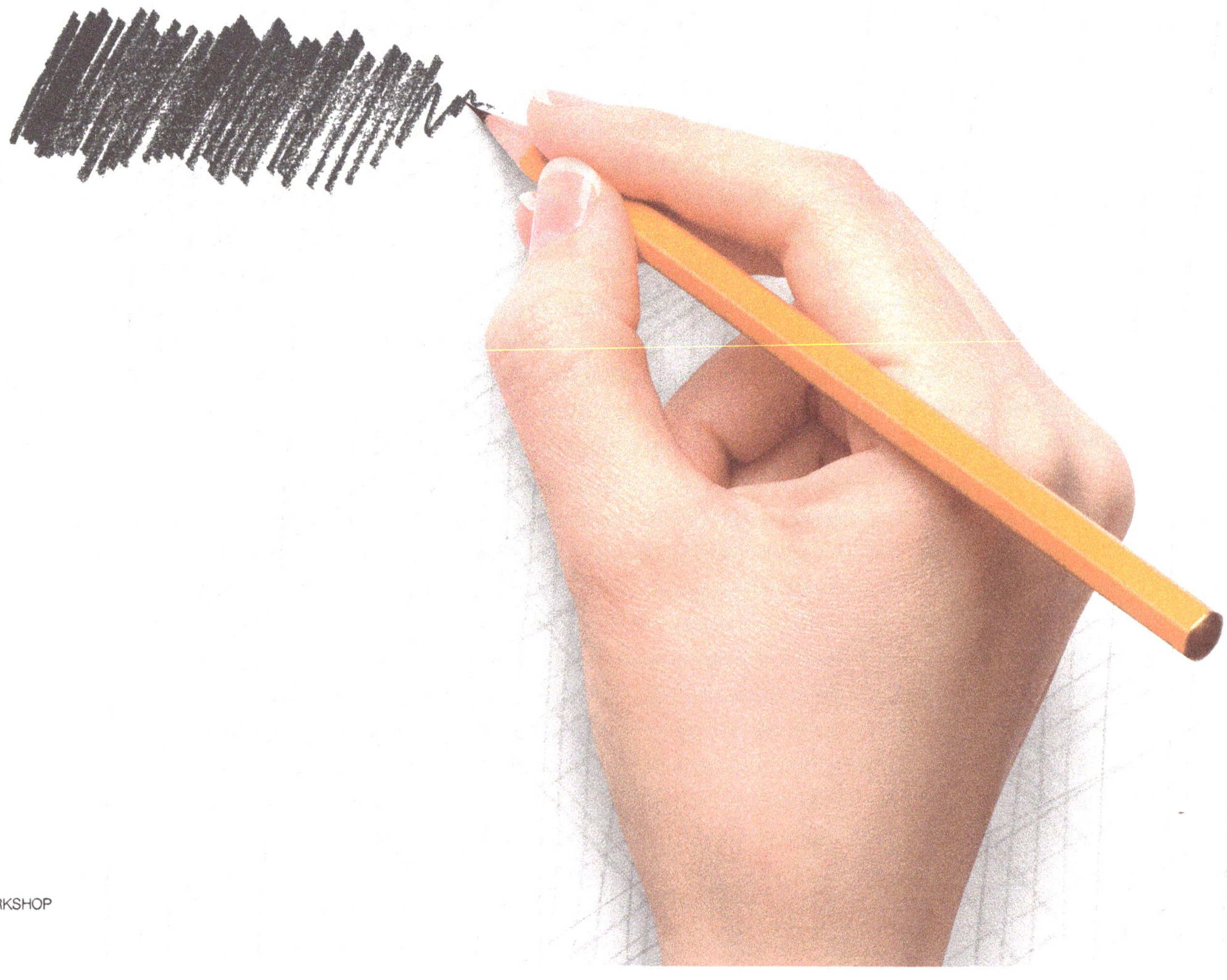

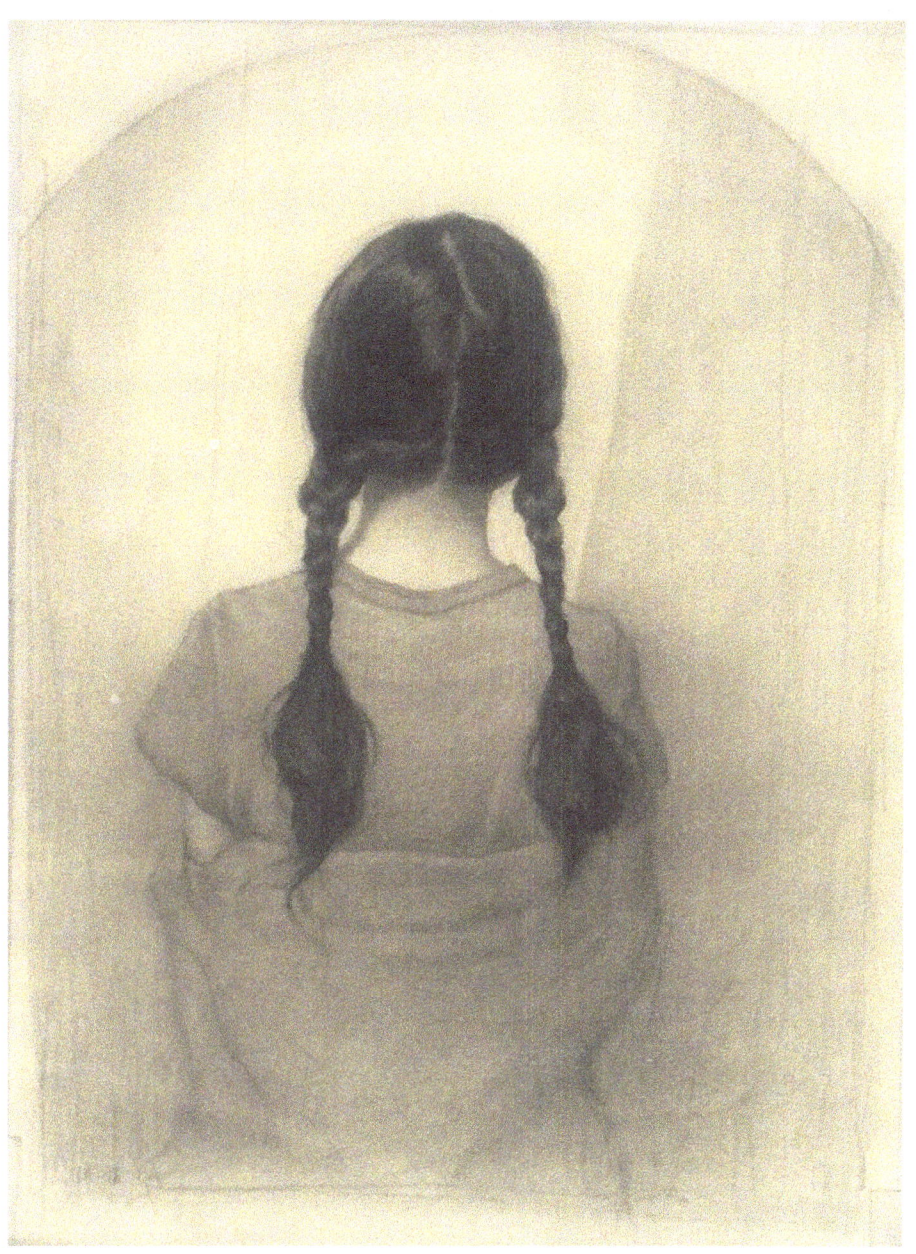

Isaac Pelepko,
Mako with Braids,
pencil on paper

Tonal drawing is based on the observation of light and how it defines what we see. The world is visible to our eye through the perception of light and shadow, but in order to draw the world the way the eye actually sees it, an artist has to overcome the instinct toward line.

Understanding tonal drawing is to understand how to interpret the value relationships within the subject being drawn. In other words, it means understanding the relationships between black and white, highlight and shadow, and interpreting these through a range of gray.

Clarity in tonal drawing is created by distinguishing the value relationship between objects and their surroundings instead of through outlining forms. In pure tonal drawing, there is no line at all, or line is created by the intersection of planes of differing values.

GETTING STARTED IN TONE

Drawing in tone forces the artist to rely on value relationships rather than line to delineate forms. It's often said that lines do not truly exist, but they are a function of the imagination. Observing tone and value, on the other hand, are reality based: Our eye interprets what it actually sees rather than what the mind understands.

I should add here that tonal drawing is not the same as photorealistic drawing. Even though photorealism relies on a similar principle of tonal, nonlinear observation, the camera is an editing tool that imposes its own interpretation of light that is different from how our eye perceives it. We will cover photorealism in a later chapter.

UNDERSTANDING TONAL RANGE (USING A WIDE RANGE OR A LIMITED ONE)

A tonal range is simply the range of gray values between the lightest light in an image, and the darkest dark. Because there is no absolute black, the range is always relative to the distance between the darkest and lightest tone, so an image can have a very wide tonal range or a very narrow one. A wide range has deep blacks, bright whites, and a broad range of gray in between.

The breadth of the range is usually determined by how dark the darkest dark is, or how bright the brightest white is. An image can have very dark darks but only marginally lighter values for the brightest tones and, therefore, a very narrow range (as in a dimly lit room). Likewise, the range can have very bright whites, but with the darkest tone being a medium gray, leaving the range very narrow but on the lighter end of the range (think of foggy morning light).

BUILDING RELATIONSHIPS WITHIN THE IMAGE

Interpreting value relationships in an image is based on a relative scale; the darkness of an object can be determined by its relationship to its surroundings. When you observe your subject, ask yourself, "Is this object darker or lighter than the object next to it? Is the object in the foreground darker or lighter than the background?" Determining these relationships should be broad at first, then narrowed to be more specific.

Start by looking at the entire image and identifying the darkest and lightest areas. Specifically, what is the darkest dark and the lightest light? You may find squinting helpful, as it reduces the perceivable information to the most general forms.

EXERCISE 1: TAKING CREATIVE CONTROL OF THE VALUES

A photograph of an image fixes the value range of a subject in relation to the camera's shutter speed and aperture. The result is not a true representation of light and reality, but a mechanical approximation. This approximation is often taken as the de facto absolute in interpreting reality: Photos are frequently used as a reference for drawings, but the camera reads light differently than the eye.

The locking in of values is significant in terms of natural observation. The eye has a far more relative system of interpreting light. The pupil is constantly opening and closing to let in more and less light, so it adjusts value relationships based on the focus of the eye.

If the eye focuses on a shadow, the pupil opens wider, letting in more light. It can allow the eye to see higher contrast and a wider value range than when the eye refocuses on a wider expanse of space.

For instance, in drawing a portrait, looking at the face as a whole will dilute the details but give a sense of the overall light and shadow. The details in the shadowed portions of the portrait will be obscured in low contrast when the face is looked at as a whole. Yet the eye, unlike the camera, can focus on specific details in the shadows and perceive them with a heightened contrast. Drawing the heightened details without returning your focus to the whole face can lead to over-rendering the details and losing the overall tonal relationships in the portrait.

All of this is to say that in drawing from life, the value range is never fixed and is always relative. This can be tricky to overcome, but realizing that a value range is not fixed can also be liberating. It allows you to create a tonal drawing using an arbitrary value range: the value range can be as narrow or as wide as the artist decides.

For instance, by establishing the darkest dark in an image as a middle gray, and a whitest white at the opposite end of the scale, the values in between will exist in the usual proportional relationship, but will be lighter on the scale, resulting in a lighter-contrast image. The reverse will be true if the lightest light is middle gray, with darkest black at the opposite end of the scale: the image will be interpreted as shadowy, in a darker range.

This choice and control gives the artist liberty to go beyond capturing reality accurately, but to interpret it emotionally as well, suggesting mood and drama in a subject.

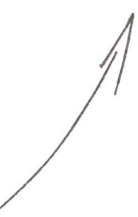

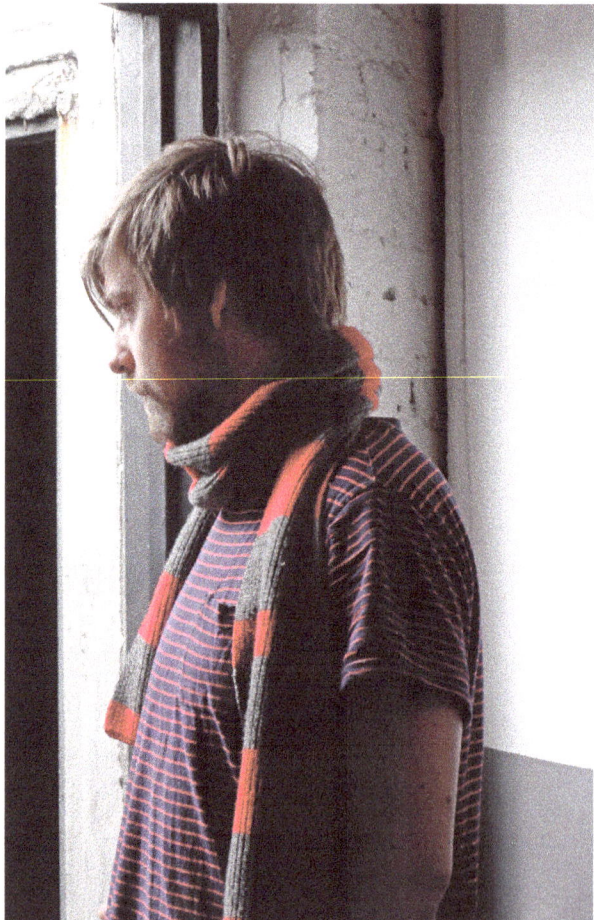

Photo reference
for tonal drawing

Tonal drawing—light range

Tonal drawing—dark range

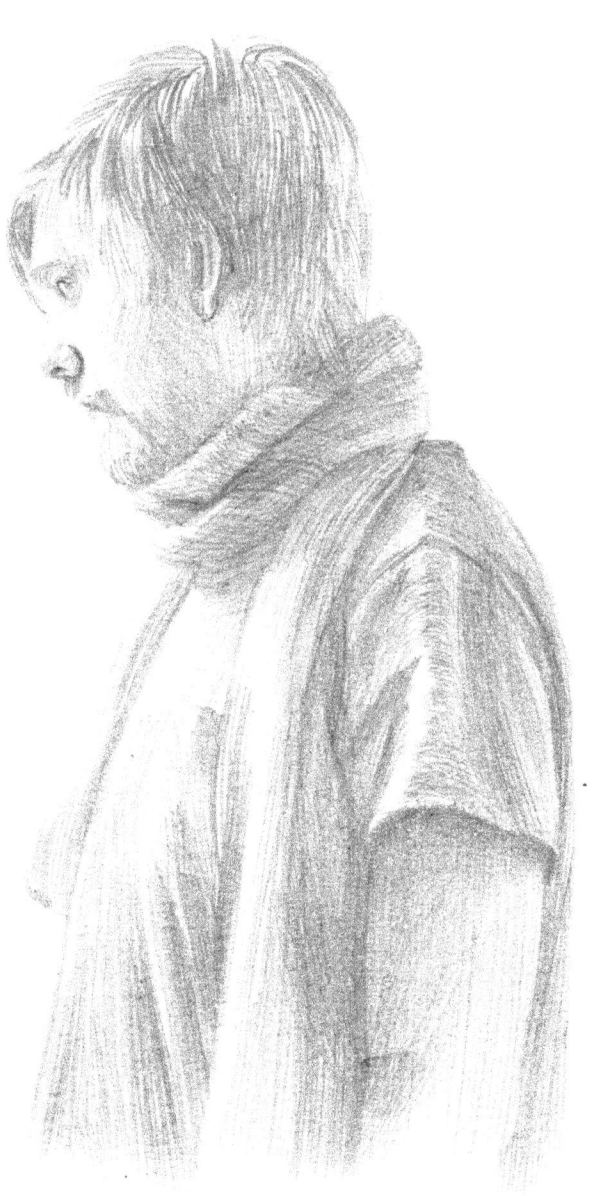
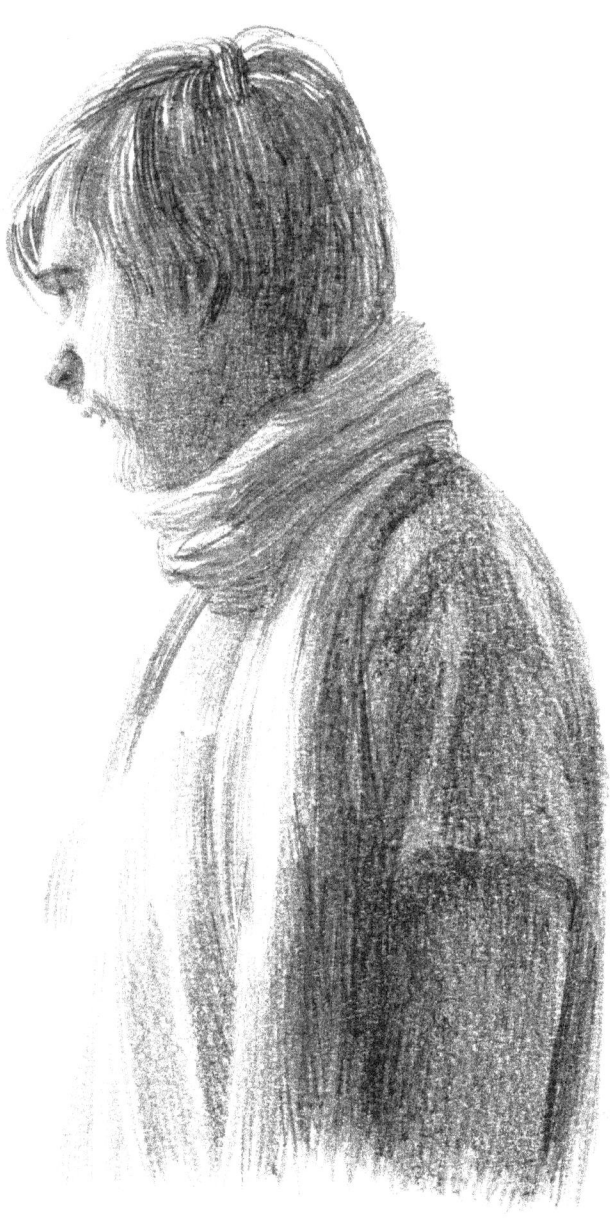

EXERCISE 2: GETTING STARTED

This exercise presents a method for creating a tonal portrait using a photo as a reference. The process starts with creating an even graphite middle tone, extracting the highlights with an eraser, then going back and drawing with the pencil to create the full range of tones that make up the details in the shadows of the portrait. You'll need pencils between the range of 2H for the lighter range and 2B for the darker shadows, plus a chamois cloth or paper towels for blending, and both a kneaded and a plastic eraser.

CREATE AN EVEN TONE

Holding the pencil at about a 45-degree angle to use the broadside of the pencil point, draw in wide, broad strokes over the page. Try to keep the tone even. Work the marks over the entire surface, covering as much of the paper surface as possible.

Once the page is covered, use the chamois cloth to smudge the graphite into an even tone. Hold the cloth as you might hold a dish rag. Smudge the pencil as if you were polishing the page, but without using too much pressure (don't scrub the paper with the cloth). Blend the pencil strokes as much as possible so the surface is as smooth and even as it can be.

If the tone appears too light in some areas, use the pencil to darken those areas further, then blend in the new marks with the cloth to even the tone.

Pencil marks with chamois smudge

Right:
Create an even tone. Begin the smudge from left, working towards the right.

Once you've established an even tone on the paper, study the portrait in the photo. It may help to squint at it to identify where the lightest highlights fall. These are the areas that you will establish first with the plastic eraser, removing areas of the graphite-tone you've created.

Start to pull highlights out of the graphite with the eraser. Avoid using it to draw lines: instead, look at the shapes of the highlights and re-create them. This will take some practice, but it's essential to seeing tone instead of line. Squinting at the drawing will help you see the broad shapes of highlights — stick with the broad shapes to start, the details will come later.

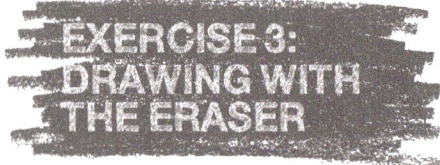

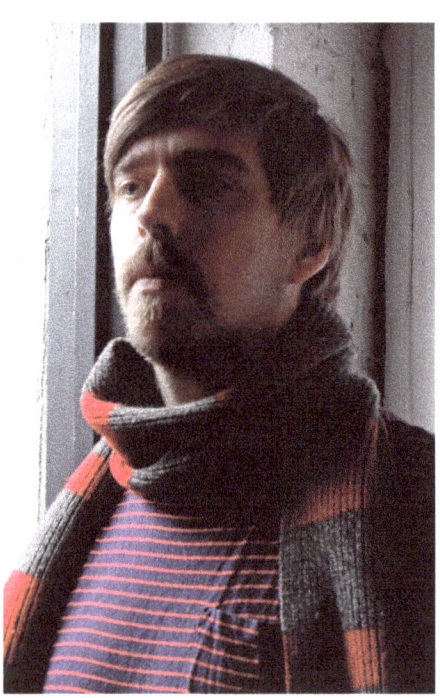

Photo reference for tonal drawing

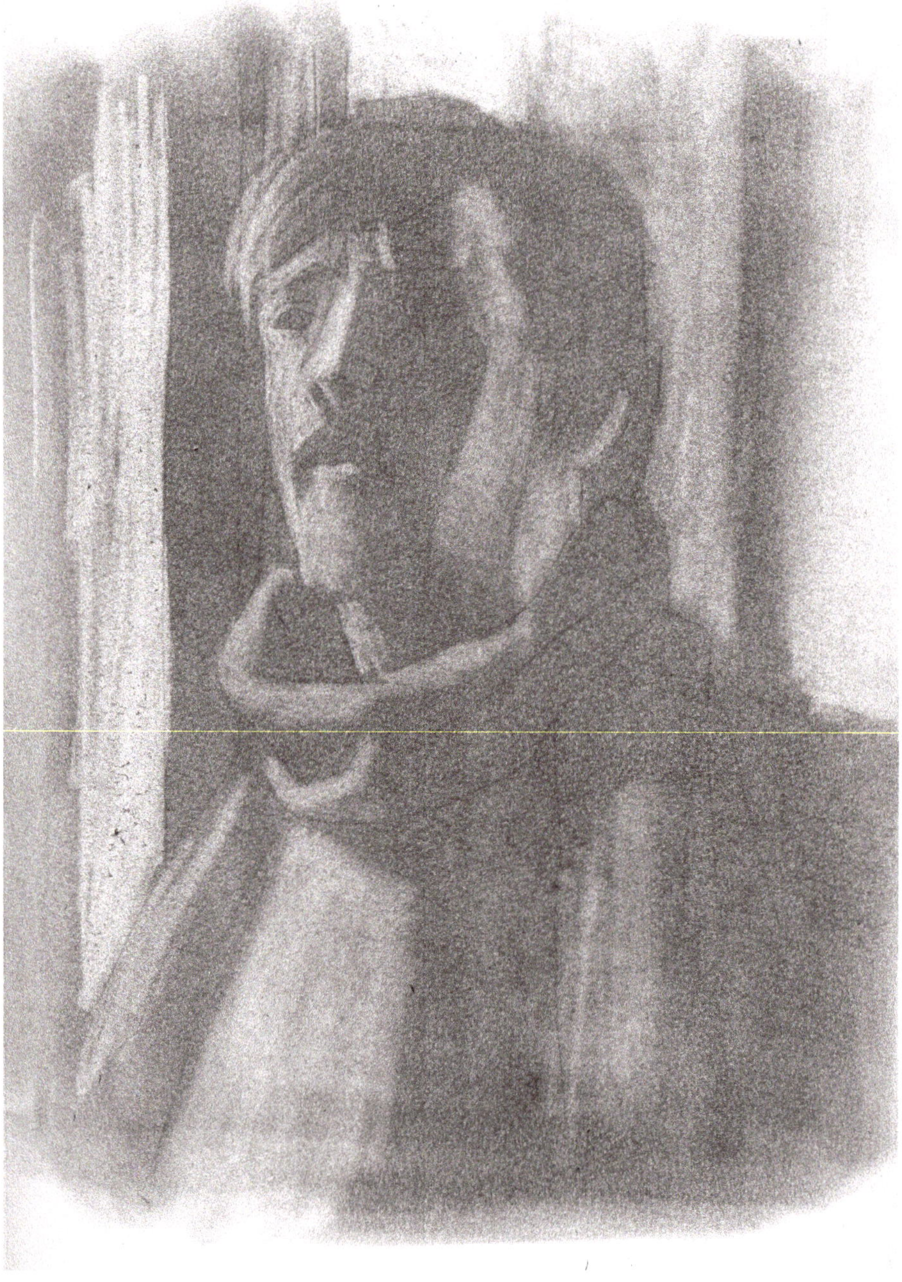

Removing tone with an eraser

If the highlights look wrong, or you removed too much graphite with the eraser, use the chamois cloth to reapply tone to the paper.

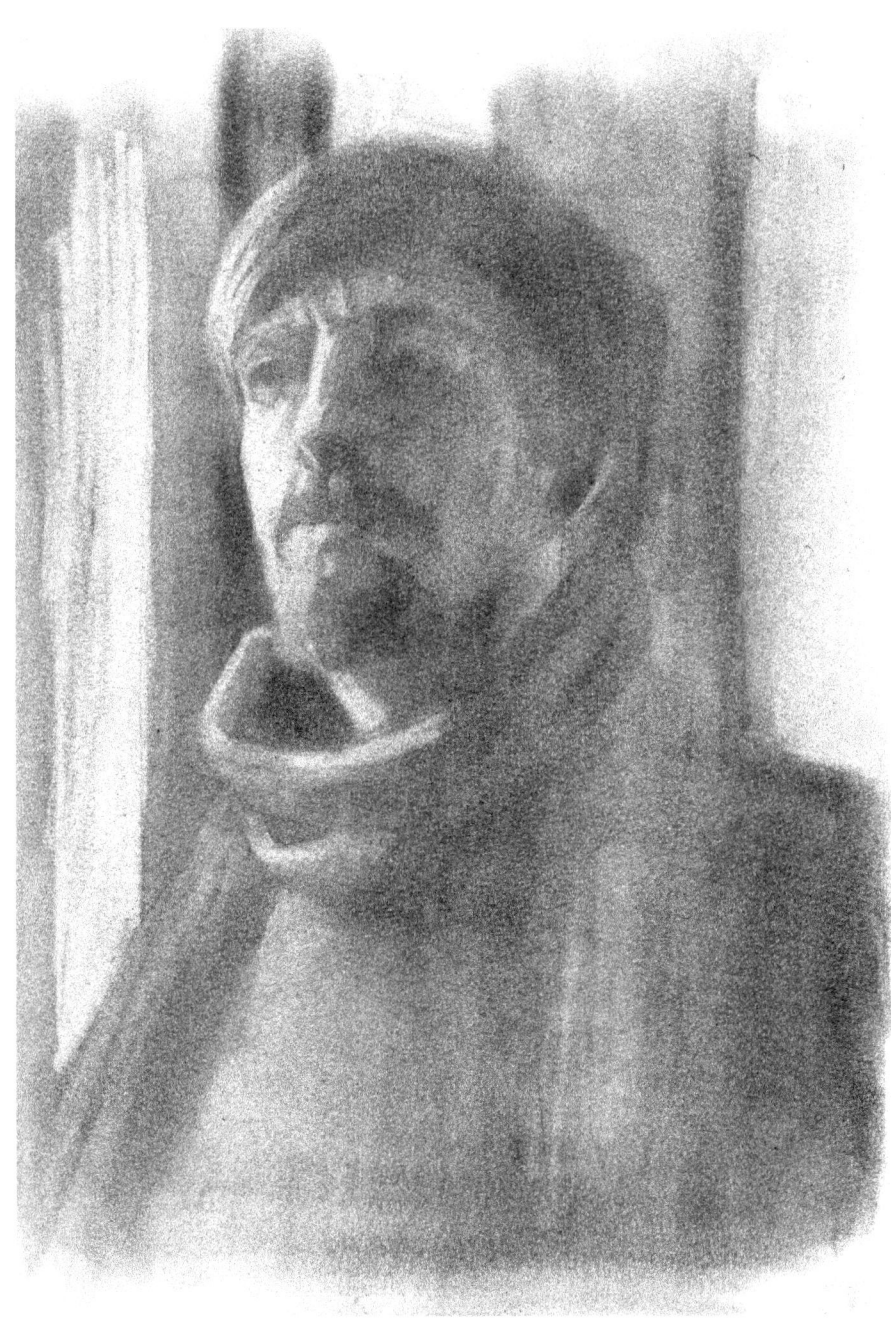

Adding darker values with a pencil

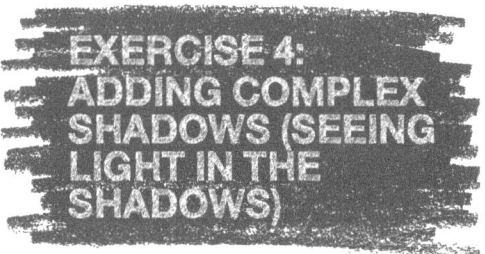

EXERCISE 4: ADDING COMPLEX SHADOWS (SEEING LIGHT IN THE SHADOWS)

Once the initial highlights are pulled out of the graphite, the drawing will consist of two tones: a medium dark shadow in the darker half of the value range and the highlights in the lighter half. You'll now work with a pencil within each tonal area to create a greater range.

Within the highlights, add details using mainly the H-range pencils. Depending on how delicate the details are, use the point of the tip and light pressure on the pencil. For a darker mark, use more pressure on the pencil. For a darker grade, depending on how dark the shadow needs to be, consider using a different pencil. You might move, for example, from a 2H to an HB.

While you add details in the highlighted portions of the portrait, try to prevent them from becoming as dark as the initial graphite tone. To soften the details if the pencil work becomes too dark, use the kneaded eraser: flatten one edge of the eraser and lightly tap it on the details to lighten them. Tapping on the drawing will lift small amounts of graphite, lightening the details without erasing them.

Adding line

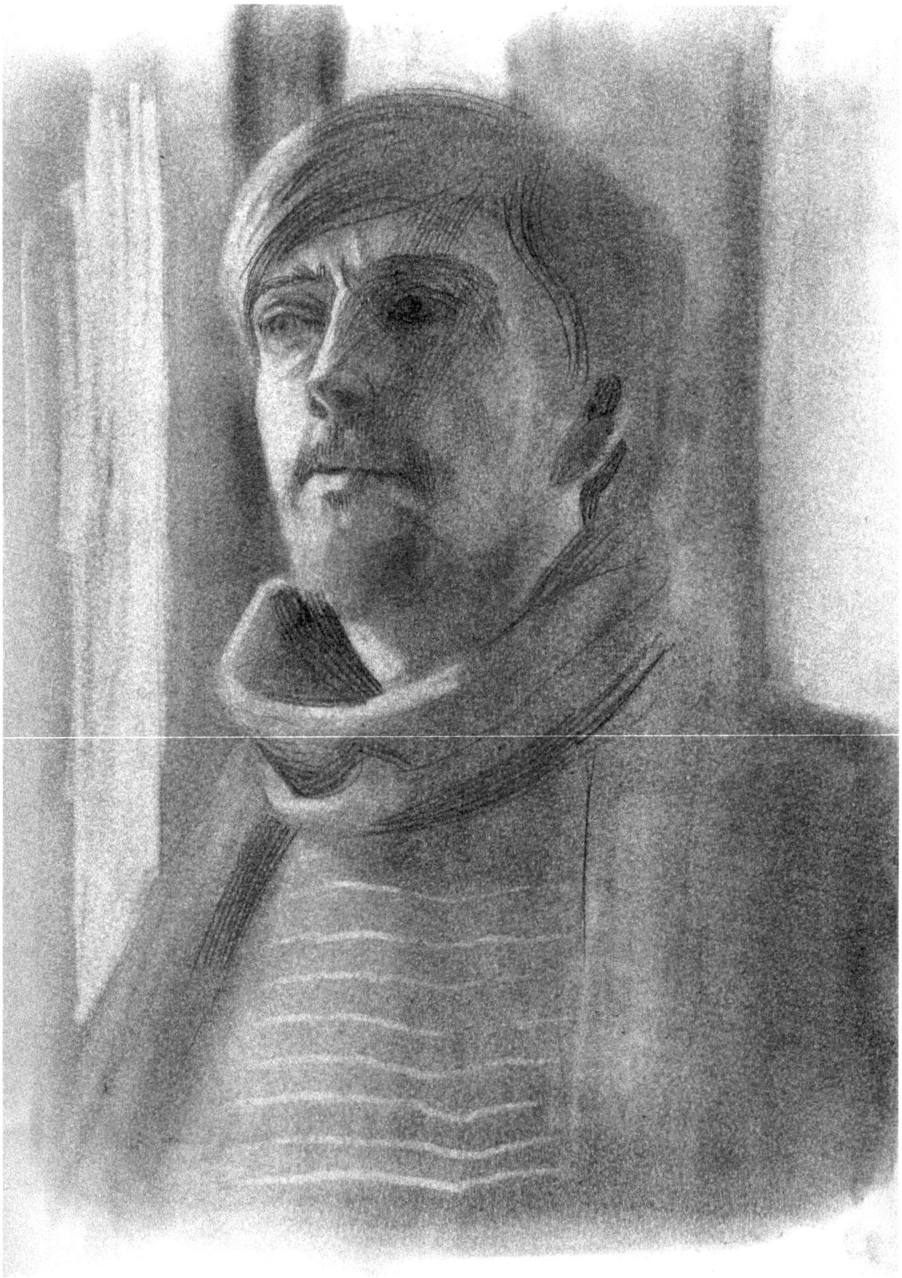

When darkening and adding detail to the shadow portions of the portrait, creating deeper and more dramatic shadows, use the darker range of pencils, such as those in the B range. For adding more subtle transitions, use the lighter range, such as those in the H range.

This system allows for precise detail and adds a great degree of depth and volume in the drawing. At the same time, it keeps the value range organized and all of the details clear.

Finishing with line and texture

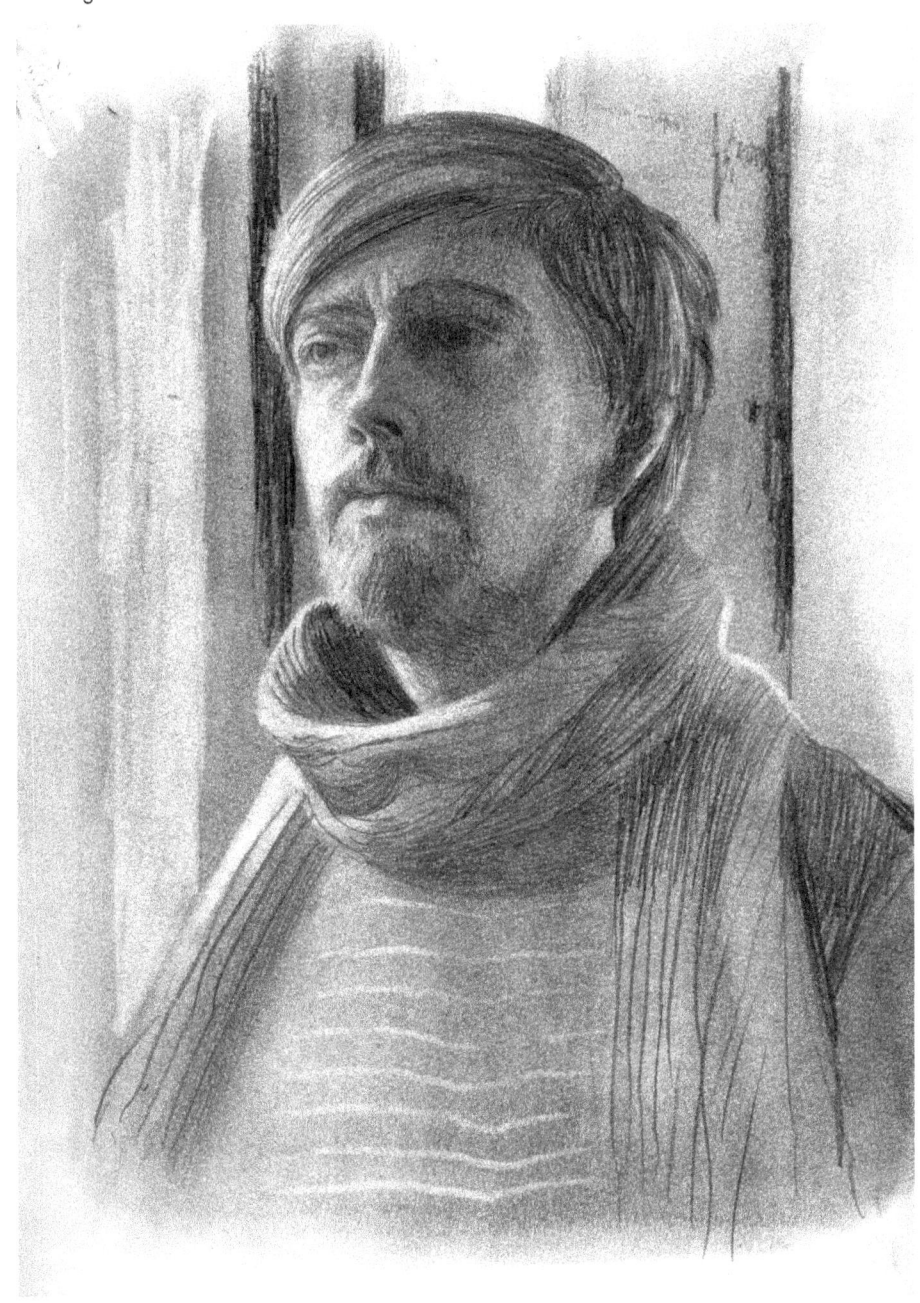

EXERCISE 5: FOLLOW UP: BUILDING TONE WITH MARKS

Drawing with tone, using a chamois cloth, and pulling out the highlights with an eraser will show you how to draw without relying on line. Through this technique, you'll understand how tone works in a drawing, how to control value, and how to see light correctly. Once these foundational points are clear, using other techniques to draw with tone becomes easier and can be used to create more expressive drawings.

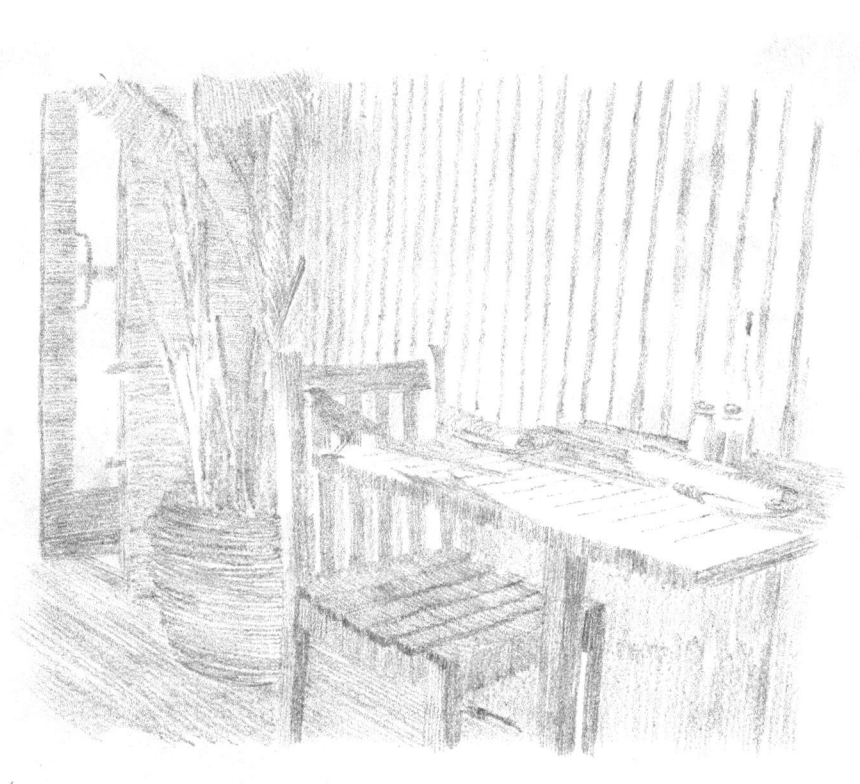

Use lines to create a light tone.

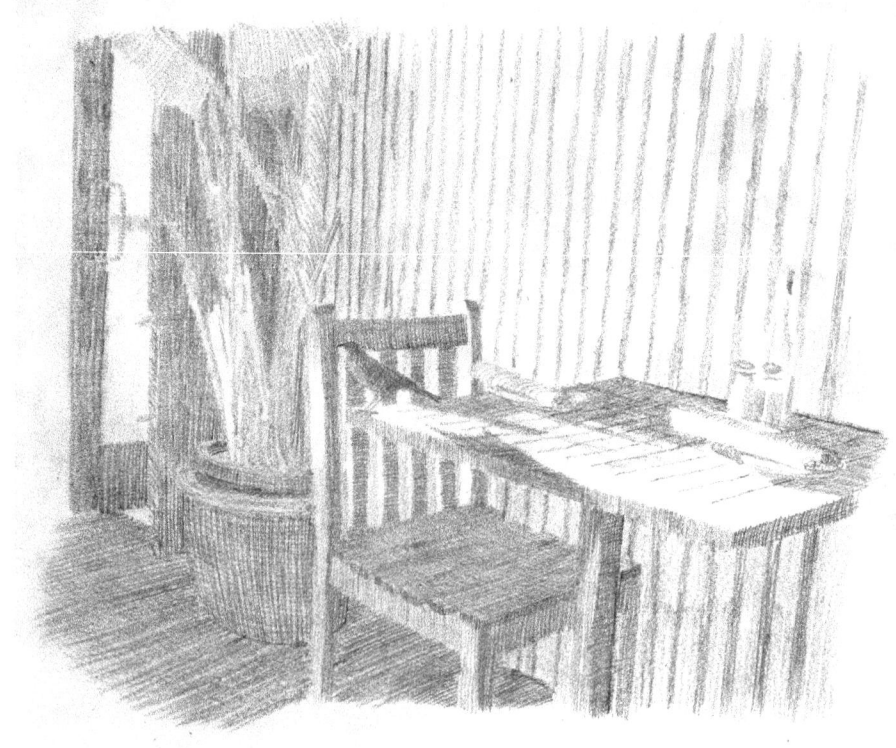

Use crosshatching to create middle tones.

For instance, you might combine line drawing with tonal drawing. Start by creating a line drawing that is simple, has no shading, and is made with basic contours. Start adding shadows, creating the shadows as an even tone at first. Focus on the larger, more general shadows. Again, squinting will help direct your attention to the general elements of shadow and light and away from the details that should be dealt with later.

Once the general areas of shadows are drawn, work further into the darks. Look for the details within the shadows and describe those with an even darker shadow. The depth of the drawing will increase with each new pass at the shadows, but the idea is to not get caught up in one area of the drawing. Keep moving across the entire image, developing it as a whole.

The last step in the drawing is to add the darkest darks. There should only be a few parts of the drawing that have these dark punctuations. It's these spots of highest contrast that attract the eye the most. They will help control how the eye is led through the drawing.

Add the darkest darks—there should only be a few. They will help lead the eye through the drawing.

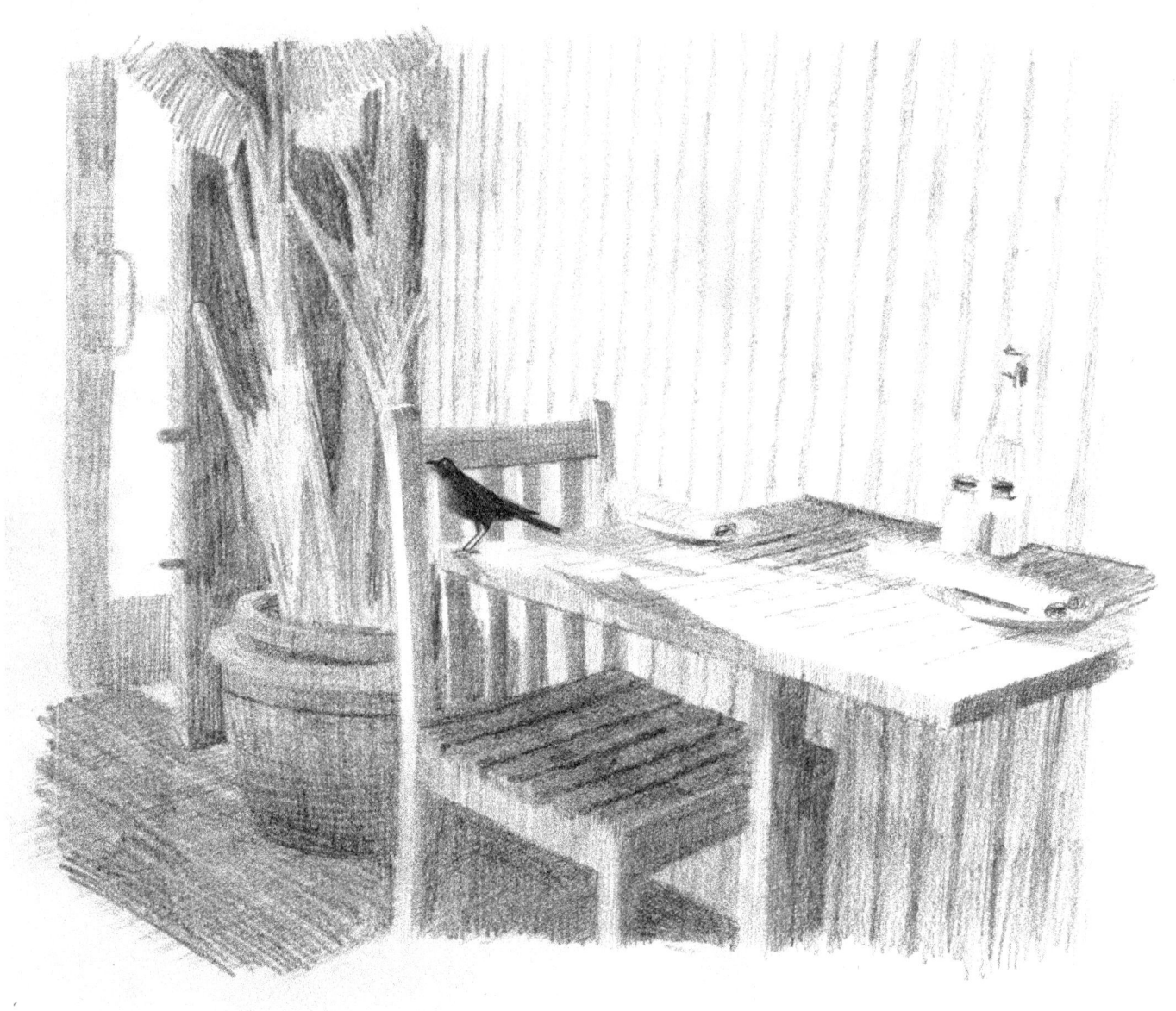

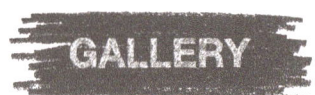

Isaac Pelepko,
Antonia's Hair,
pencil on paper

Isaac Pelepko,
Raven with Rope,
pencil on paper

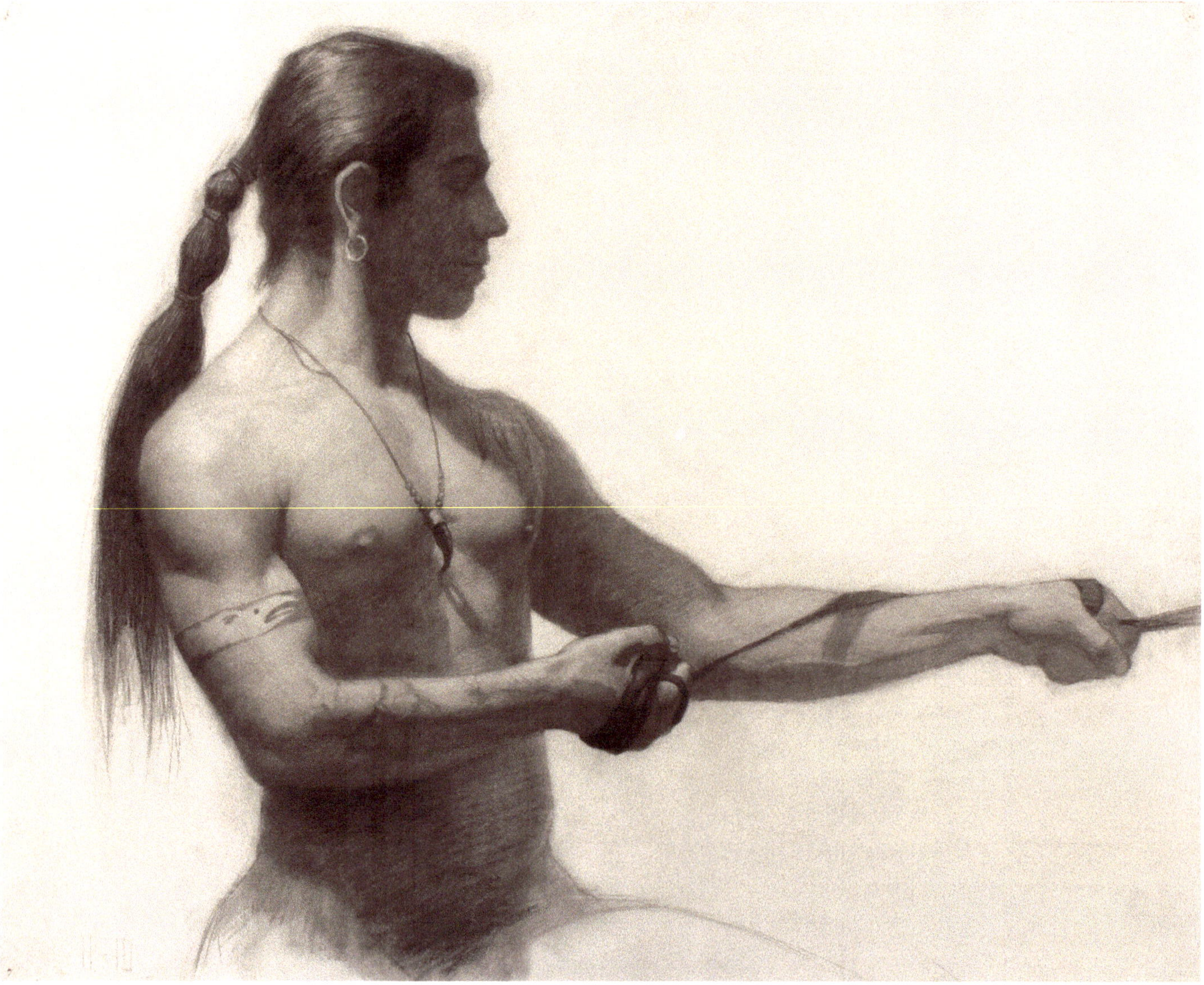

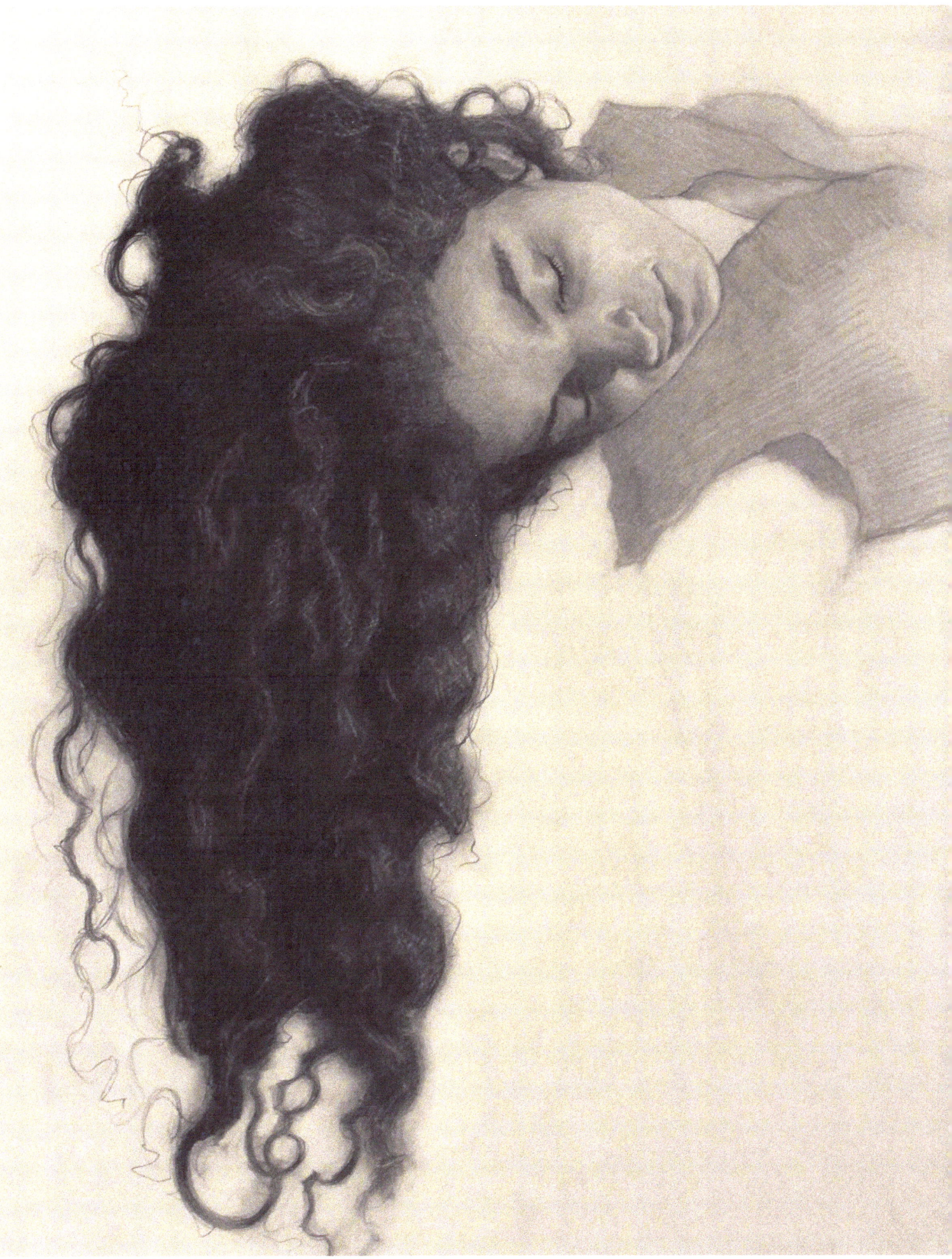

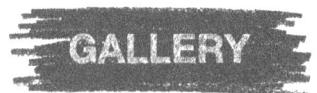

top:
Henrique de Franca,
Torpor #10,
pencil on paper

bottom:
Henrique de Franca,
Torpor #13,
pencil on paper

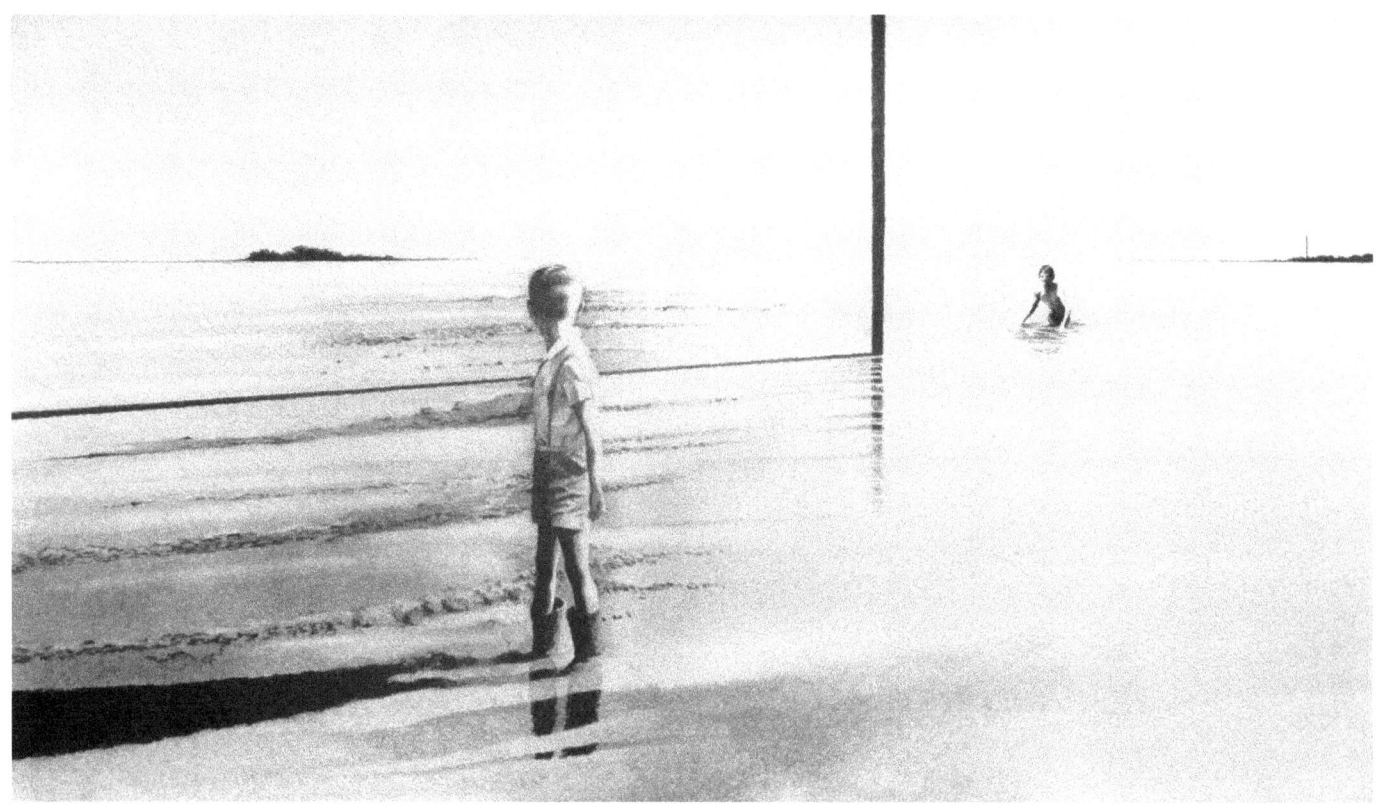

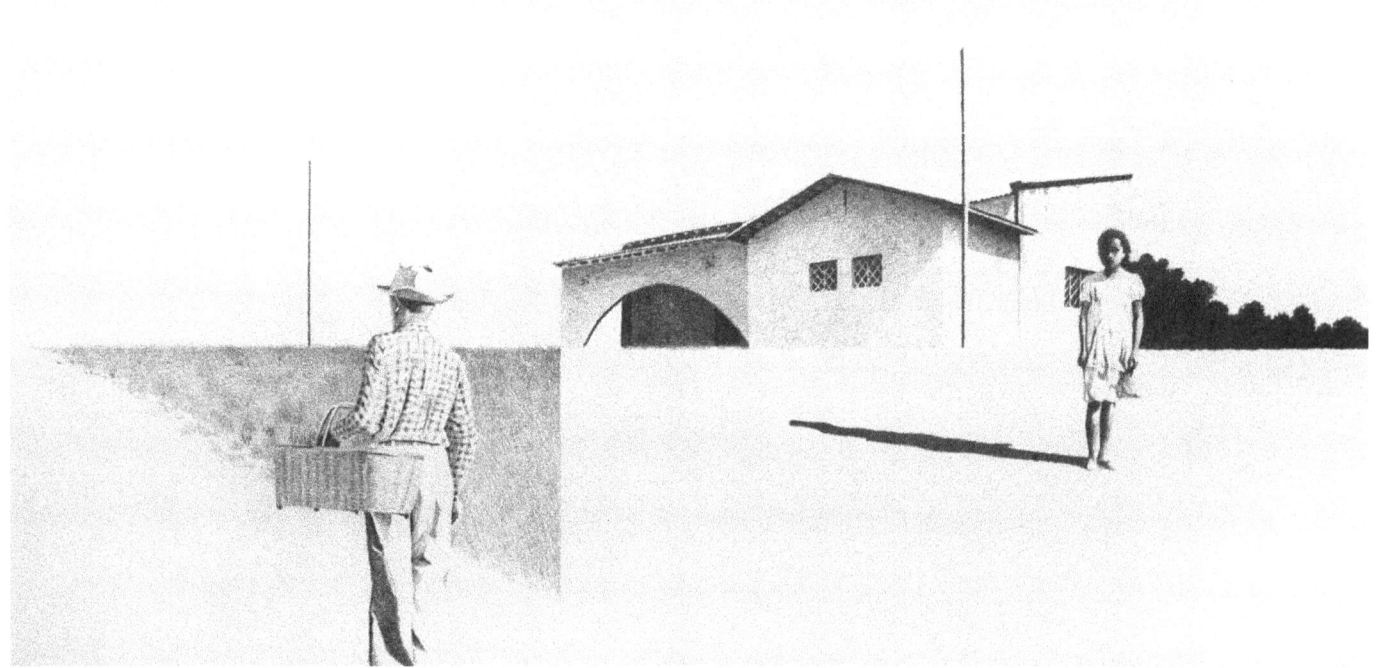

top:
Henrique de Franca,
Torpor #11,
pencil on paper

bottom:
Henrique de Franca,
Torpor #12,
pencil on paper

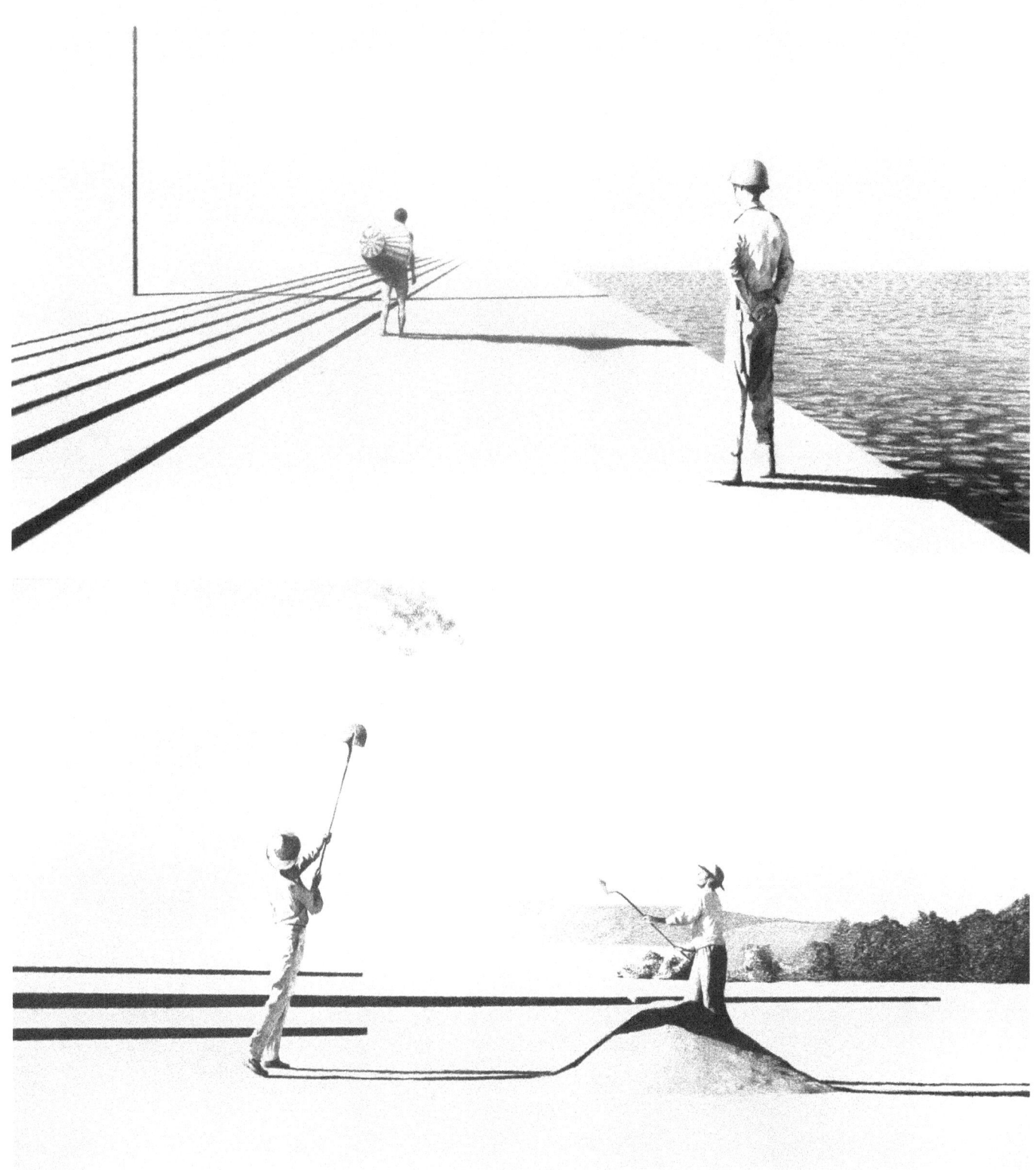

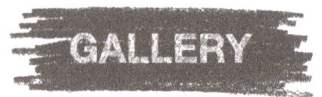

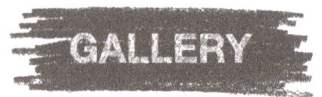

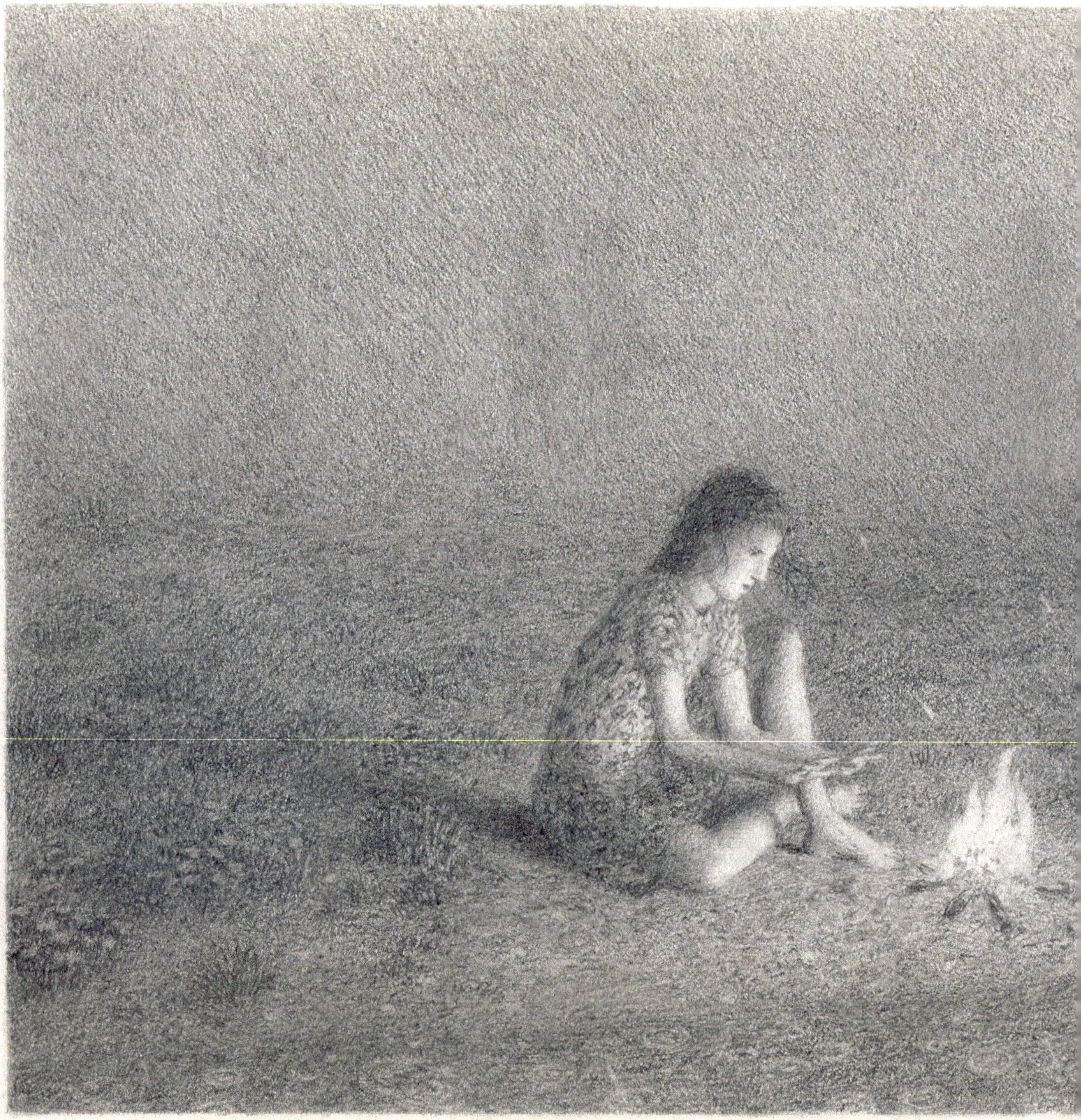

WIESENFELD

Aaron Wiesenfeld,
Refugio,
pencil on paper

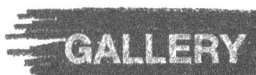

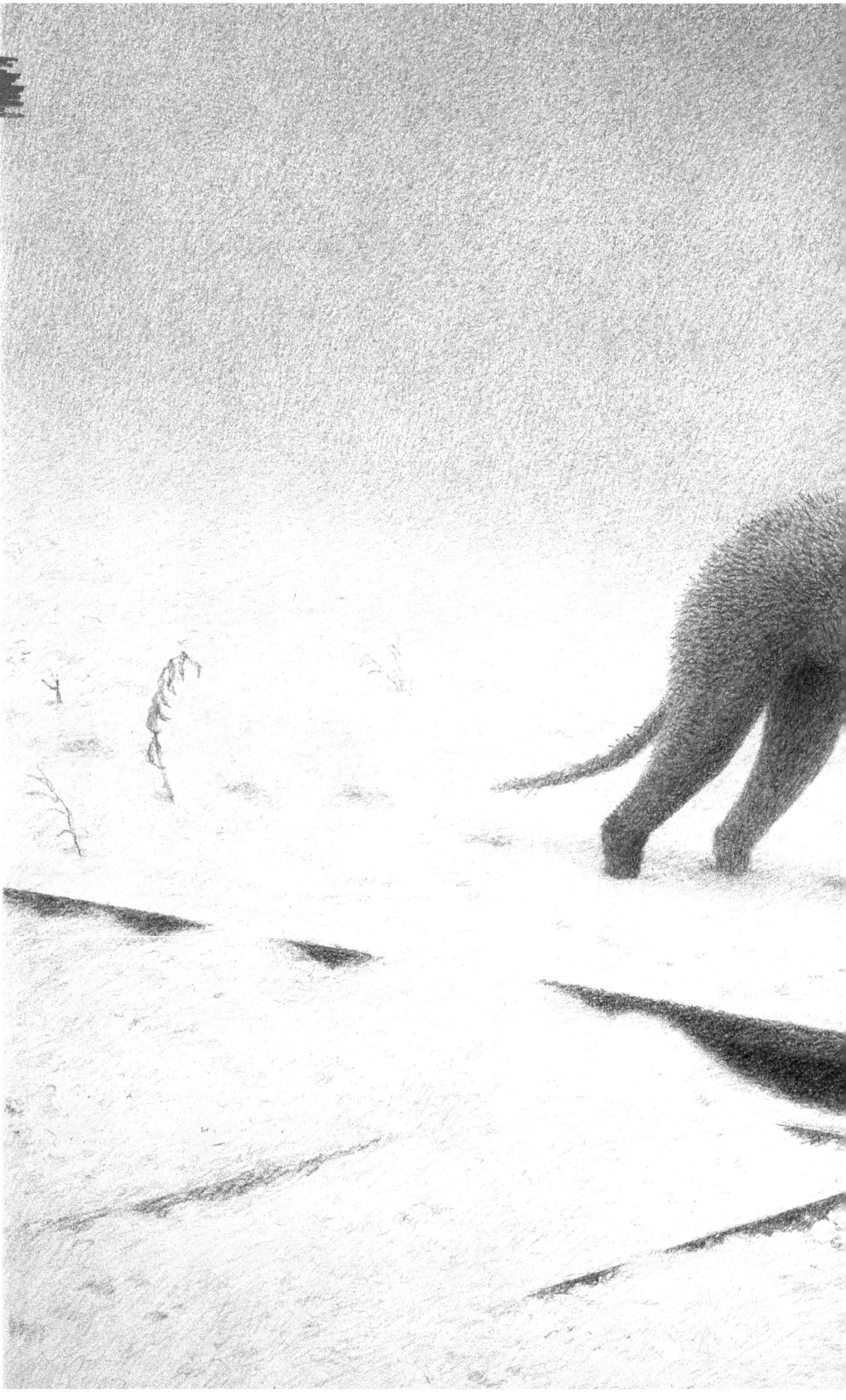

Aaron Wiesenfeld,
Tracks,
pencil on paper

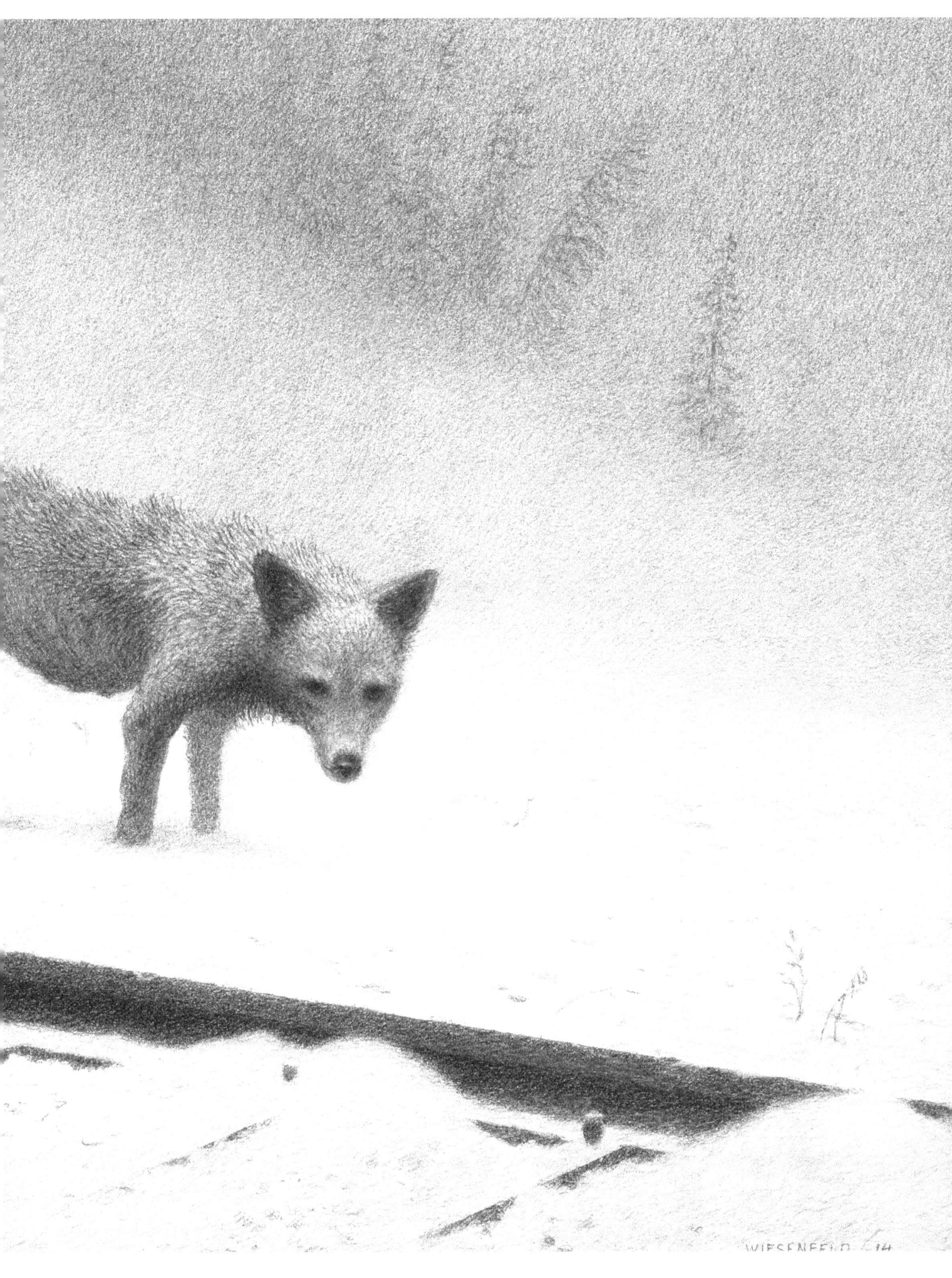

WIESENFELD '14

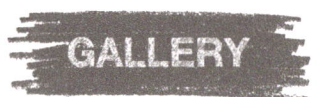

Amaya Gurpide,
Saudade (detail),
pencil and chalk
on paper

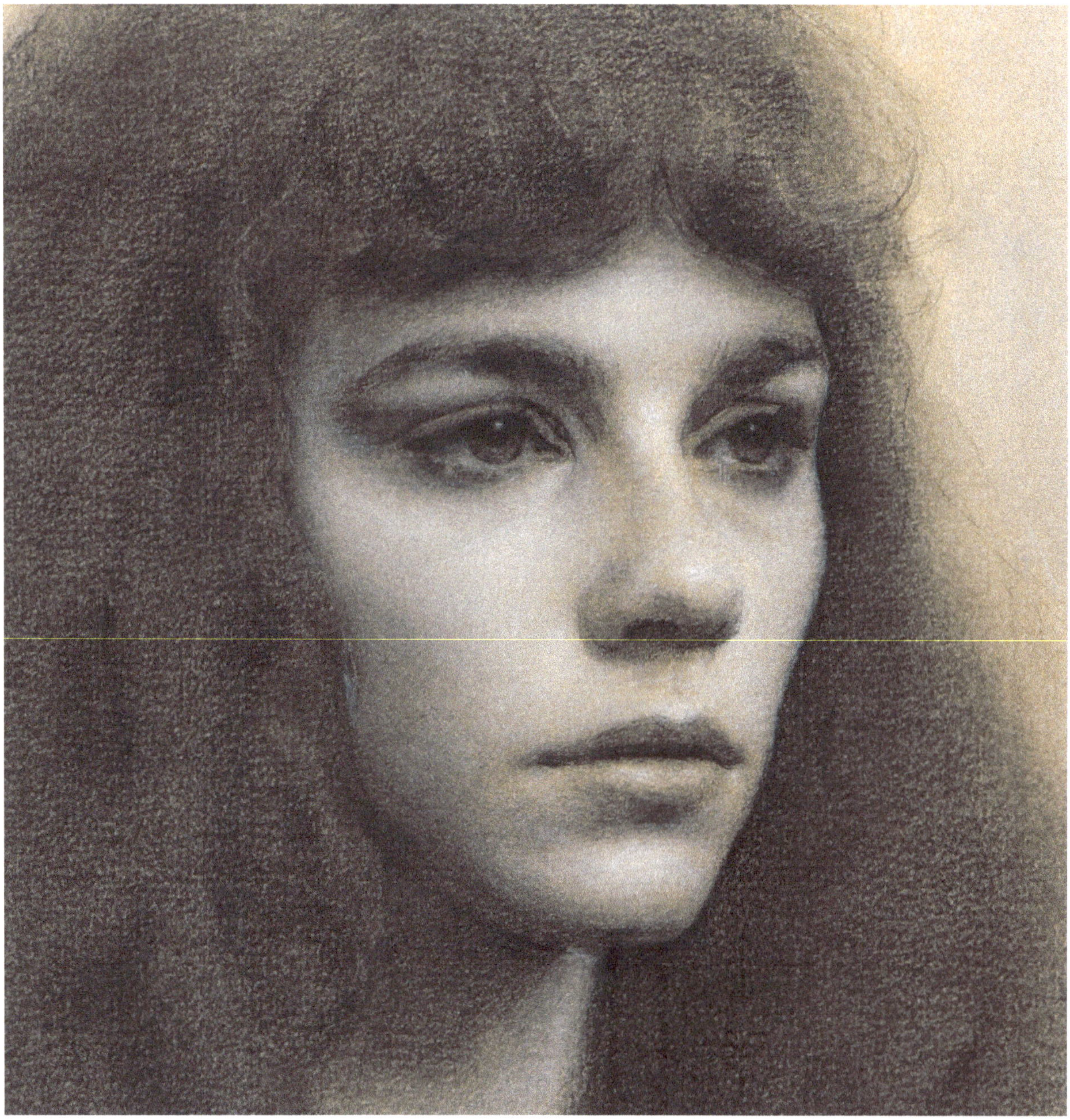

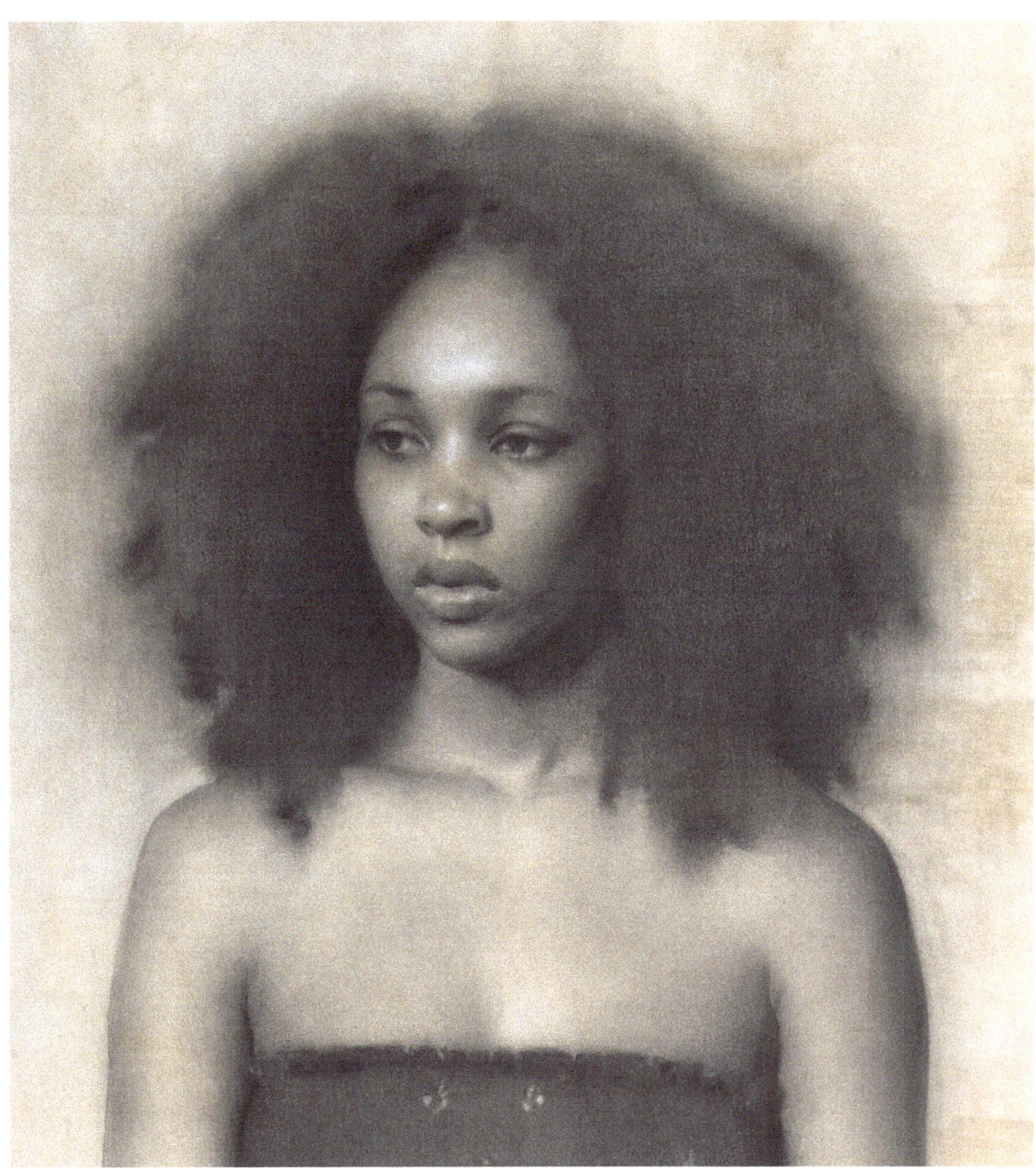

Amaya Gurpide,
Maryum (detail),
pencil, conte, chalk,
and gouache on
paper

CHAPTER 3

DRAWING QUICKLY

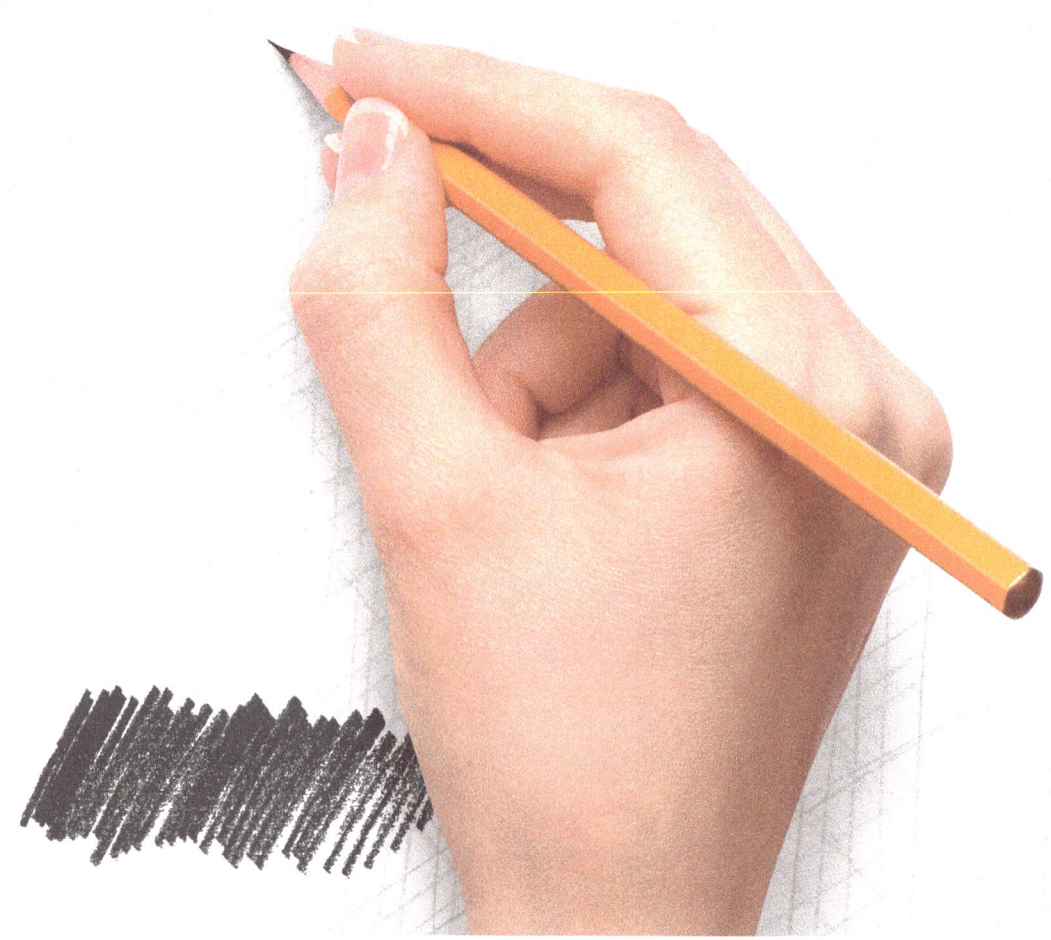

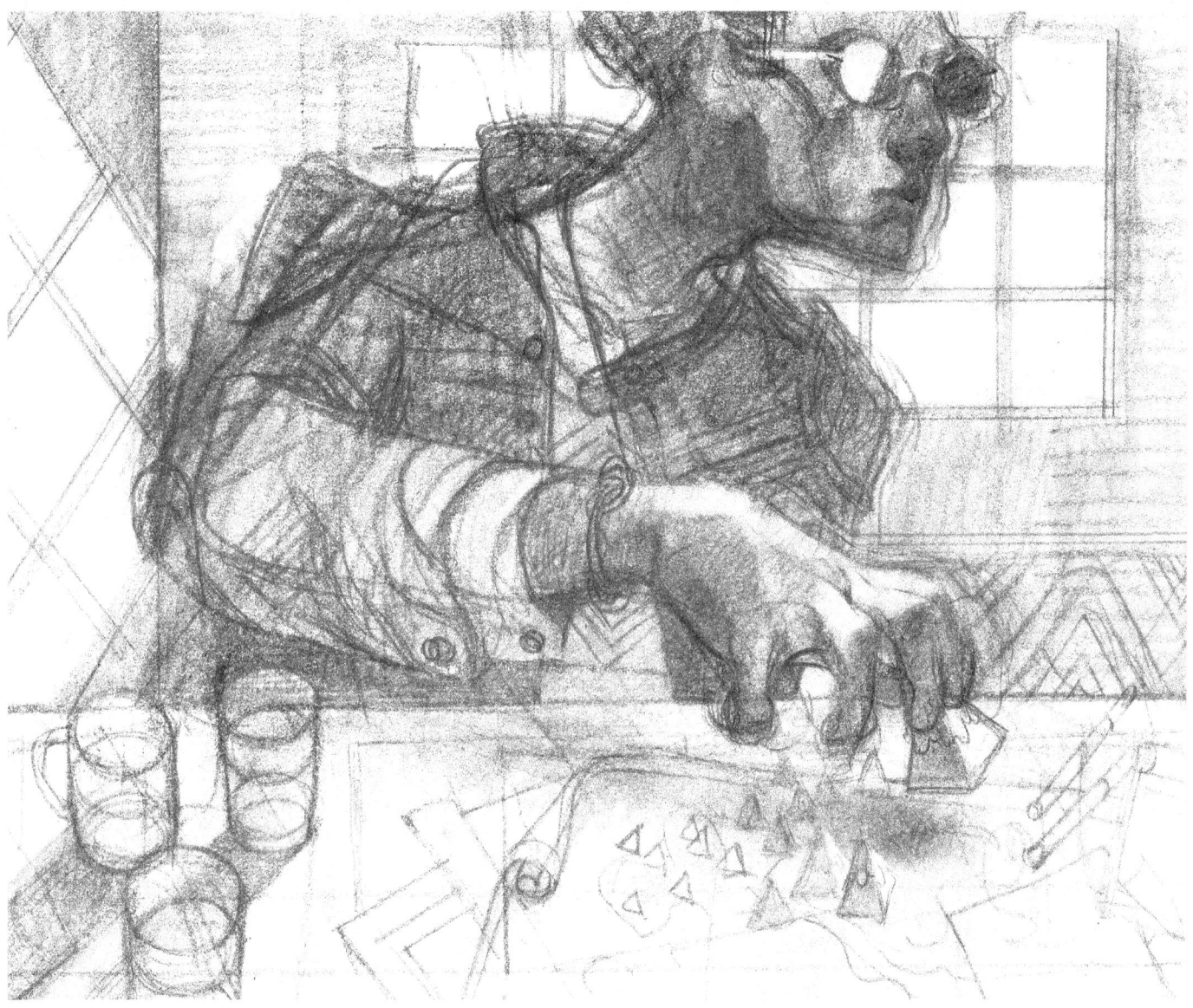

Anand Radhakrishnan,
rough draft for *The Dewarists*,
pencil on paper

Learning to draw quickly means learning to use a single mark with economy and using that mark to capture an impression of the subject.

Capturing a subject in motion—a moving person or animal, for instance—comes down to focusing not on the details of the subject, but the essence of a pose or gesture. In drawing quickly, you convey the personality of the subject, capturing as much with one line as quickly as possible.

This is not a style of drawing where you'll want to get hung up on the details. Work down to the details from the initial impression or gesture.

FINDING THE ESSENCE OF A FORM

Photo reference
for drawing quickly

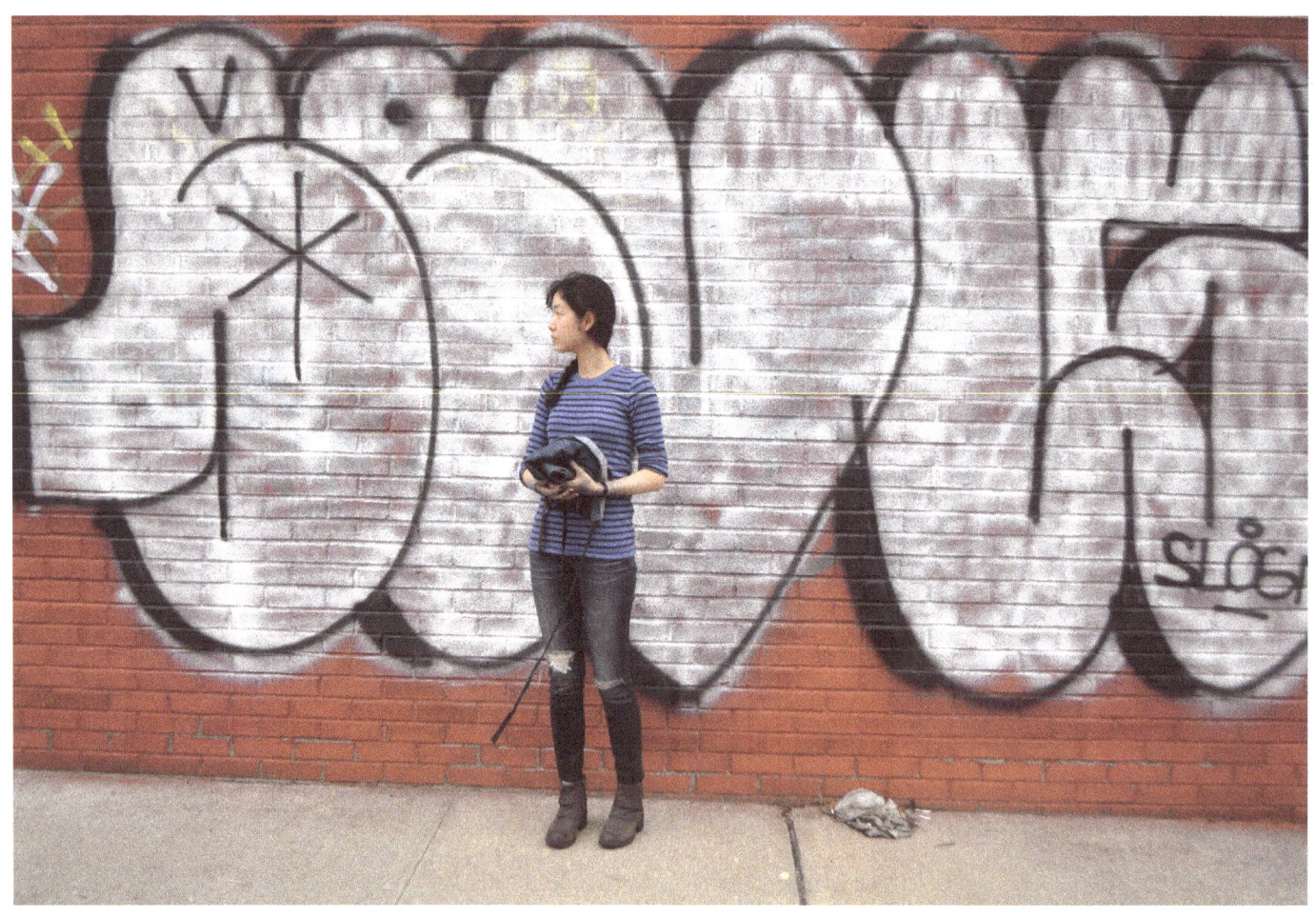

A fleeting subject—such as a moving person or animal—requires capturing an image quickly. This is not so much a trick, but more of a practice—the practice of capturing as much with one line as quickly as possible. In drawing the figure quickly, it's essential that you lift the pencil from the page as little as possible and allow the line to follow your eye across and through the figure.

Allow the line that might start with an arm or the head to be the same line that travels down and describes the folds in the shirt, and then the pants, and the legs and feet. Do not immediately try to separate parts such as clothing and limbs, but use the line to connect these elements in the overall flow of the figure. Then build from this initial impression. Do not get hung up on the details: Work toward details from the initial impression or gesture.

A good warm-up practice is to start by allowing yourself only 30 seconds and as few lines as possible to draw a figure. Every 30 seconds, switch to a new drawing and pose. Do about ten drawings at this speed: It will put you in the mindset to stop thinking so much and just respond to the subject with the pencil. This may be something to try at home or at a life-drawing session where the model is staged, rather than in a public space where you will be drawing strangers.

For these sketches, use a softer pencil, 2B and up. The softer graphite moves easily across the page, leaving a bolder mark, which makes it a good choice for the quick nature of the drawing. Because much needs to be captured with a simple line, you do not need

a finely sharpened tip. A broader tip works well because details are not overly important. The broad tip covers more space and is good for bold marks. The tight, detailed marks of a harder, pointed tip take longer to draw and do not flow as smoothly.

You might find it helpful to pause before starting a drawing. Take just a moment to think about the flow of the form before beginning. Jumping in without first looking closely at the figure can lead to a more generic impression. Try moving your eyes from head to toe on the figure, following the motion of the form first. Then look again, this time following with your eyes while drawing. This will help you create a more specific impression with more individual character to the gesture.

Once you have confidence capturing the initial impression, begin to spend more time focusing on a specific area. Spend time working out more specific details of the face or hands, for instance.

Once you have confidence capturing the initial impression, spend time working out more specific details.

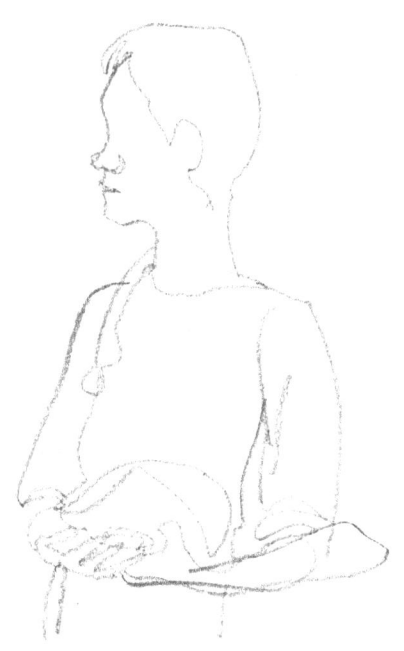
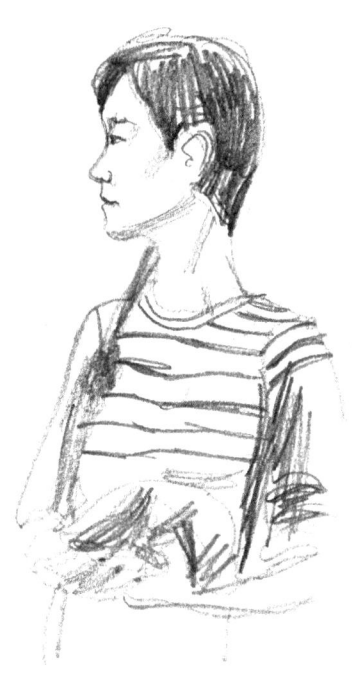
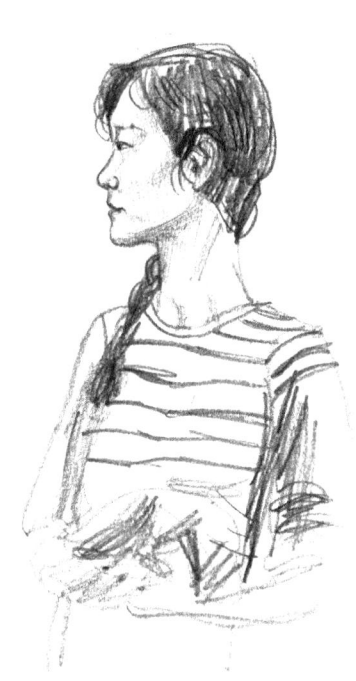

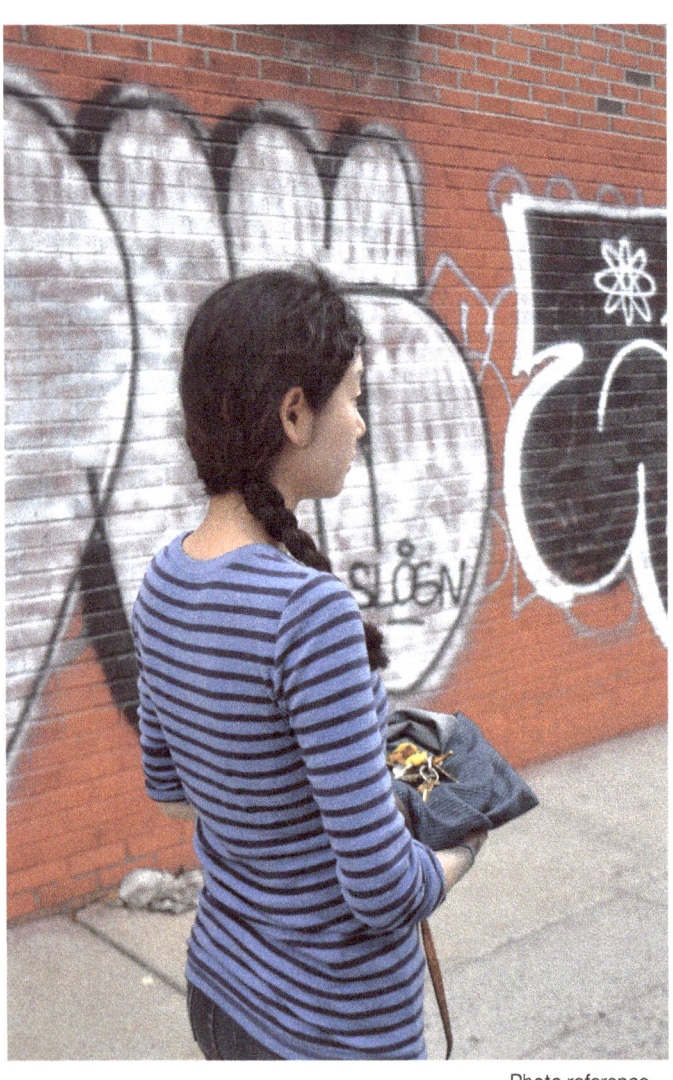

Photo reference
for a quick sketch

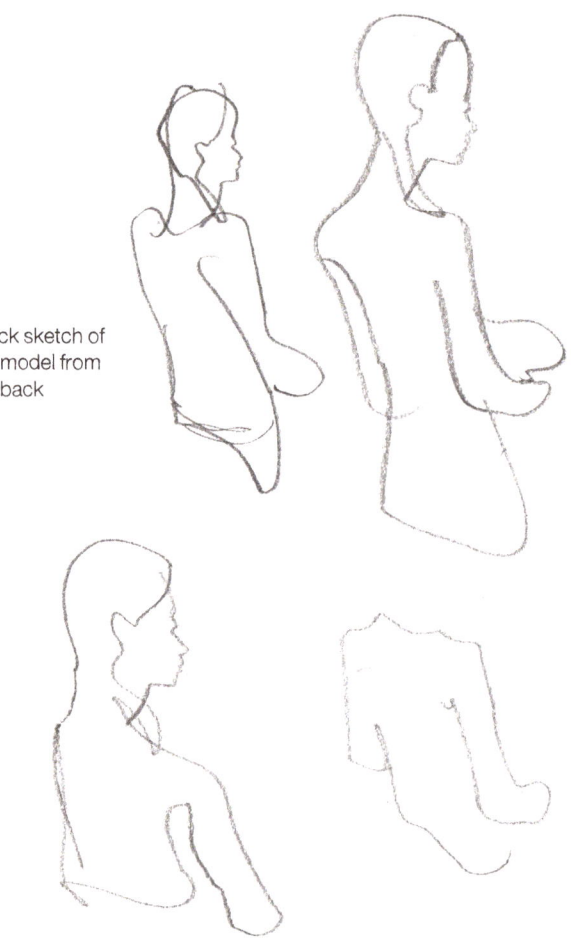

Quick sketch of
the model from
the back

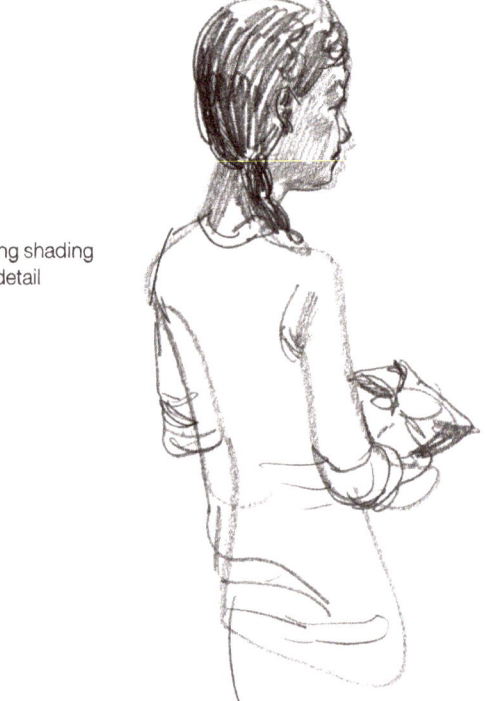

Adding shading
and detail

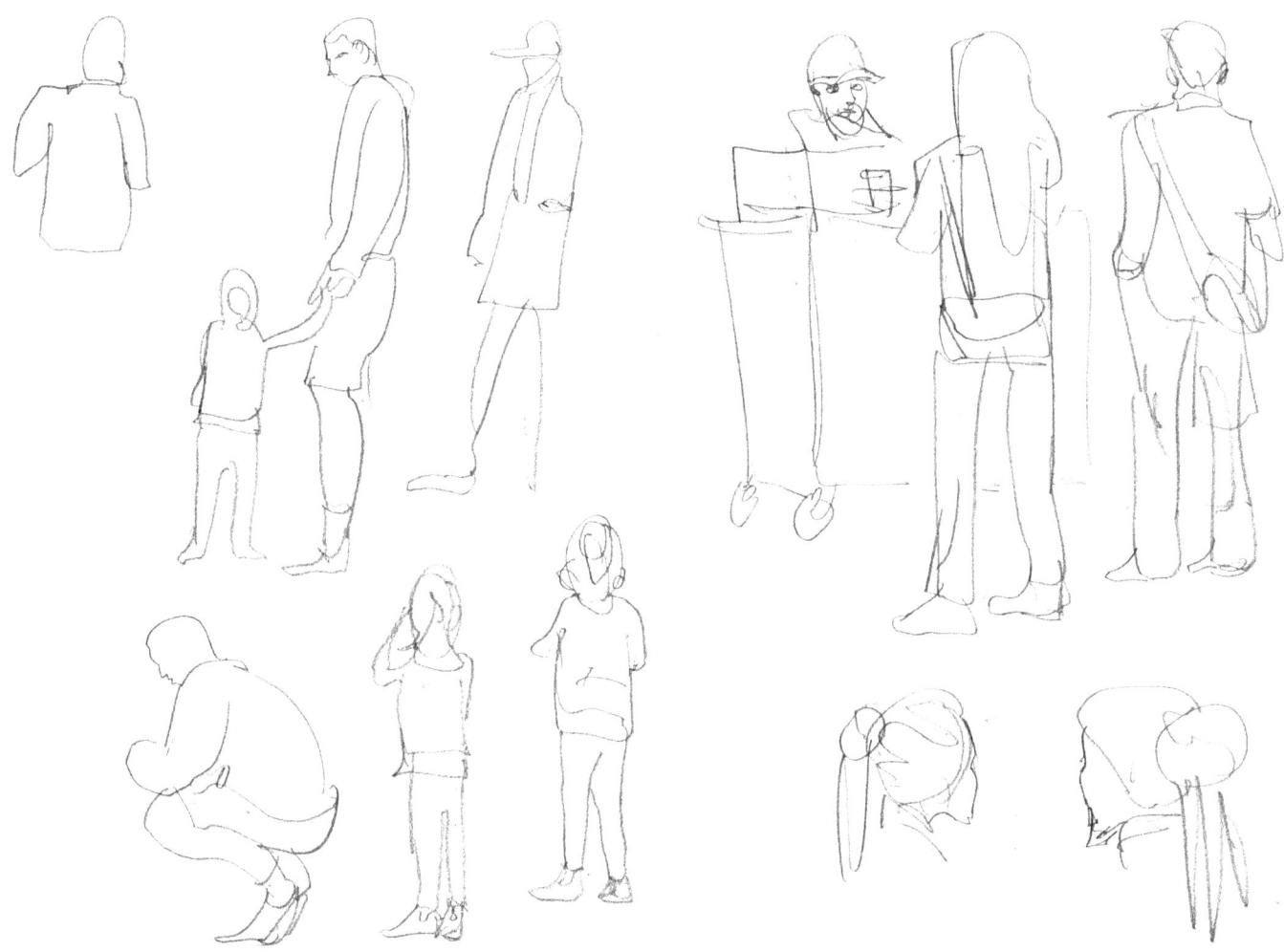

Quick drawings
of people on
the street

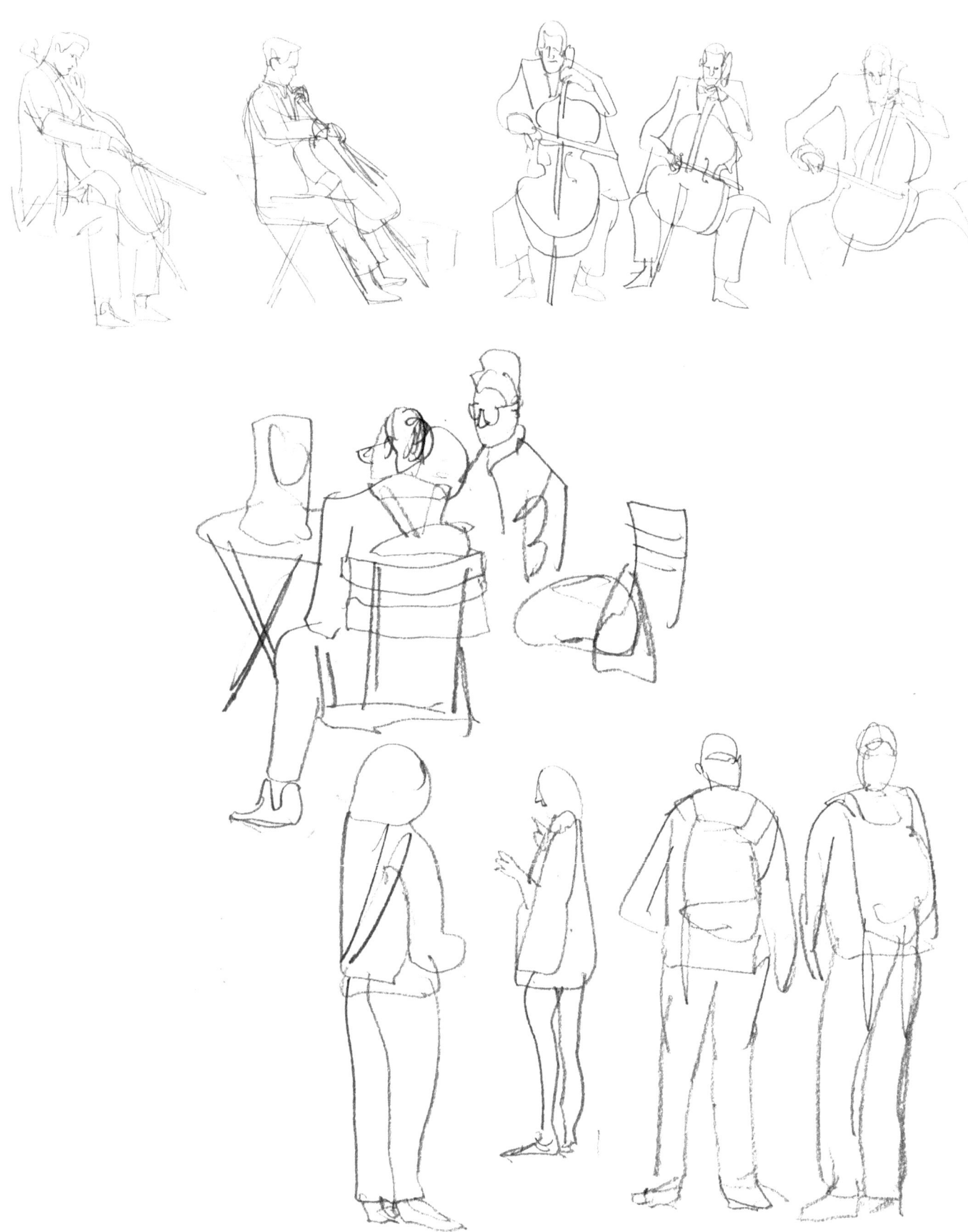

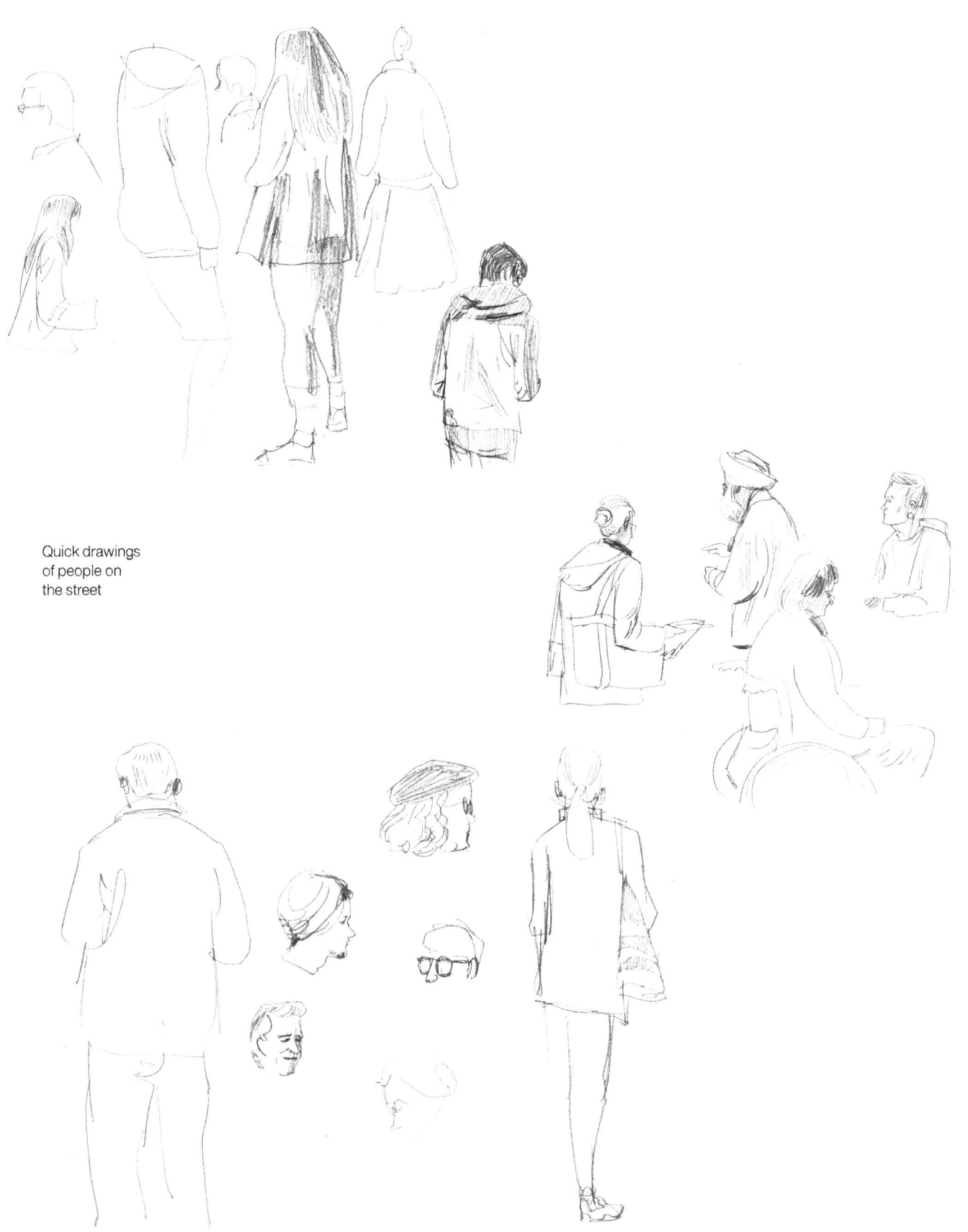

Quick drawings
of people on
the street

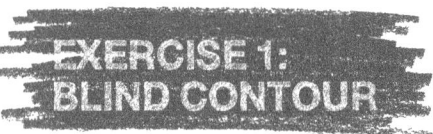

EXERCISE 1: BLIND CONTOUR

One of the hardest parts about drawing a subject quickly is learning to let go of what you know in your mind about a subject. Those things might include the general, nonspecific look of a nose, or an eye, or hand. Letting go of assumptions leaves room for you to learn to really look at a subject carefully while allowing the pencil line to follow your eye.

A starting point for letting go of familiar habits is an exercise called blind contour drawing. A blind contour requires the artist to use a single line to draw the subject without lifting the pencil from the page and without looking at the page. The line must move in creative ways around and through the drawing to capture all the details. Not looking at the page leads the eye toward a more uninhibited style of observation, forcing the artist to really take in the specific details of the subject.

Spend a moment looking at the subject before starting. Mentally map out a course for the line to follow, establishing the best starting point for the smoothest path through the drawing. The final drawing will be uninhibited and is not meant to be beautiful or accurate.

The goal of this exercise is to break the habit of trying to make a beautiful work of art instead of a visual response to what is in front of you.

The tendency to idealize or beautify a drawing distracts from the quick reaction needed in the process of drawing quickly. It creates an artificial filter instead of an automatic response to the subject. Reaction and intuition are more important than overthinking in this case.

Blind contour
drawing made with
a single line

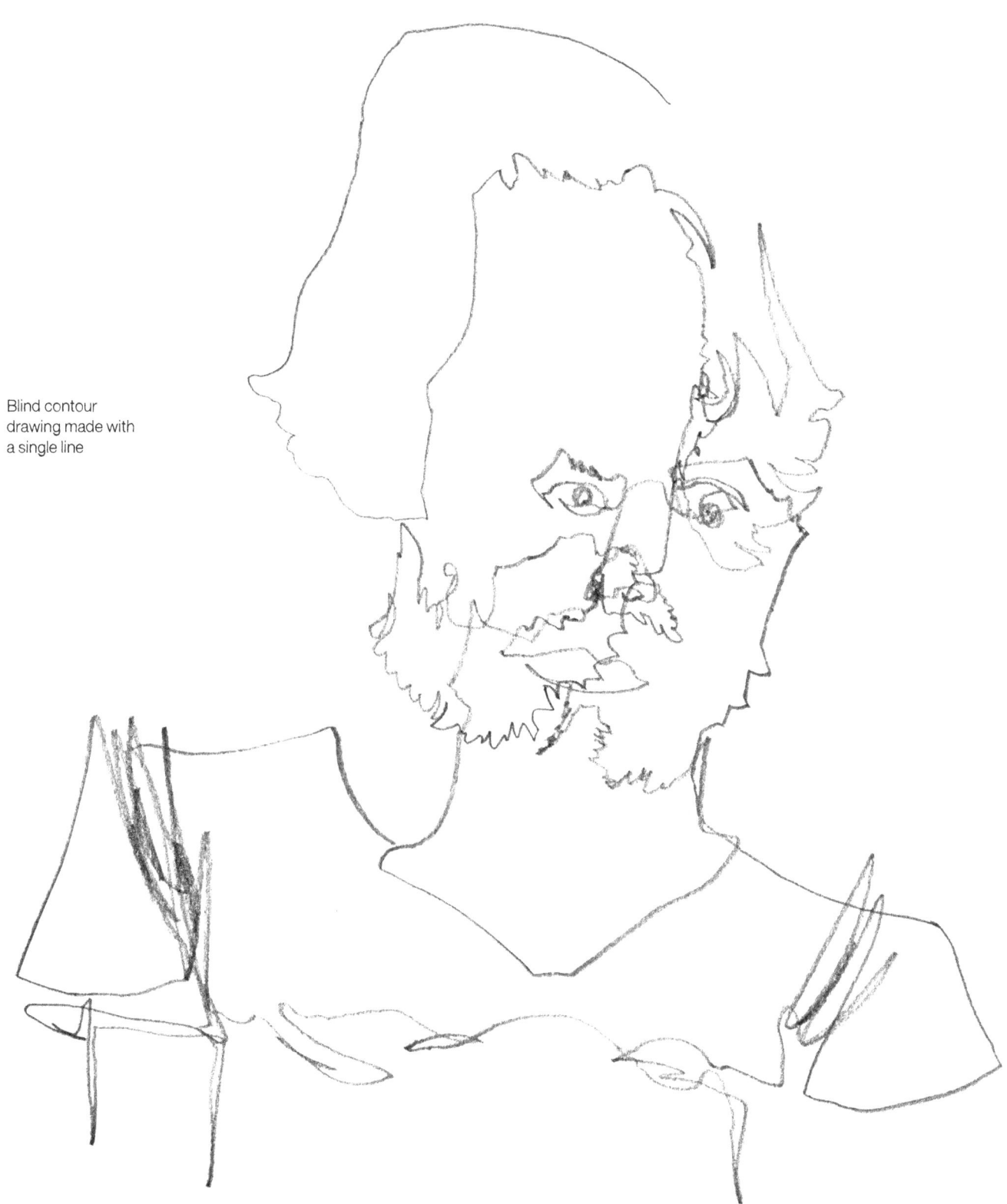

EXERCISE 2: DRAWING IN A BUSY PUBLIC SPACE

Find a public place such as a park, museum, train or bus station, airport, zoo, or public market. Bring a sketchbook and pencils to observe and draw the location and people there. The challenge of drawing on location is having no control over the circumstances and environment—and not knowing when someone will move.

The shifting nature of a public space forces you to improvise and let go of a drawing as a delicate or finished work. You learn to move around the drawing, focusing on some areas, while not worrying about the others.

Find a subject (a person, tree, dog, cat, anything) to focus on. Begin as before, by finding the essence of the subject with quick gestures and few marks, and build outward from there.

Photo reference for a figure in motion

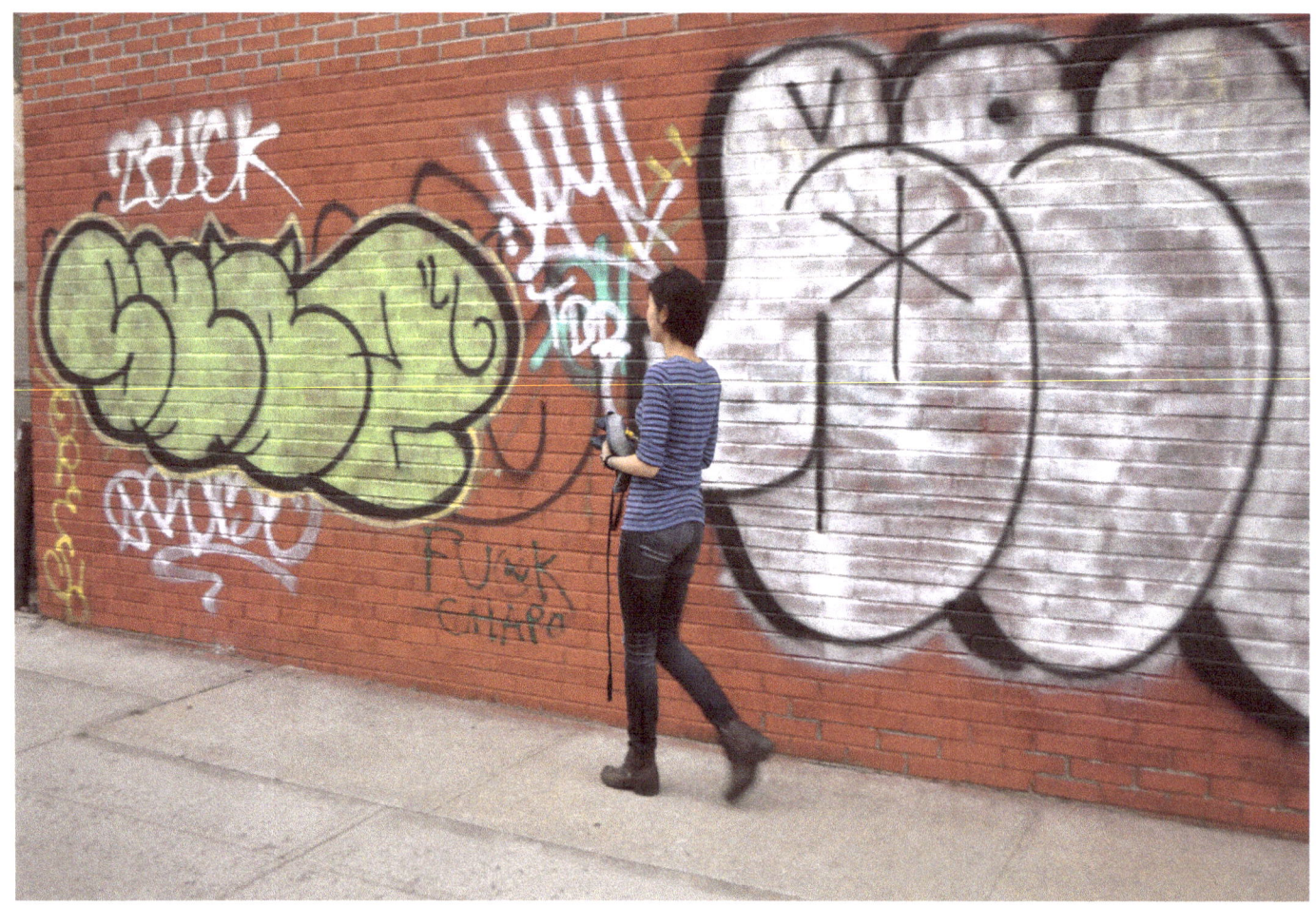

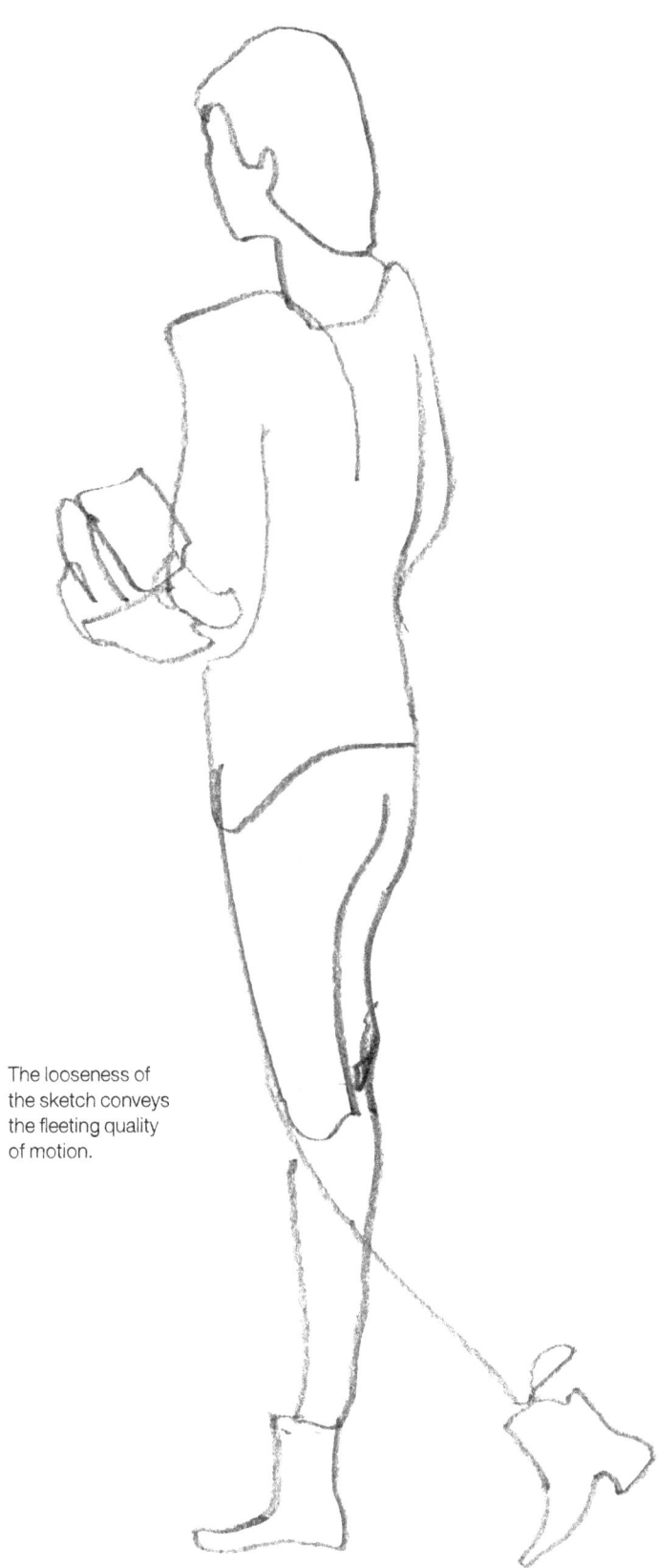

The looseness of
the sketch conveys
the fleeting quality
of motion.

Drawing a person who is not stationary is a challenge. After capturing the initial gesture, watch as the person moves around, perhaps walking or moving in a contained area or sitting and shifting positions. Focus on one part of the person at a time. Draw the face and head until they shift, then move on to another area—the hand, torso, legs, or feet. If the head shifts back to its original pose, resume drawing the face, adding more details, such as a shadow, the texture of the hair, and a refined, more accurate expression. Build all of this on top of the initial gesture, and erase the original drawing as you slowly refine it.

Try drawing someone walking by. Capture the impression and then continue to fill in details as the person walks—the style of clothing, shoes, haircut, and facial expression. Apply all of these details to the initial gesture, even though the pose continues to change as your subject walks.

Drawing a figure in motion is not like capturing the exactness of a stationary person. The looseness of the sketch conveys the fleeting quality of motion. If the walking figure is drawn as precisely as a stationary person, the drawing will feel frozen and stiff and not in motion at all.

Stick with the figure as long as possible (and as long as is polite). Capture as much detail as possible. Portions of the drawing will be more complete than others. If a hand or head moves, don't avoid redrawing it; you may end up with several outlines of the same object—a sort of document of the shifting position of the figure, which can be interesting. These should not be treated as precious drawings; correcting, adjusting, overlapping, or starting a section and then abandoning it are all part of the process.

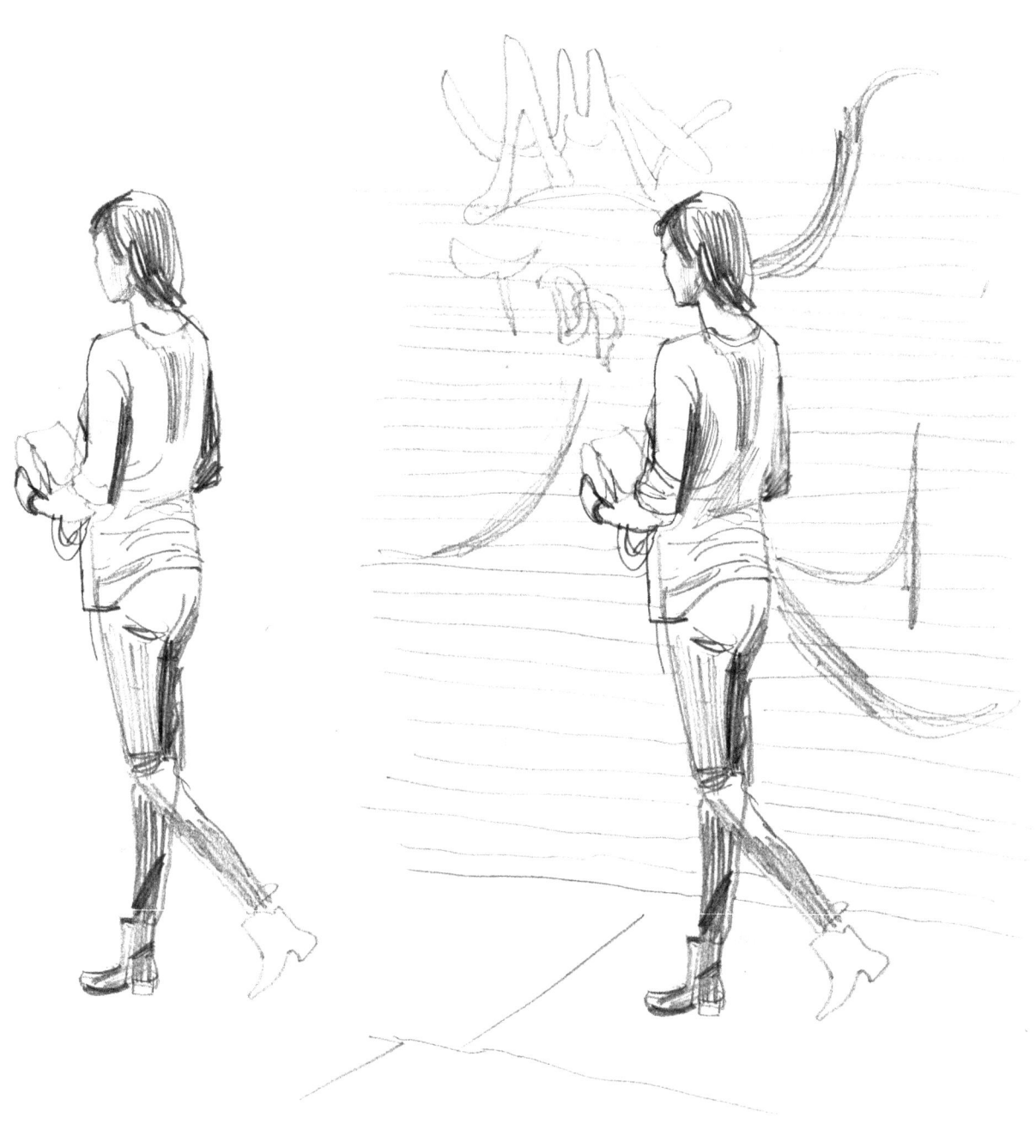

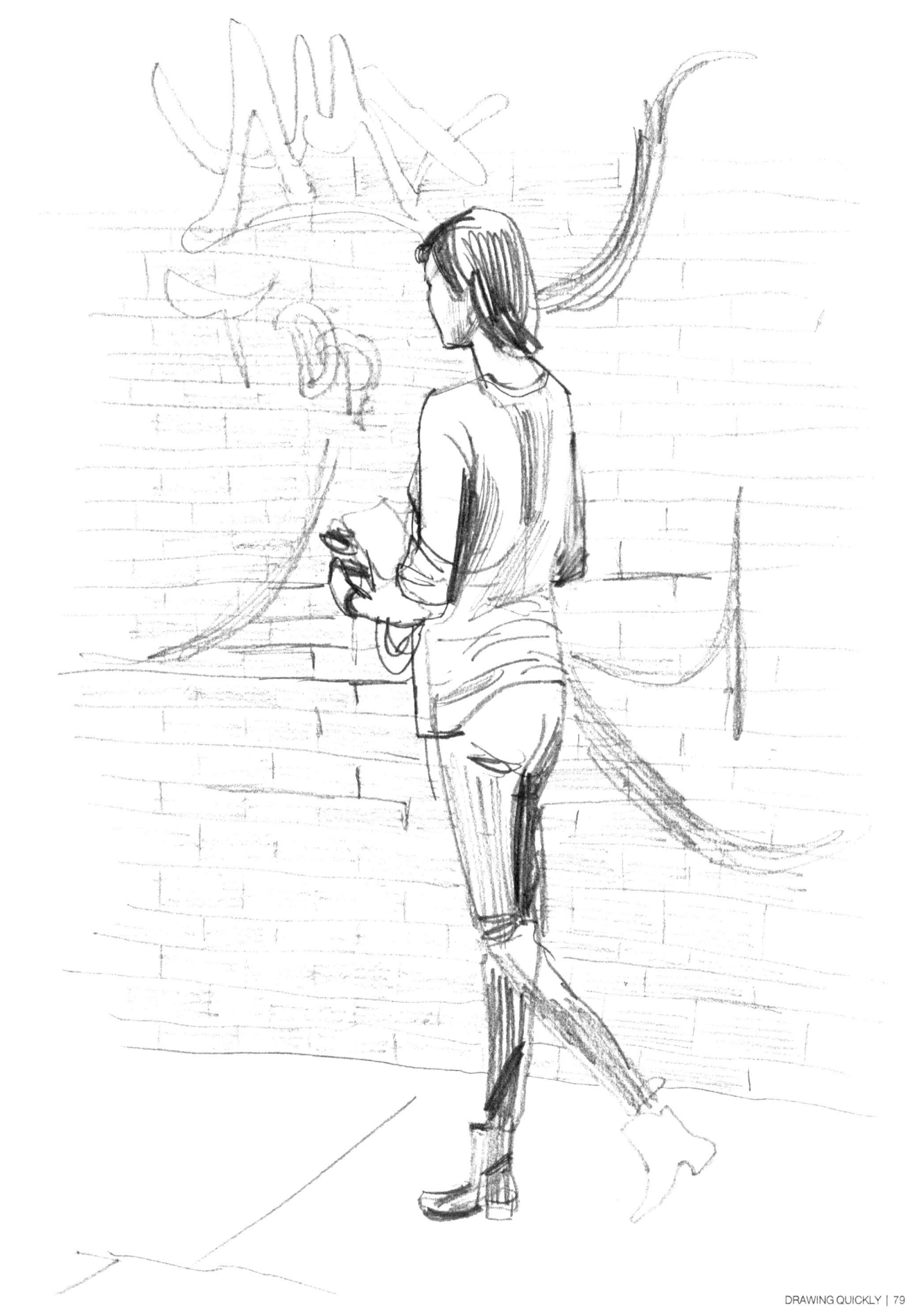

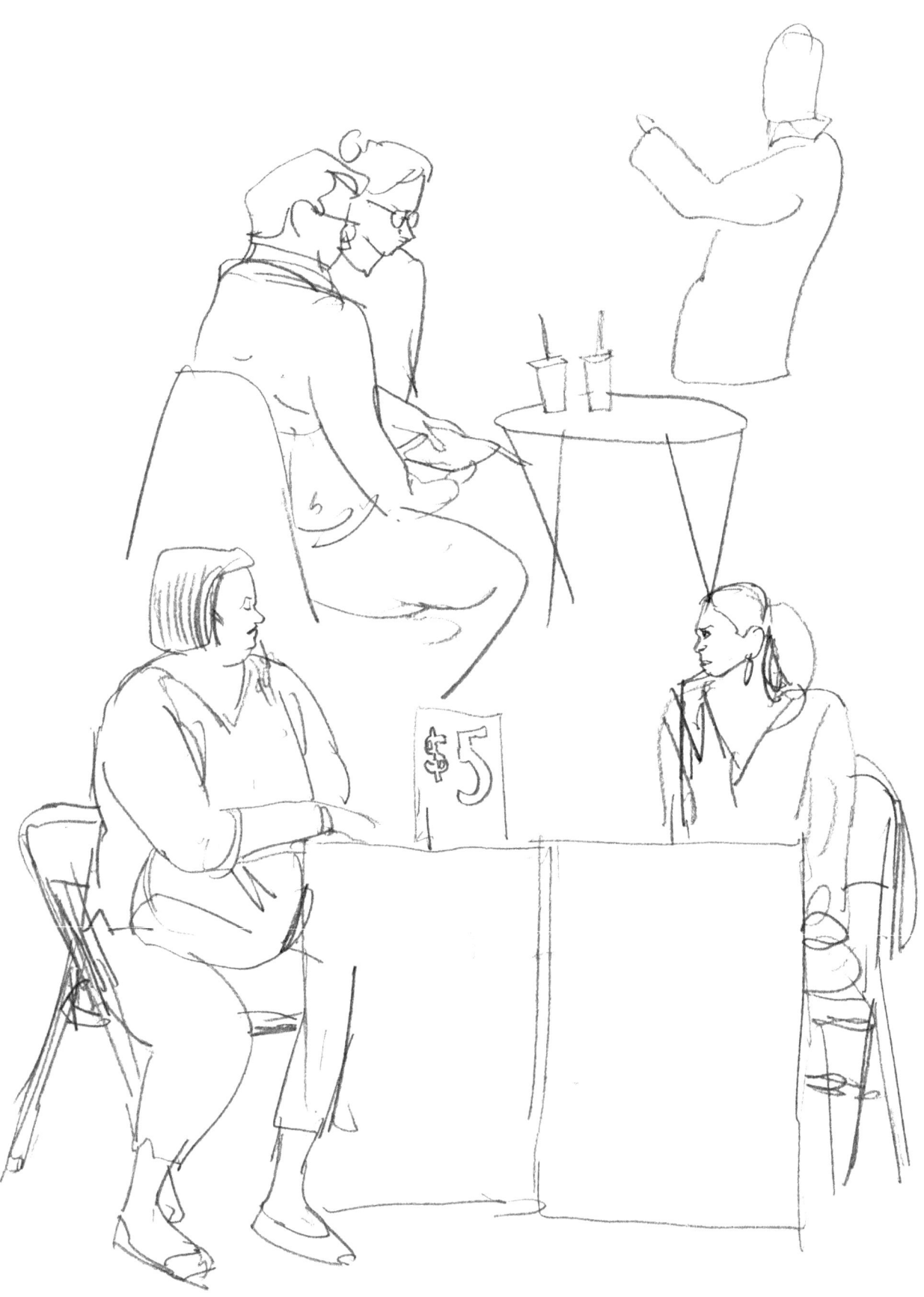

Palm Reader, pencil on paper.
Capturing time as it passes with
a quick sketch on the street.

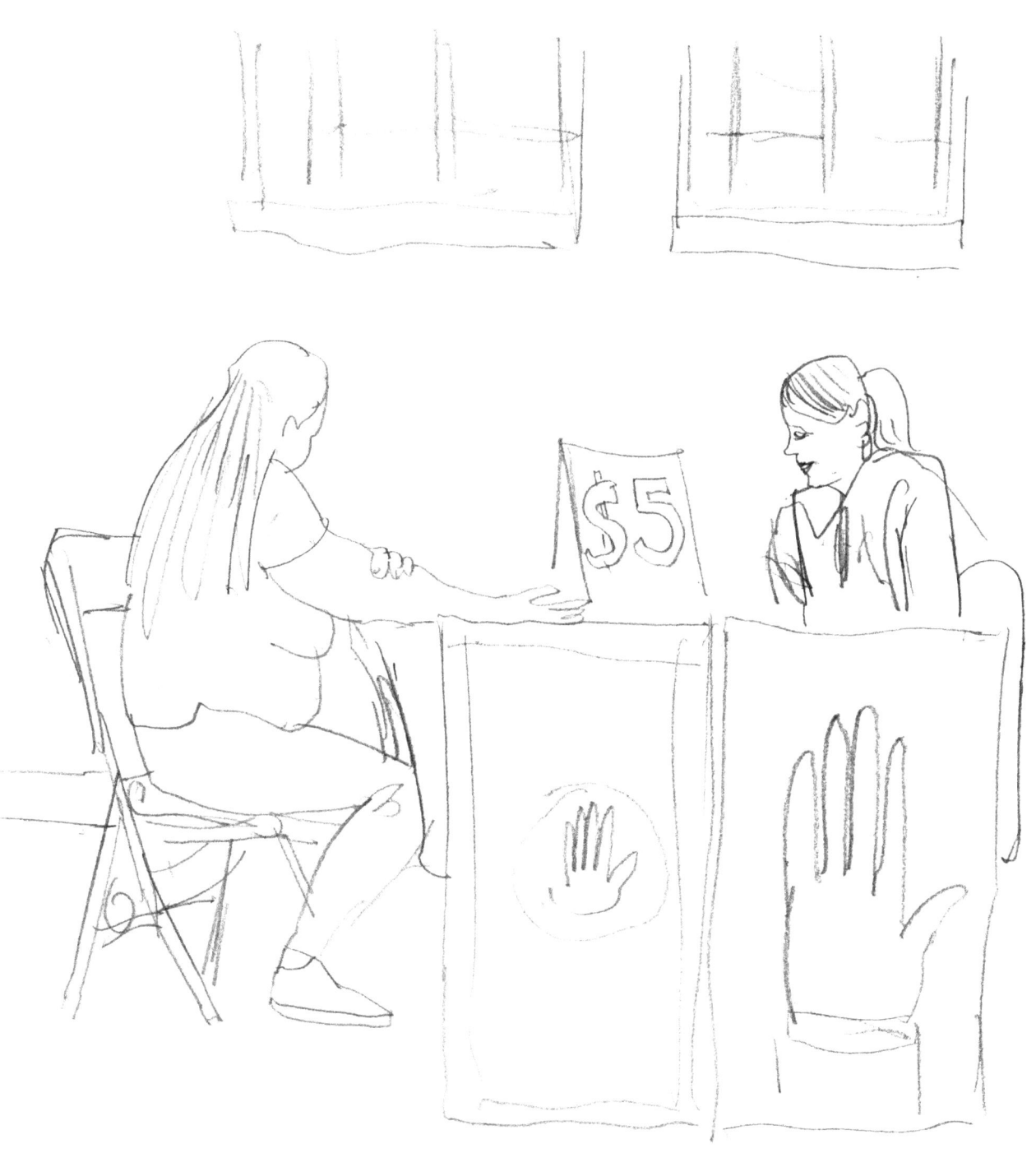

EXERCISE 3: ADDING A BACKGROUND

Once you're comfortable with individual subjects and people in motion, expand your drawing to include the environment such as plants, cars, and architecture.

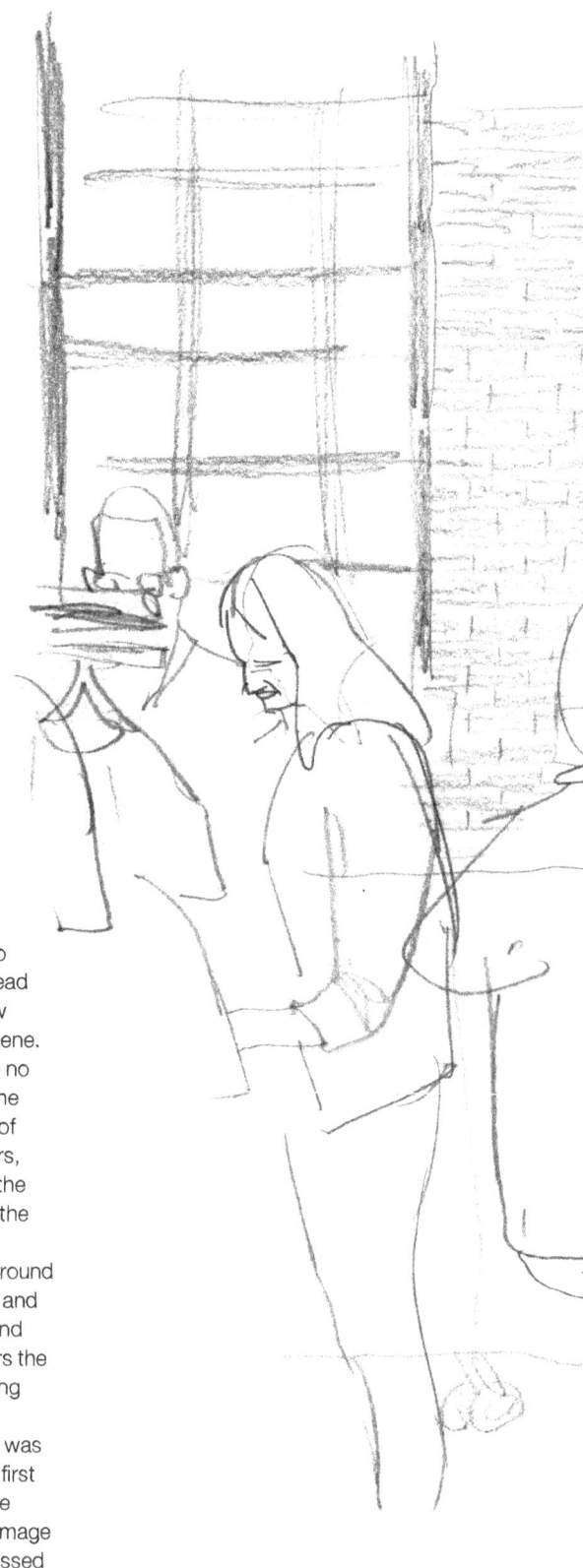

Start, for instance, with someone standing. Draw the person as quickly as possible, and determine where different parts of the body line up with the scene in the background. What do the shoulders line up with, a window? What do the knees line up with, a table? Briefly mark those points while you continue to work on the figure. Then, when your subject moves, return to the background and develop it in more detail.

Think back to the blind contour style of drawing as you work on the background. Follow the background as it leads through the scene, but don't immediately get caught up on resolving them—allow a table to lead to a window and follow the window to the ceiling. The way these pieces line up and overlap will become a pathway around the space that you follow quickly with your eye and pencil.

Stationary objects are always easy to return to, but you can also use them to lead to other people in the composition. Draw people as they come and go from the scene. Return to the background when you can no longer focus on a person. Begin to use the architecture to figure out the proportion of the figures. Line up their heads, shoulders, torsos, and legs with the proportions of the background to accurately place them in the environment with other people.

Add shadows and value to the background as you switch focus between the setting and the people. Again, don't avoid layering and overlapping the subjects. If a figure enters the drawing and then abruptly leaves, allowing you only enough time to draw an outline, that outline can be filled in with whatever was behind the figure. Or, draw on top of the first subject with another figure that enters the drawing and stays longer. The resulting image will record the history of time that has passed while completing the drawing.

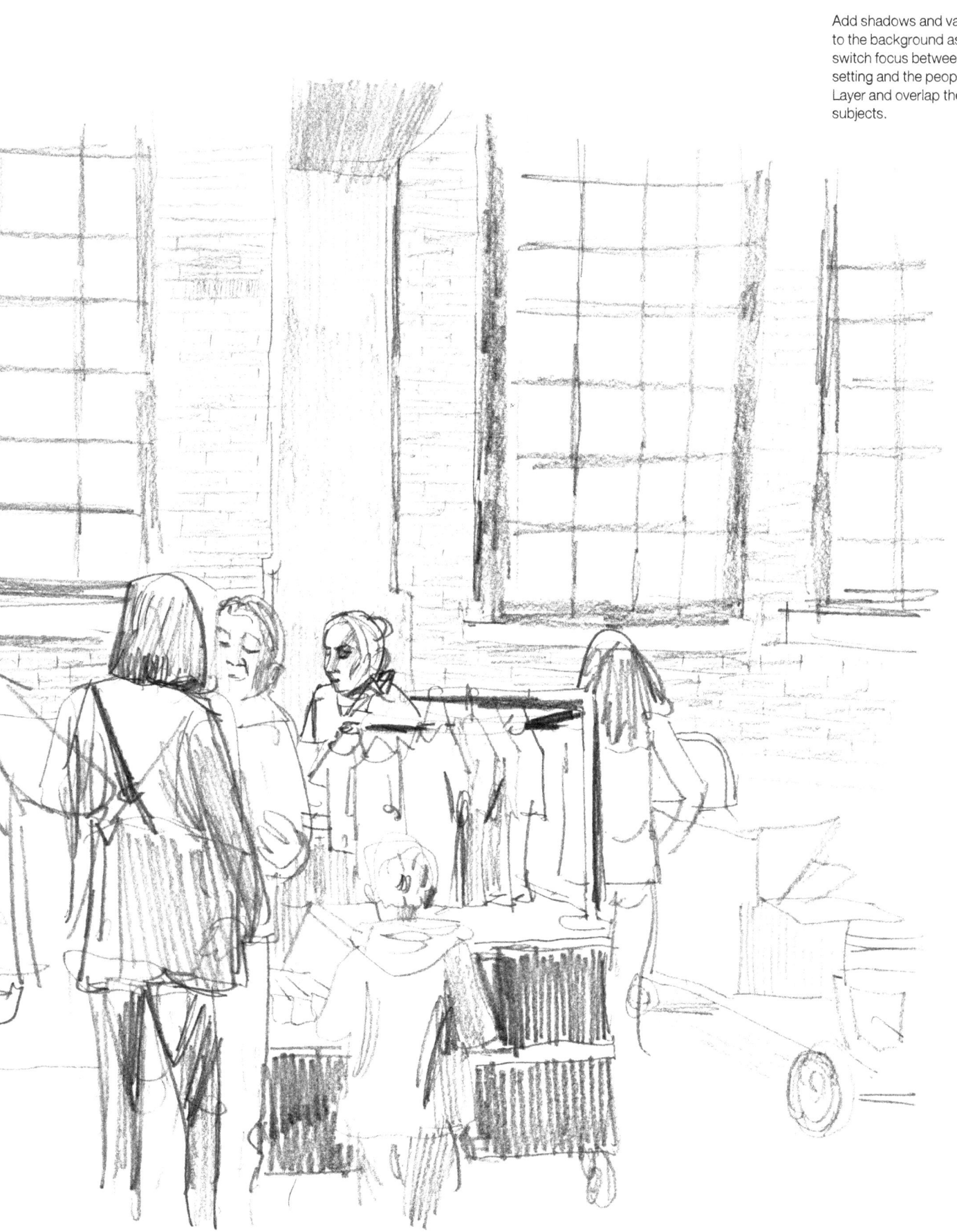

Add shadows and value to the background as you switch focus between the setting and the people. Layer and overlap the subjects.

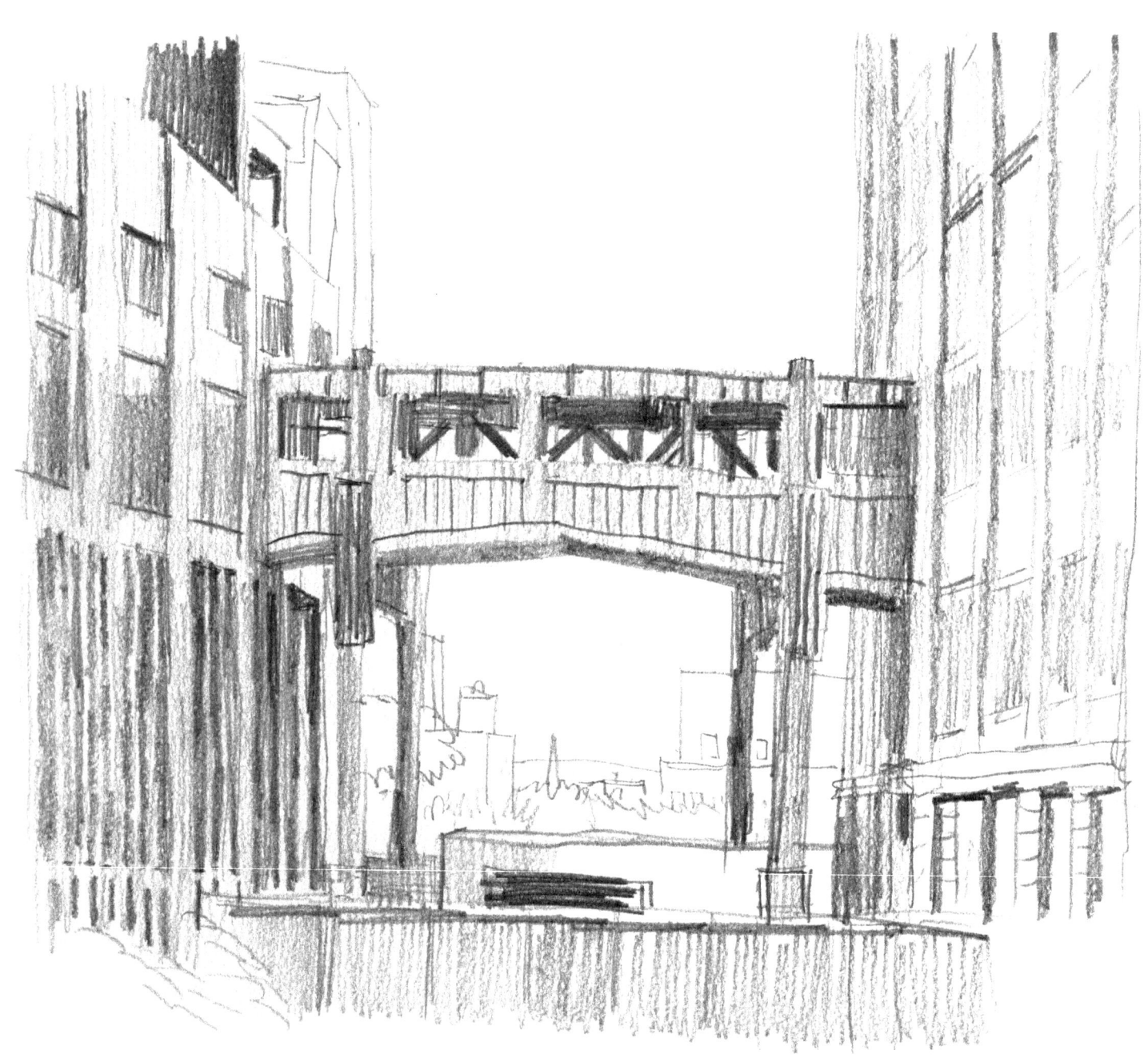

Start with the quickest
outline sketch, then go
back and add shadows,
details, and contrast.

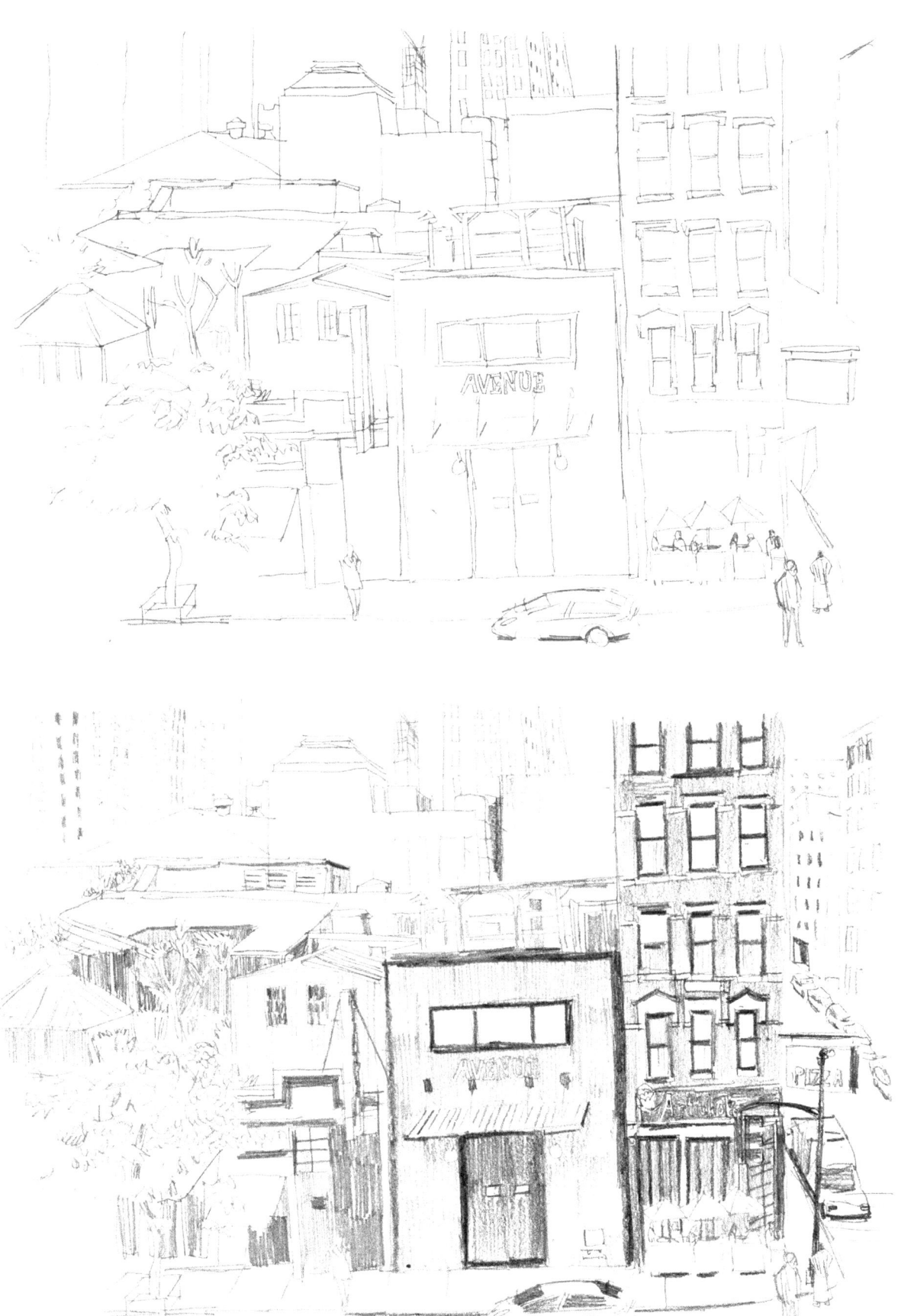

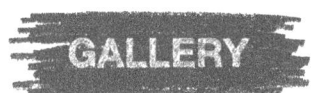

Benoit Guillaume,
Art Gallery in Berlin,
pencil on paper

Benoit Guillaume,
Roads in Bangkok,
pencil on paper

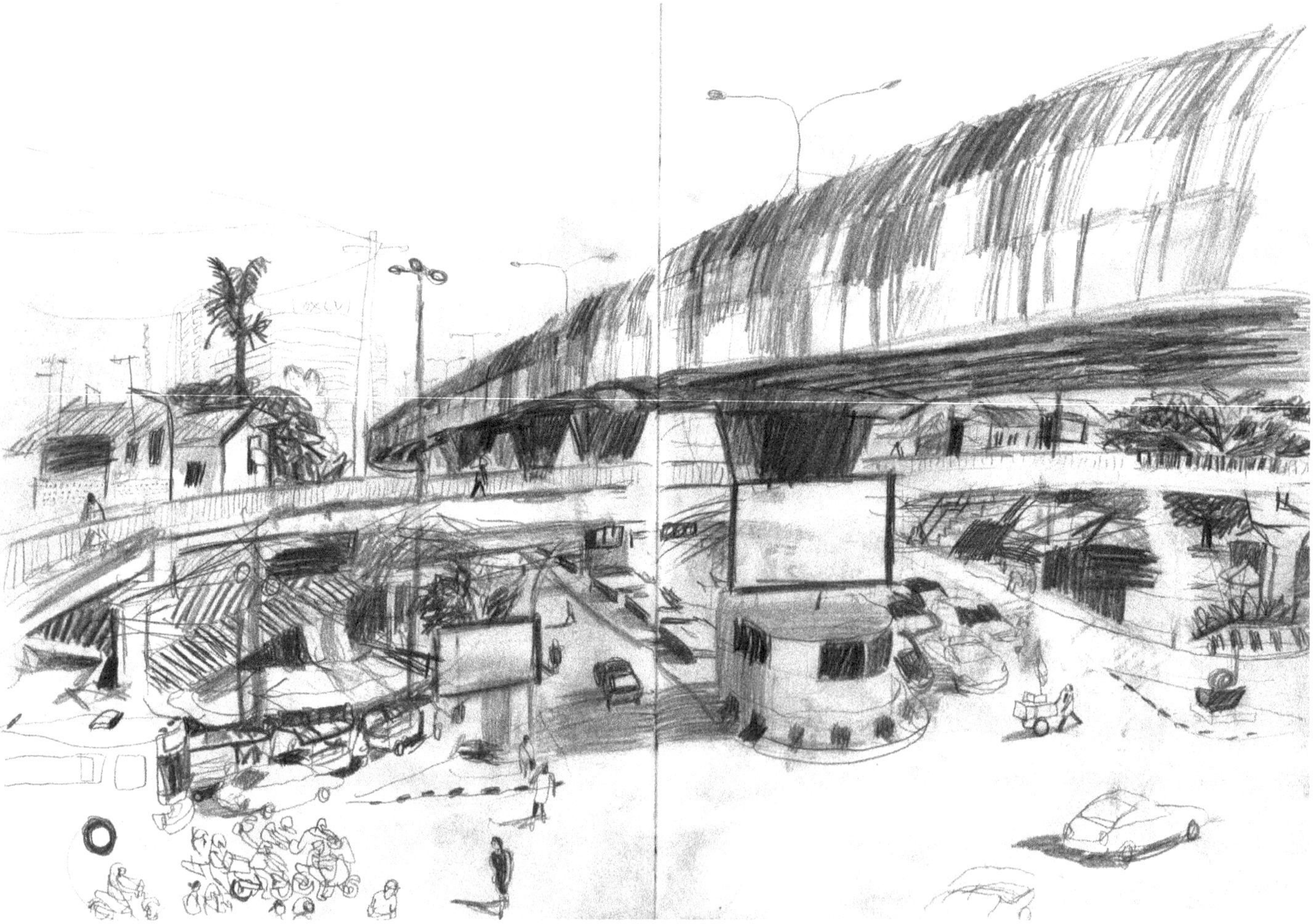

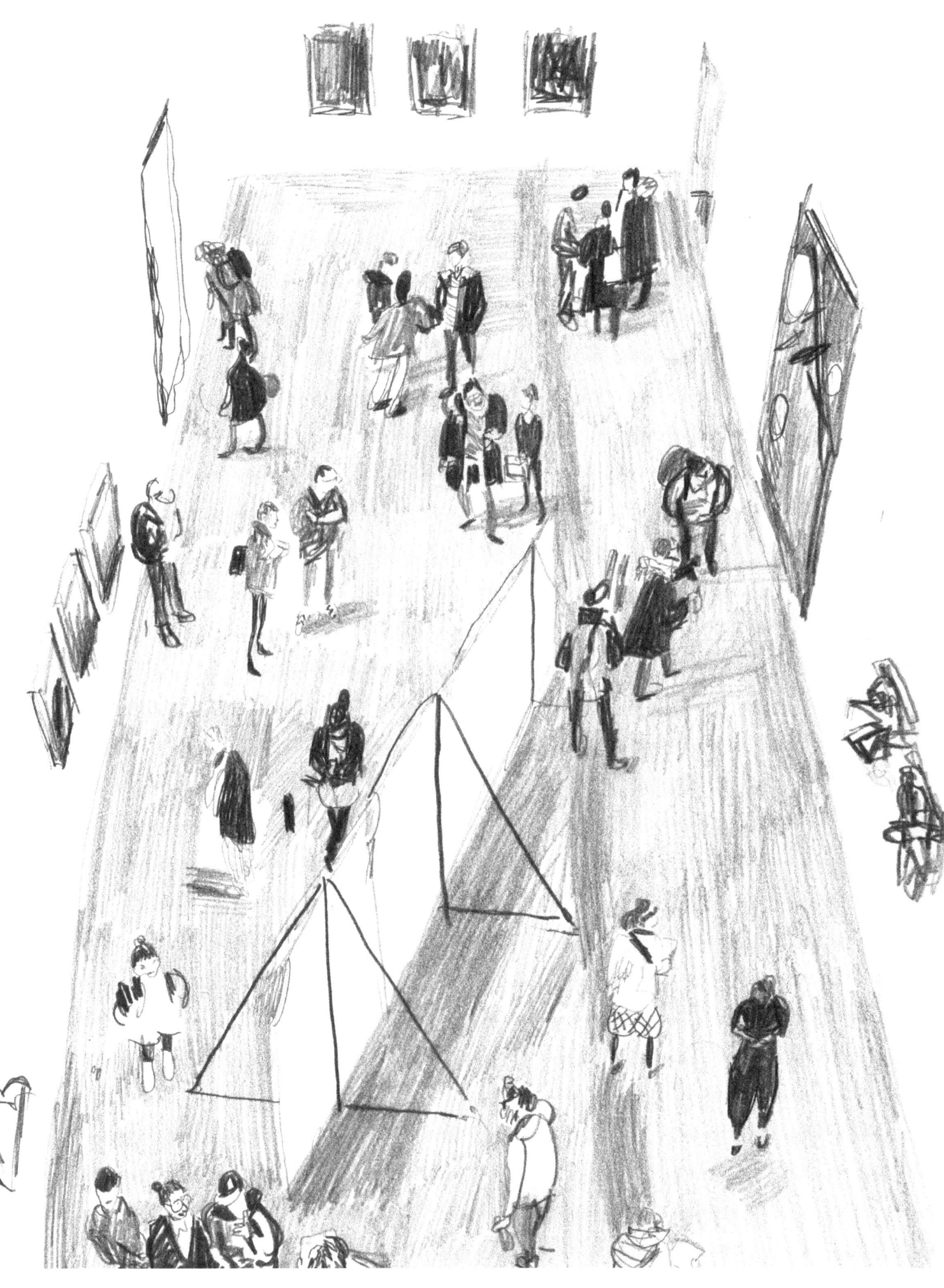

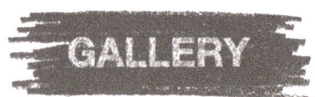

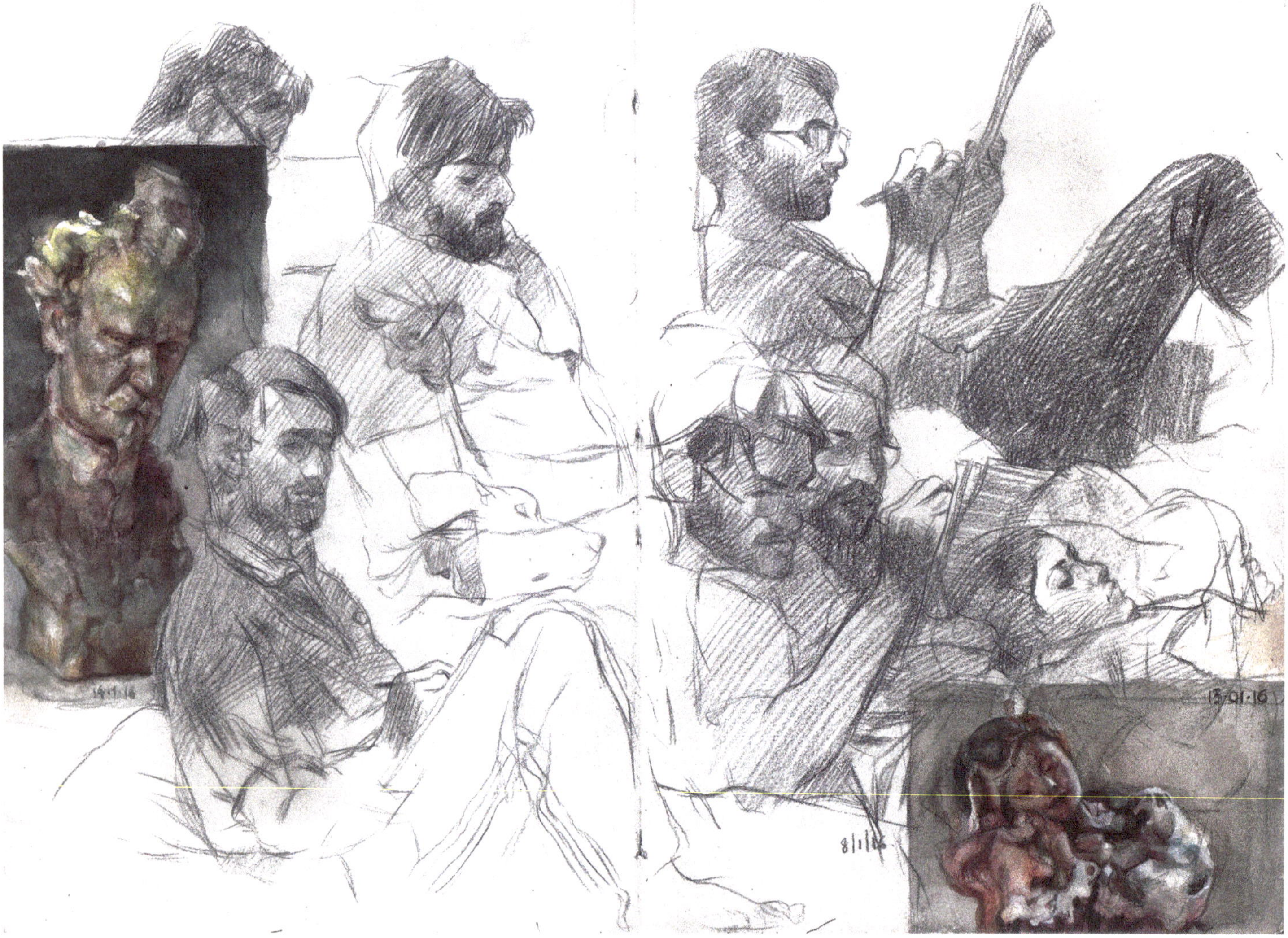

Anand Radhakrishnan,
sketchbook spread,
pencil and watercolor
on paper

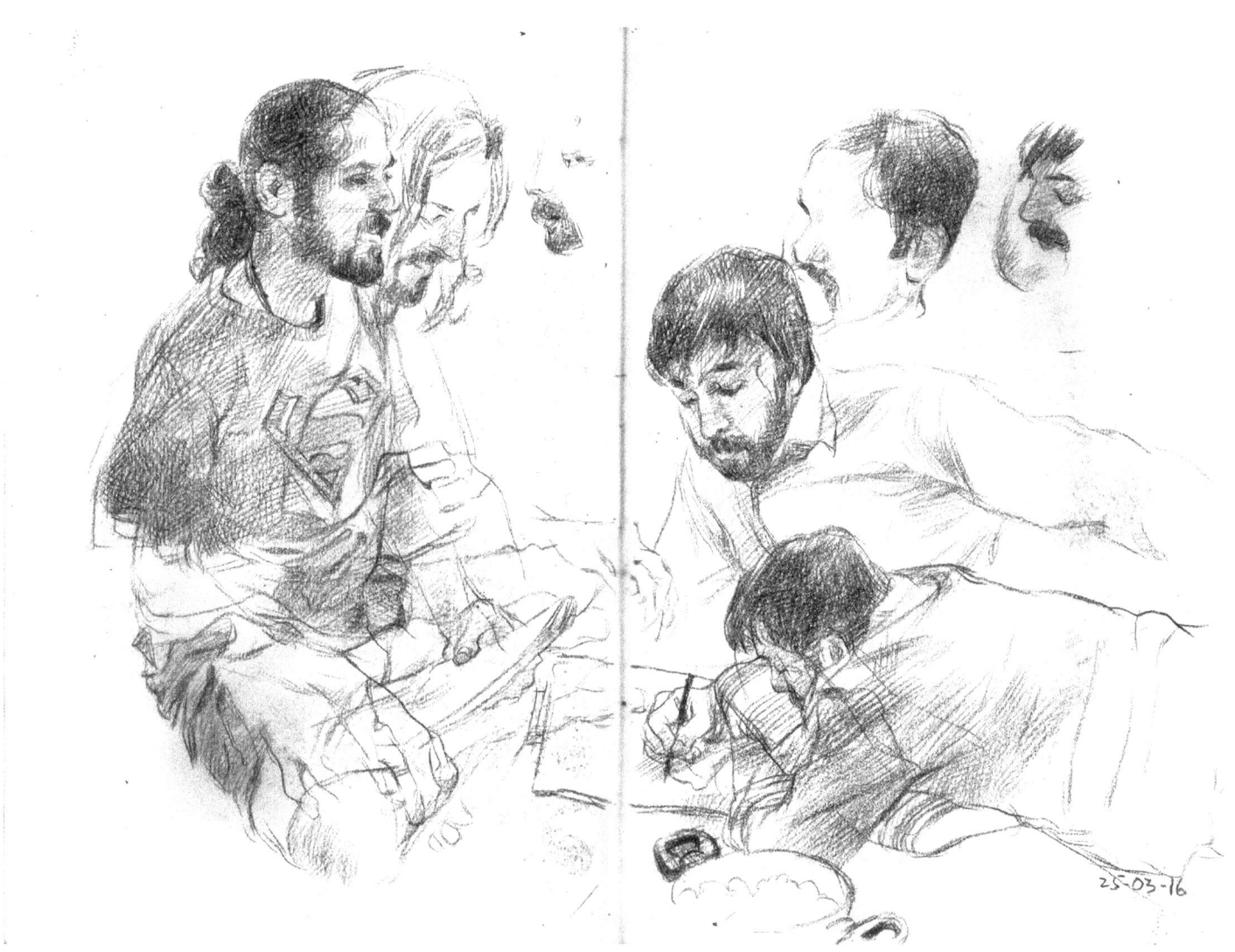

Anand Radhakrishnan,
sketchbook spread,
pencil on paper

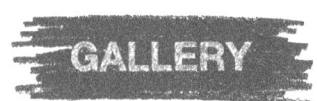

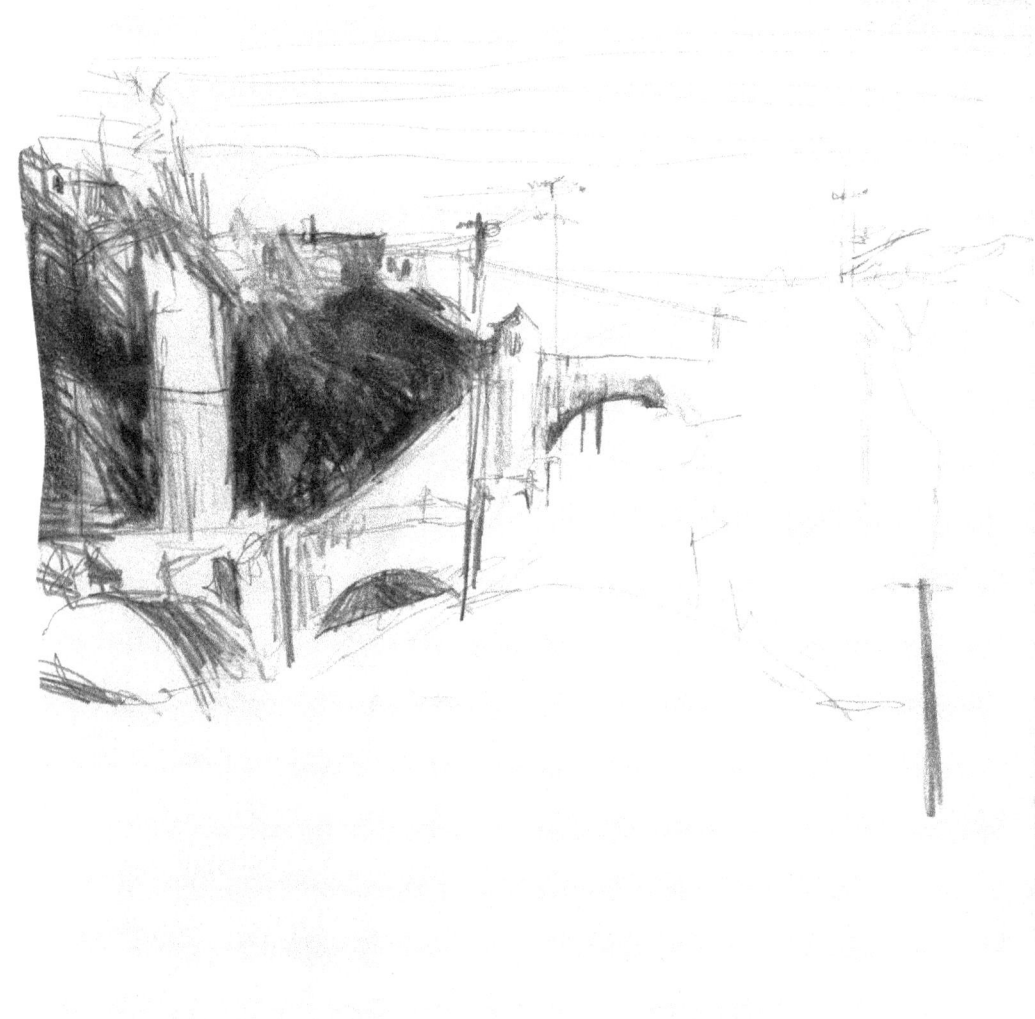

W L   california 1965

Warren Linn,
California '65,
pencil on paper

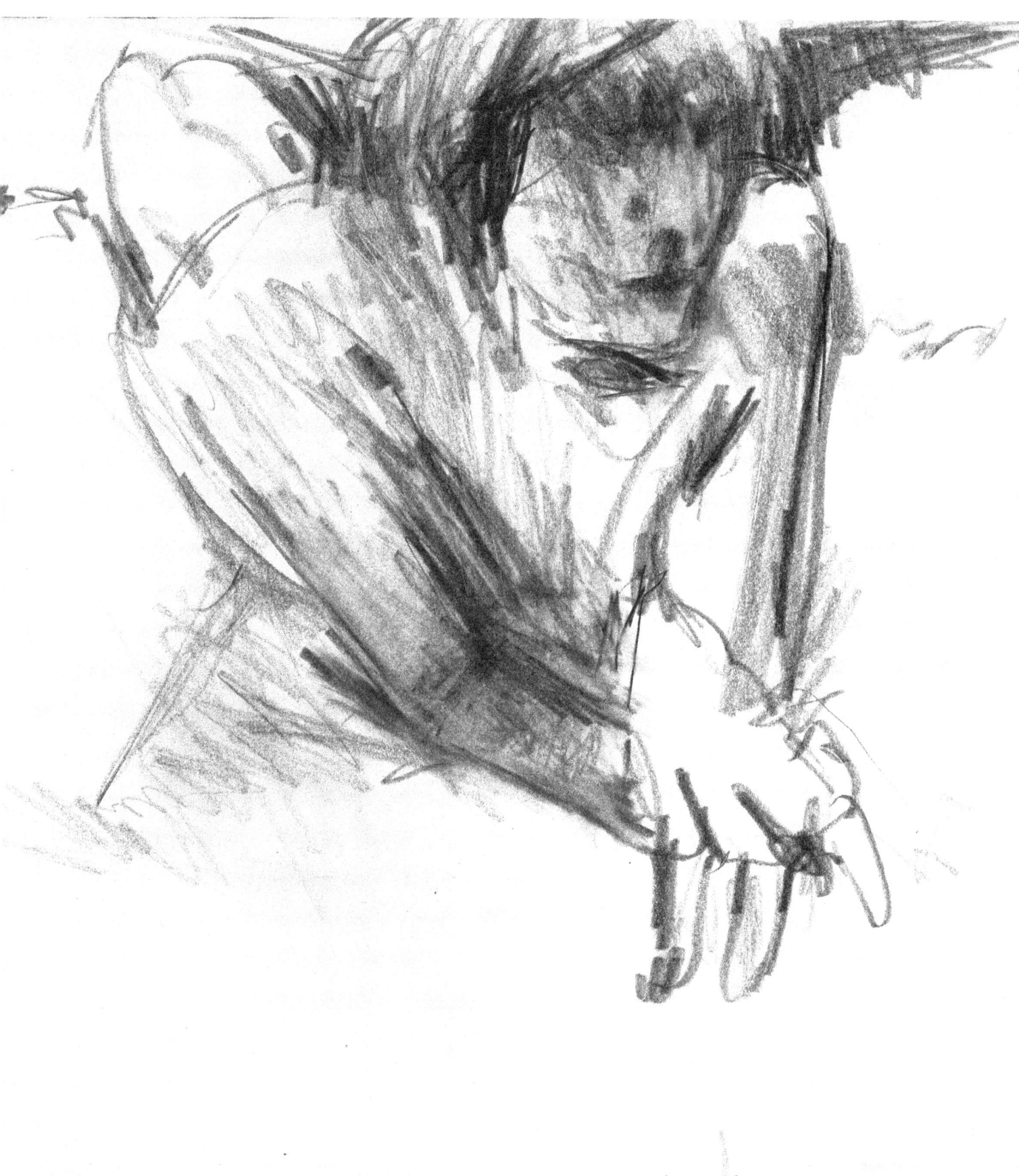

Warren Linn,
Sally '67,
pencil on paper

CHAPTER 4

PHOTOREALISTIC DRAWING

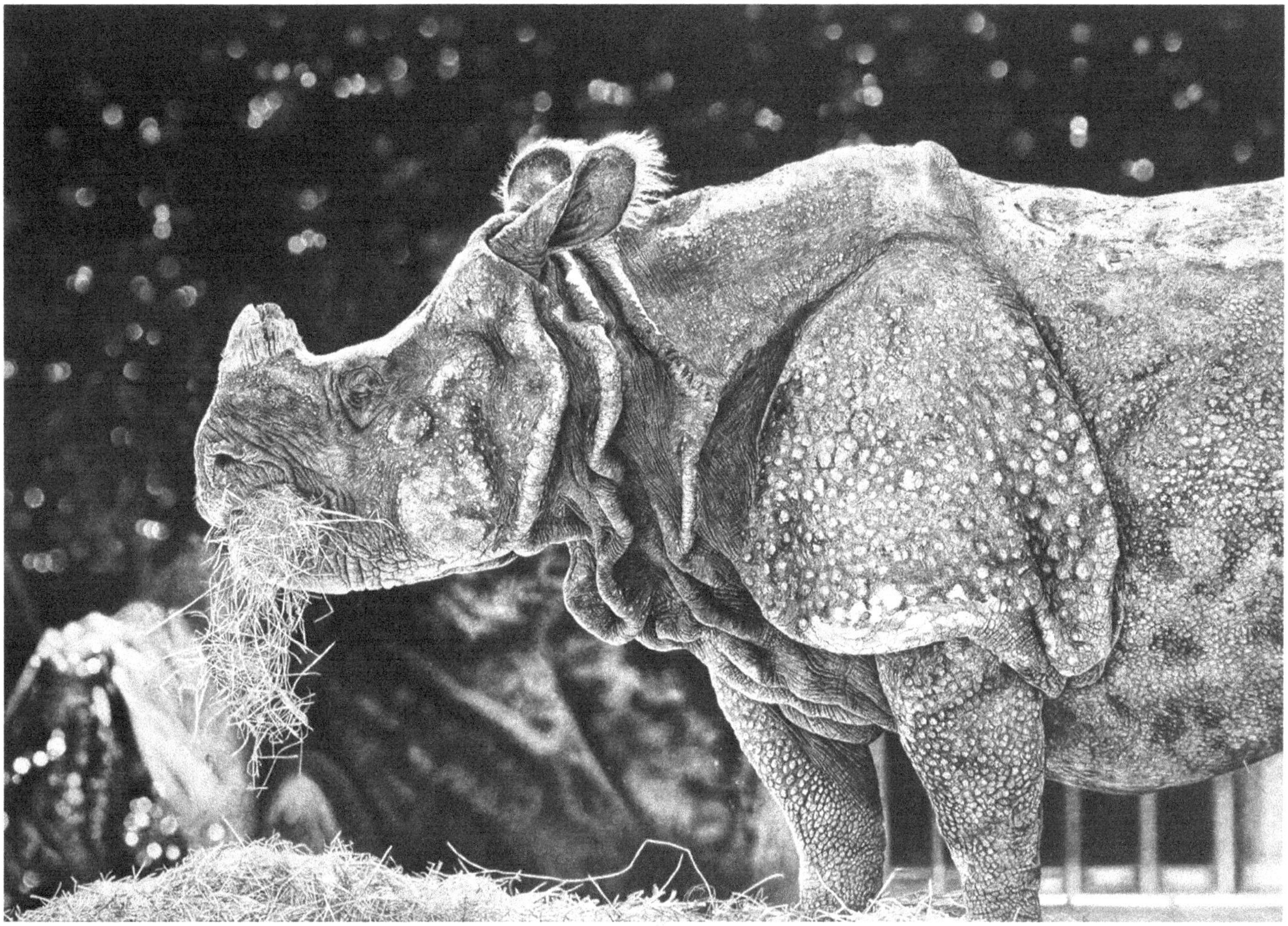

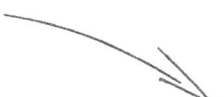

Monica Lee, *Rhino*, pencil on paper. Photo by Emmanuel Keller.

The art of photorealism is a unique form of realism in drawing and painting because it references specific qualities found in photography.

As a term relating to art, photorealism has been around since the 1970s. It centers mostly on the work of artists like Chuck Close, John Baeder, Richard Estes, and several others. Photorealism distinguishes itself from other forms of realism, such as the nineteenth-century realist and naturalist movements, in that it focuses on the specific interpretation of reality as seen through the lens of the camera.

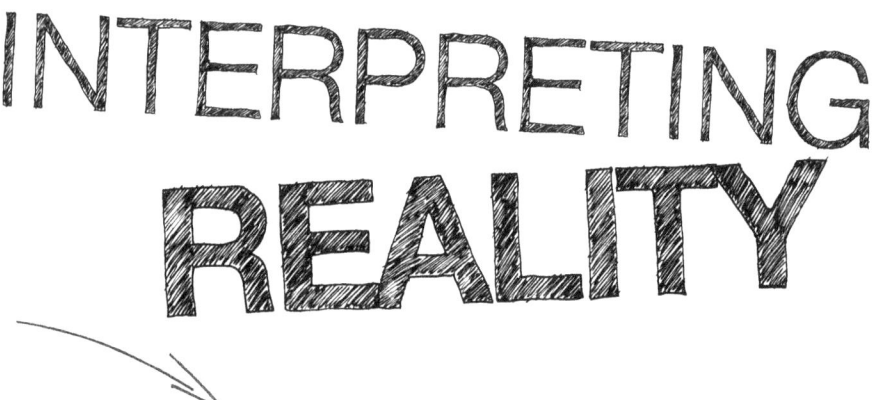

INTERPRETING REALITY

At first glance, a photo might seem a more accurate depiction of reality than a painting: It captures and records light in a way similar to the eye. The camera lens is like a mechanical eye, simply capturing whatever it looks at when the shutter opens and closes with its indifferent gaze.

Before the use of the camera, the depiction of realistic images was left to the highly refined skills of a painter. The invention of the camera allowed anyone to click and capture an image. To the untrained eye, a photo's reality is accepted as the truest depiction of reality in two-dimensional image making. However for trained image makers, painters, and drafts-people, photography is still a distortion of reality. In other words, photo reality in an image is not absolute reality and does not represent absolute truth in depicting reality. Photo reality still differs greatly, if subtly, from both what is perceived by the eye, and what can be detailed through a drawing or painting.

The type of lens in a camera, the aperture, and the shutter speed can all be set to determine the depth of focus of a photograph. With a wide-angle lens, a camera can create a sharp focus in a deep space such as a landscape. It can maintain focus on an image close to the camera, as well as details far behind it, however, the curvature of the lens can disproportionately enlarge objects around the edge of the image. A telephoto lens can zoom in on a subject from a distance and focus sharply on the subject, but it also creates a shallow depth of field around and behind the subject, leading to a distinctly sharp subject and blurry background. The very idea of blurriness or out-of-focus imagery is attached to photo imagery, and did not exist in drawing or painting before the camera, because it is not how our eyes work. Previous to the camera, space was depicted through linear and atmospheric perspective, but not focus.

The compression of values and contrast—the value range in a photo—are determined by the brightness of light in the subject and speed of the camera shutter. A photo on a bright day with a quick shutter speed could lead to a high contrast image where the mid range of values are diminished, and the shadow and highlight values are sharp and compressed. In other words, if the shadows are very dark, details within them can be hard to perceive. The same is true in the highlights. This may lead to a striking photo, but again, it is not how the eye sees light—only the camera sees light in this way.

When drawing from life, the eye can adjust to light shifts and perceive details in shadows and in highlights that a camera, under certain settings, might not. A high-contrast photo can graphically simplify an image in a way the eye would not tend to do on its own. A camera's flash is one of the most recognizable lighting effects in a drawing taken from a photo. A photo taken with a flash should not be used as a reference for a drawing unless that particular quality of lighting is explicitly part of the subject the artist is trying to achieve.

Other distortions in photography can appear in perspective and the bending of space. Photos can exaggerate and distort space in a way the eye does not. A photo of a seated figure with his legs closer in space to the viewer than his head can make the legs and feet look disproportionately large. Our eyes tend not to account for this proportional shift, but a camera will record it. It may look acceptable in a photo because it's part of the language of photography, but it will look awkward when translated into a drawing, since we know that the legs or feet of a figure are not, in fact, larger than the head. This distortion will always reference a photo quality and betray the use of photo reference.

If the shadows are very dark, details within them can be hard to perceive. The same is true in the highlights.

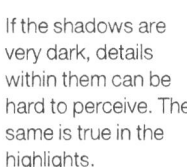

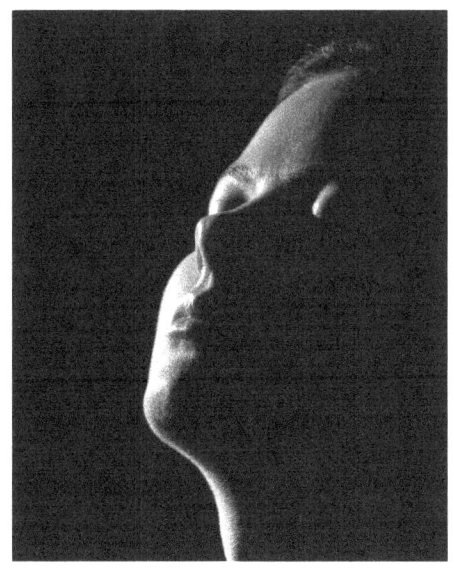

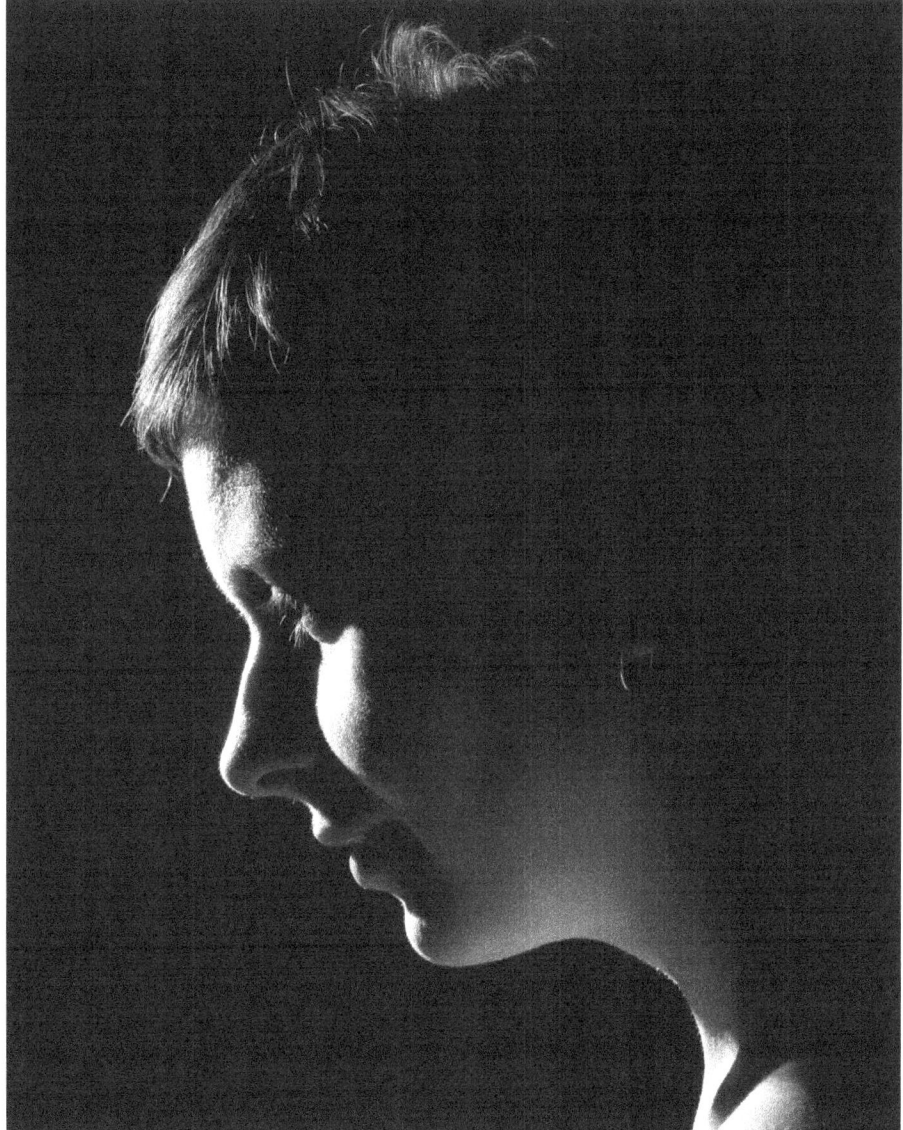

With a wide-angle lens, a camera can create a sharp focus in a deep space such as a landscape.

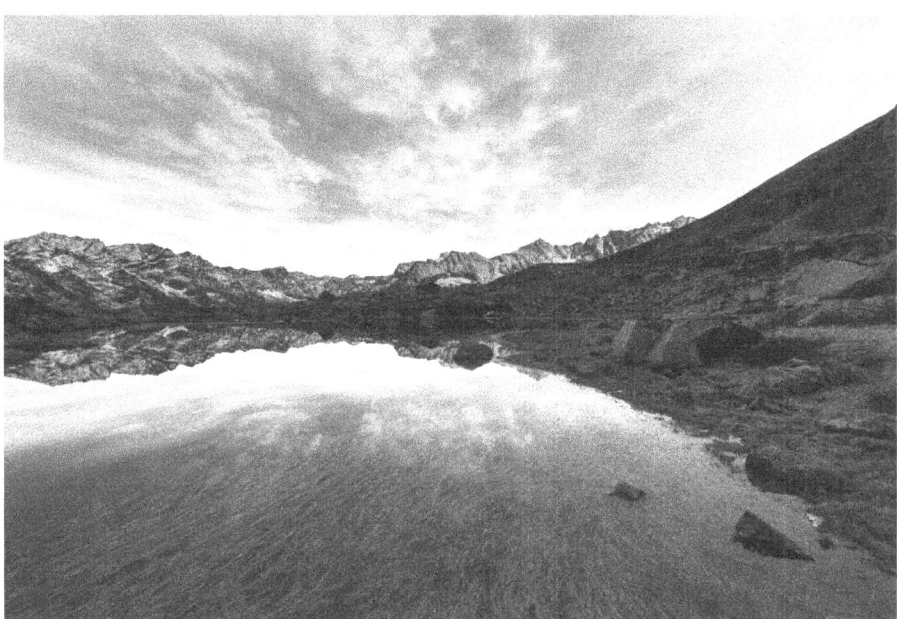

A wide-angle lens can distort the scale of images around the periphery of an image, and a fisheye lens exaggerates this distortion even more. It can cause a straight line, such as a long counter in a restaurant, or a street that is coming at the viewer, to appear to curve away toward the edge of the image. Straight lines would not curve under our natural observation, but only under the distortion of a camera lens.

An artist's decision of where to emphasize highlights, contrast, and sharpness in a drawing will help to guide a viewer's eye through it. When drawing from life, you look at a subject and decide whether the focus will be on the face, the hands, or something else. The peripheral subjects fall out of sharpness as a result of the eye's focus. Whatever the eye focuses on in real life becomes the point of highest contrast.

If the subject is a figure, but the focus is the hands, the peripheral vision will soften the details of the face, body, and background, and the highlights, sharpness, and contrast will appear strongest on the hands. This can be seen as the artist's subjective, or relative, viewpoint, which allows for organizing information in an image in a clear way.

The hierarchy of light and contrast that make an image clear and guide the viewer's eye is established by the artist's subjective viewpoint. A camera can also be subjective, but just as easily it can be objective. In a photograph, the entire image can be sharp: Highlights and contrast of even sharpness can be evenly distributed through the picture, giving the eye no obvious point of focus or importance. This can lead to a cluttered or confusing image. The eye has a tendency to edit more than the camera lens.

This photographic tendency is not taboo in image making—it's a visual cue that distinguishes the photographic language. Someone who is drawing from a photo needs to understand this as being specifically part of the language of photography. In photorealism, these are all visual cues that can be brought to the forefront of the image to be controlled and used intelligently, if the artist is conscious of them.

A trained artist can usually look at a drawing or painting and tell immediately if the image was taken from a photo reference or drawn from life based on these distortions. A photo can be used merely as a starting point or a guide to work from rather than an image to copy precisely. An artist who is aware of the distortions that come from a photo can easily control a drawing to overcome or compensate for the distortions. Likewise, if it is the distortions in the image that the artist is after, awareness of these qualities can help to emphasize them. Either way, if copying the photo exactly is the goal, then there are specific practices that will help you do exactly that.

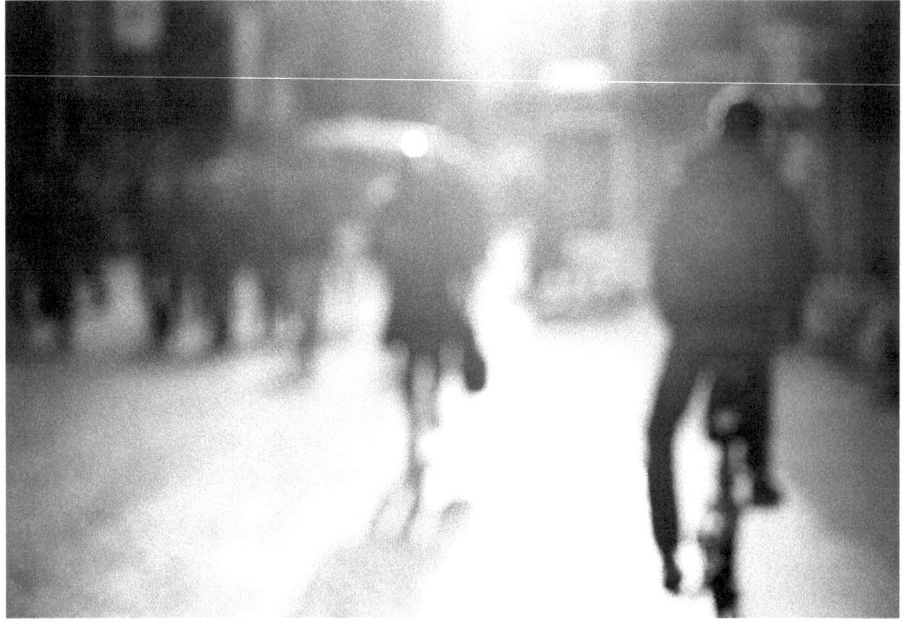

Left: An artist's decision of where to emphasize highlights, contrast, and sharpness in a drawing will help to guide a viewer's eye through it.

Right: A wide-angle lens can distort the scale of images around the periphery of an image, and a fisheye lens exaggerates this distortion even more.

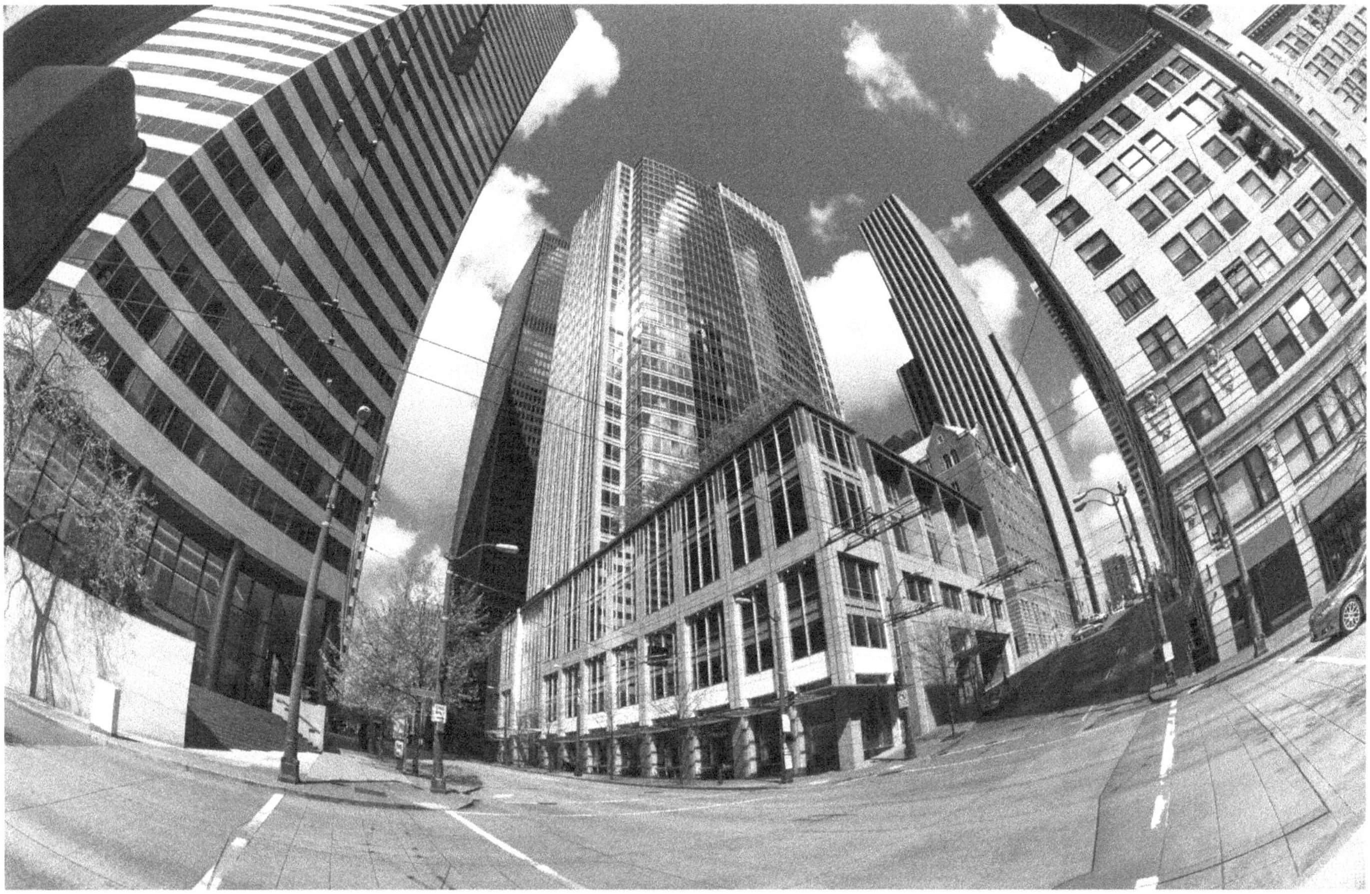

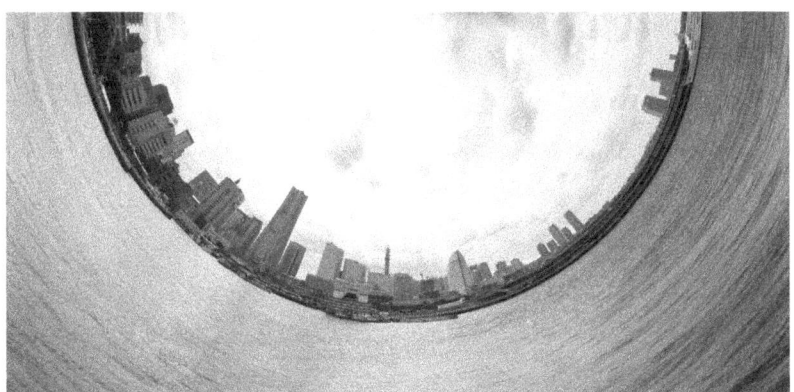

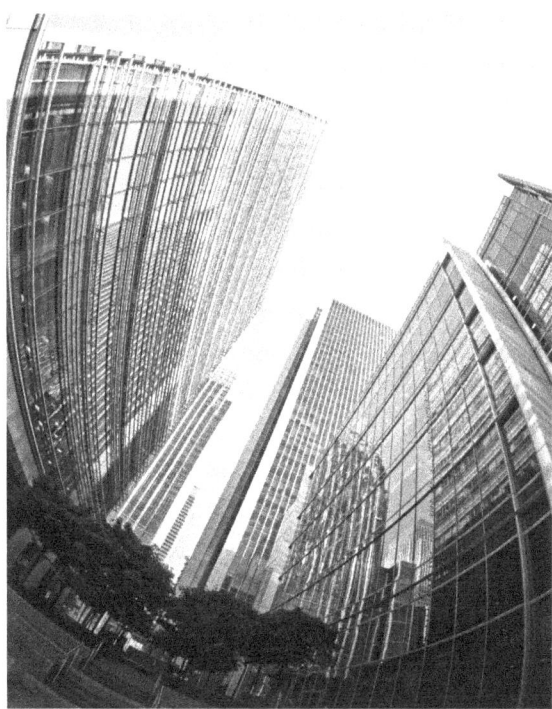

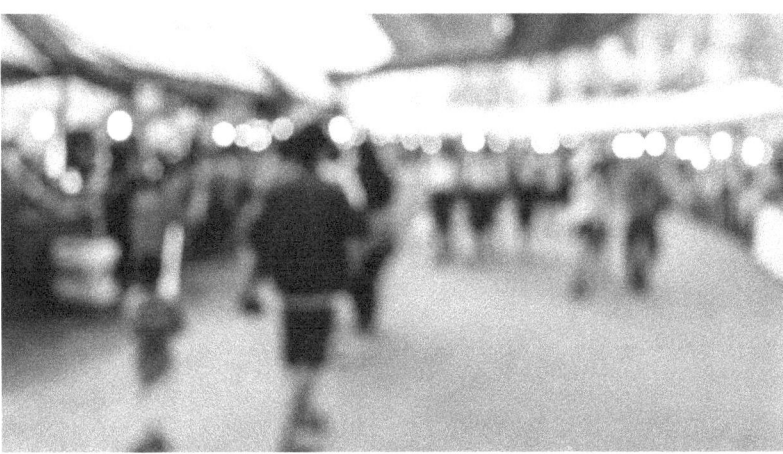

Create a grid over the photo you intend to copy. Don't make the grid too tight — keep the squares between 1/2 inch and 1 inch (1.3 and 2.5 cm). This will provide enough room to work within each square.

Draw another grid of the exact proportions on the paper you will use for the drawing. The new grid does not have to be the same size as the photo. As long as the grid is proportionally the same between the photo and the drawing, the grid can actually be used to scale up the photo quite a bit. Draw the grid lightly so it will not be visible in the final drawing.

Photo reference for photorealistic drawing

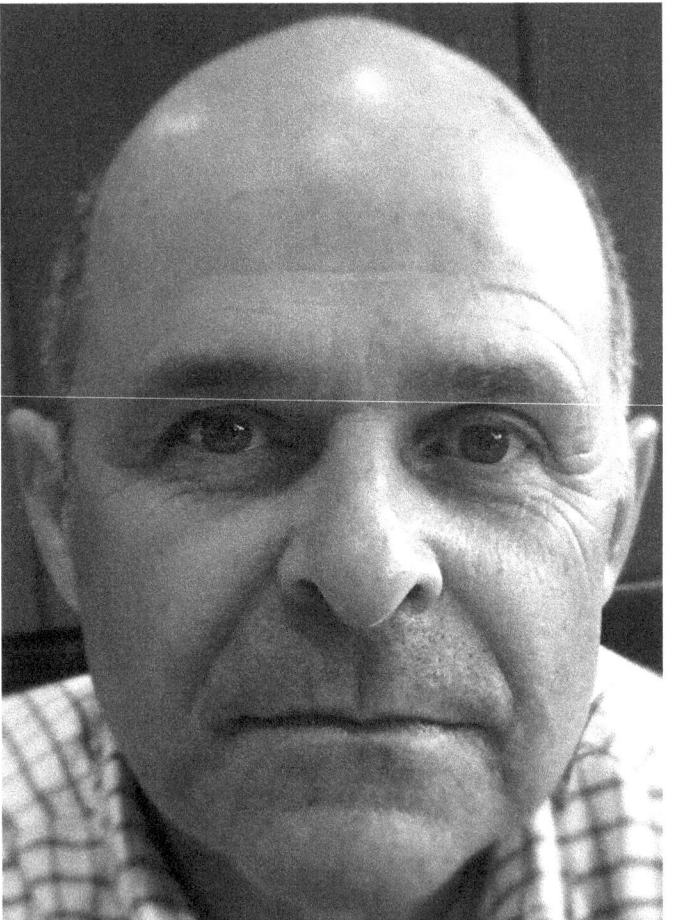

Create a grid over the photo

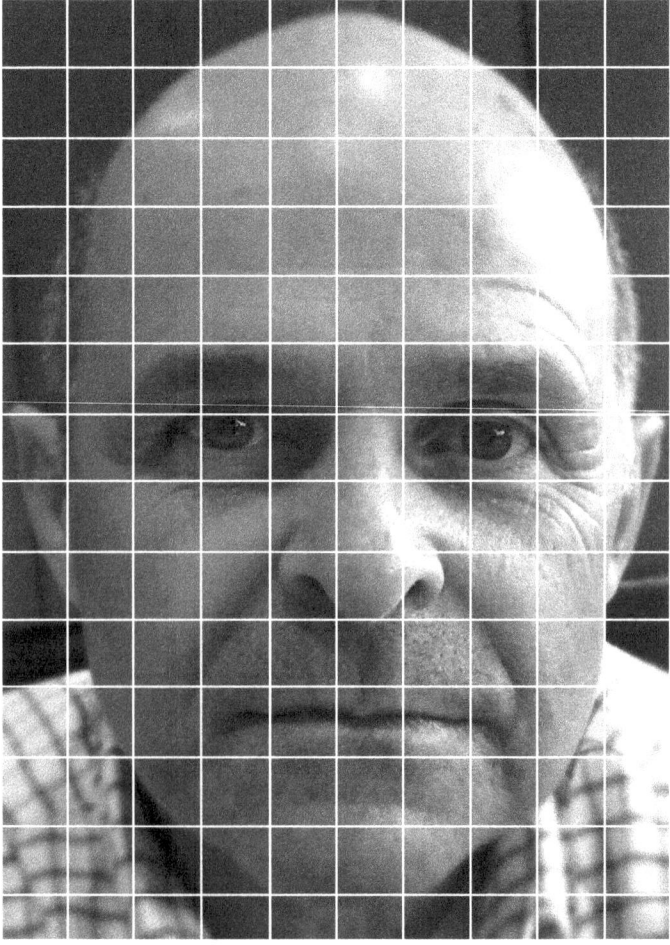

PENCIL IN THE
LINE DRAWING

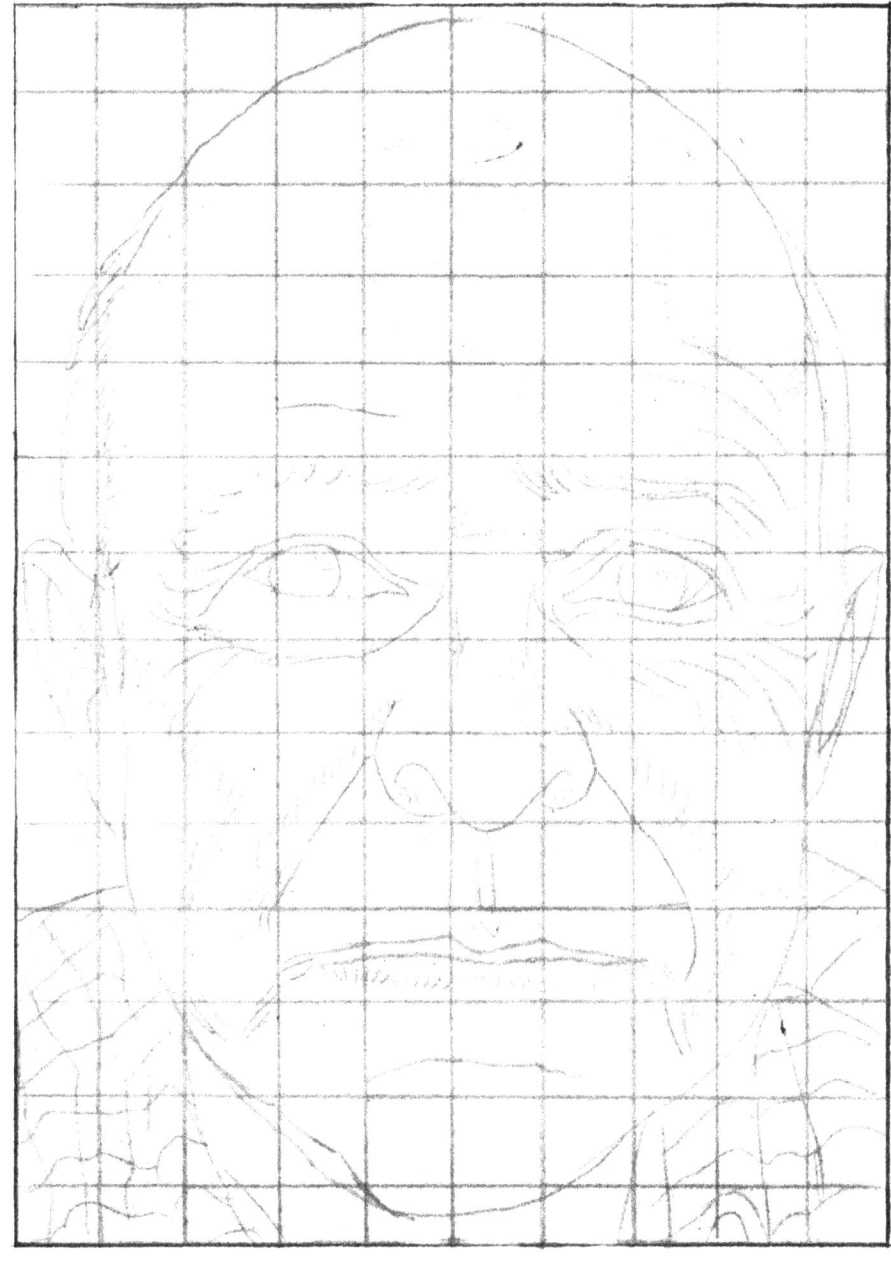

Create a line drawing over the empty grid using the squares and their intersections to align the proportions of the subject. In the example, with the left eye, look for where the edges of the eye align with the grid. Do the edges of the eye line up with the squares they sit in? Is the right corner of the eye within the square, or does it overlap into the next? Is the edge of the eye in the top middle or bottom of the square?

Mark the beginning and endpoints of the eye as it passes through the square, and then connect the points with a line. For instance, the bottom edge of the right eye passes through the center of the square it's in. The left edge of the right eye overlaps into the adjacent square and occupies the top right quadrant of that square. The eyelid arcs across the bottom of the square above and to the right of that square.

Look at the nose. The width of it takes up three squares, while the right and left nostrils take up almost an entire square each. The ball of the nose takes up the square between the nostrils, and the tip of the nose overlaps just a little into the square below it.

Draw another grid on paper. It should be the same proportions as the grid on the photo. Pencil in the line drawing.

EXERCISE 2: ADD TONE IN THE LIGHTER RANGE

Start to add shading. Keep the value in the lighter range at first. Use this initial pass to begin identifying where the highlights will go. Ideally, you will add tone to the entire drawing, excluding the highlights.

This first pass will establish the basic details and highlights without getting too dark. It will help the form if the shading uses lines or crosshatching that follow the form. Think of the shading as wrapping around the surface of the subject.

Define the background and start to add shading in the lighter range.

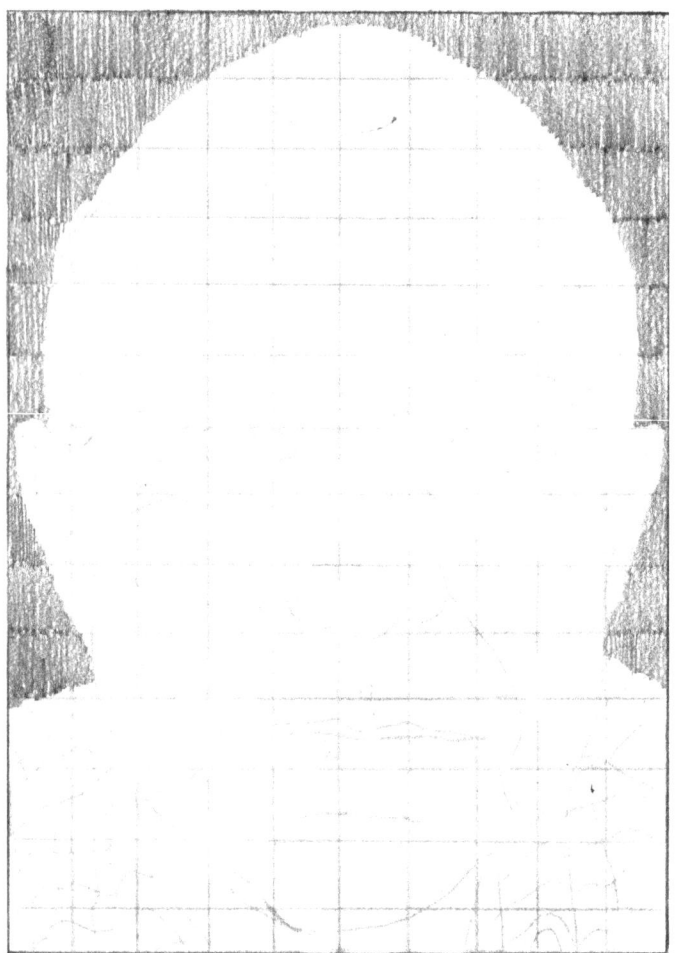

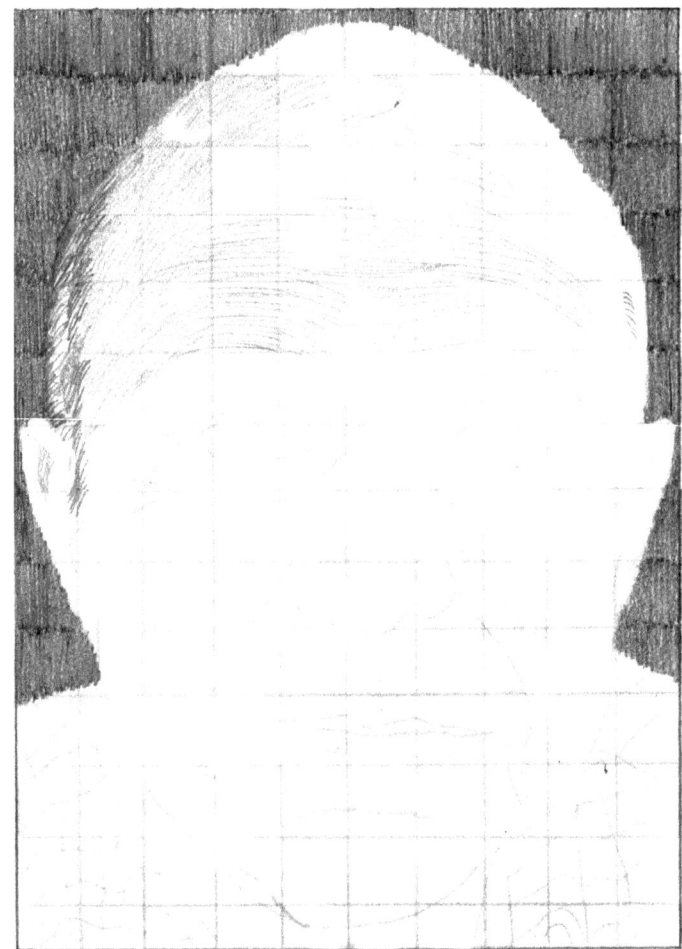

Add form to the drawing with contoured lines and crosshatching. Begin to wrap the shading around the surface of the subject.

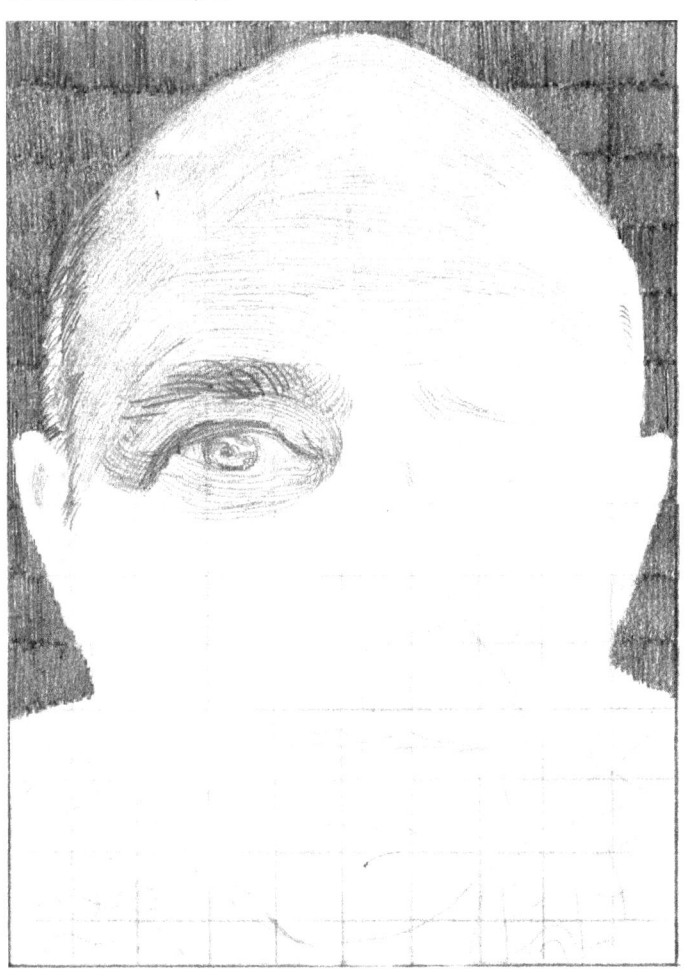 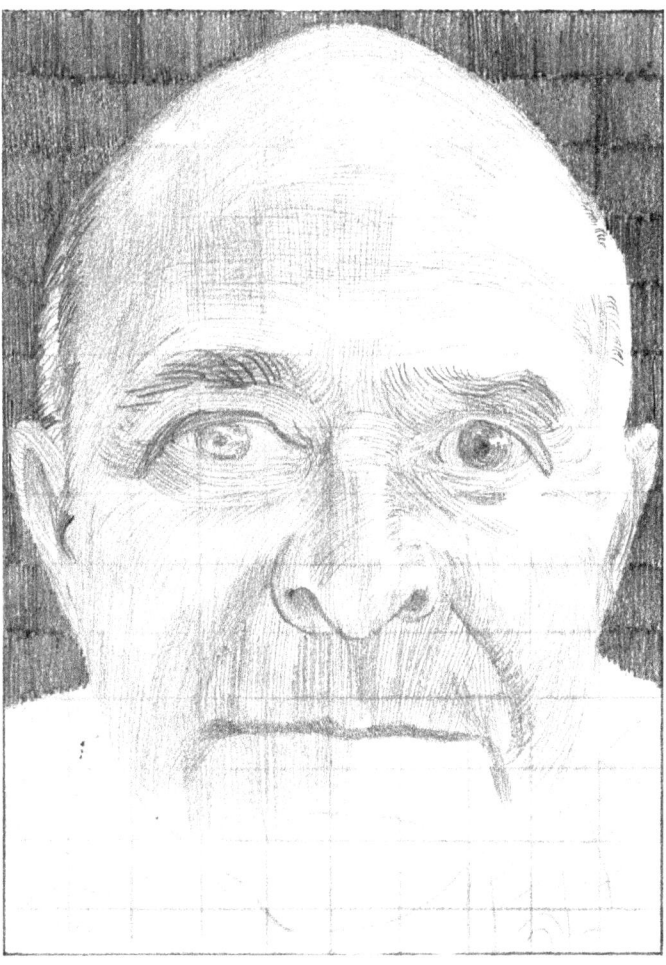

The grid can help here because you can look at the value relationships within each square and compare them to the whole of the image. Look for the darkest dark and lightest light within each square, then pull back and look at how those compare to the darkest dark in the image as a whole. If the darkest dark within a square is much lighter than the darkest dark in the image as a whole, it will help adjust the range of values accordingly within the rest of the square.

Once the basic drawing and the first light shading are done, go back into the shadow and identify the areas of the darkest darks in the image. (In this exercise, these areas will be the nose, eyes, and shadow behind the head as well as the mouth.)

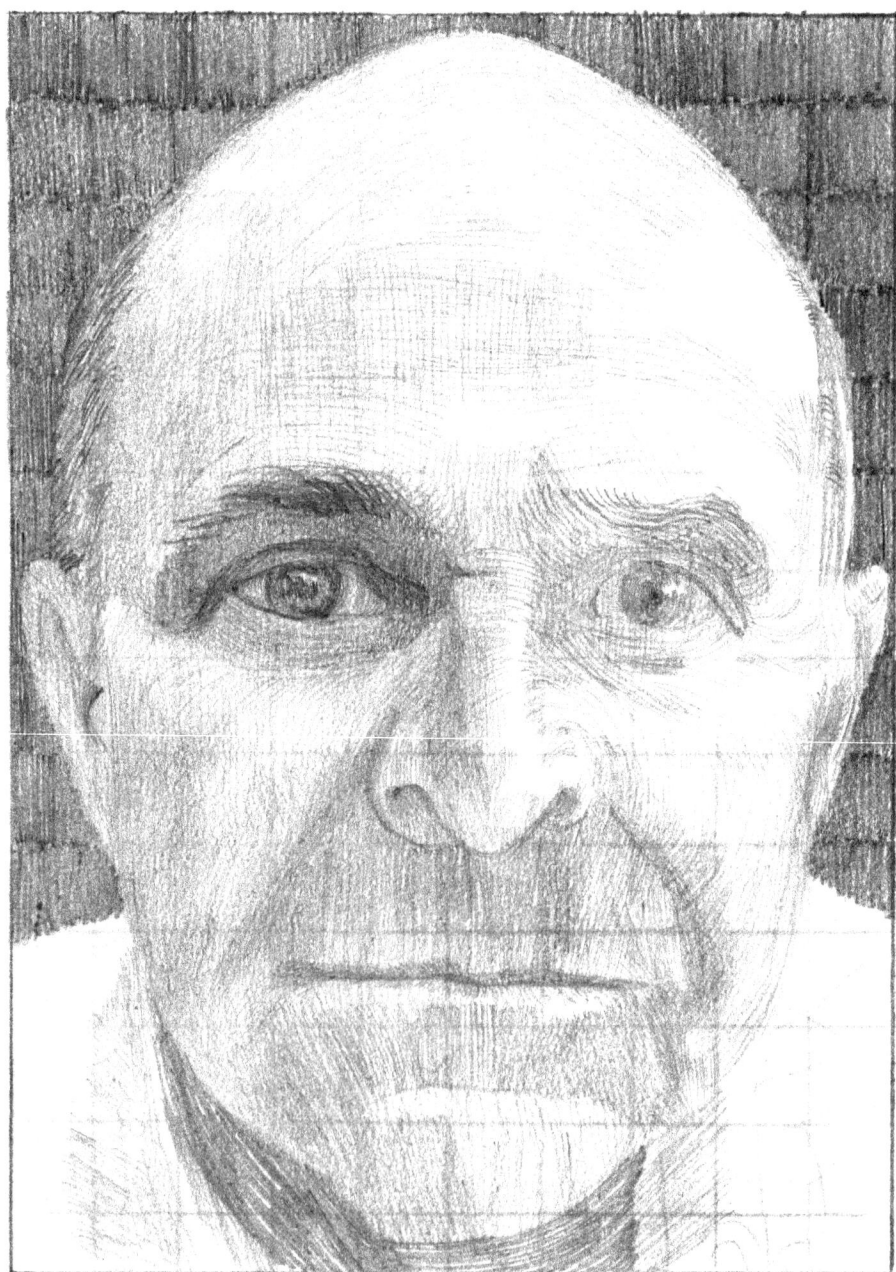

Use the grid to help you examine the value relationships within each square.

Find the darkest darks
and lightest lights within
each square.

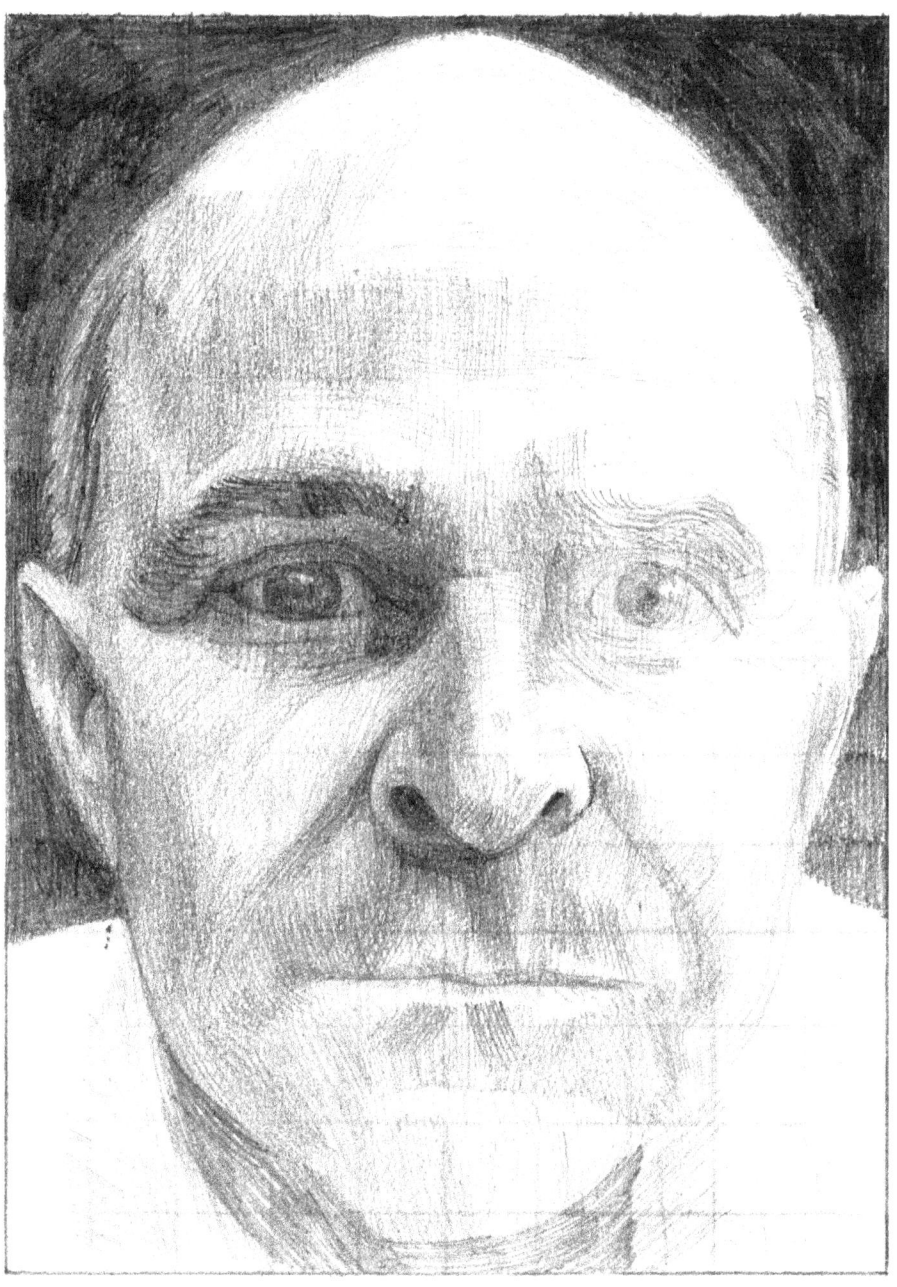

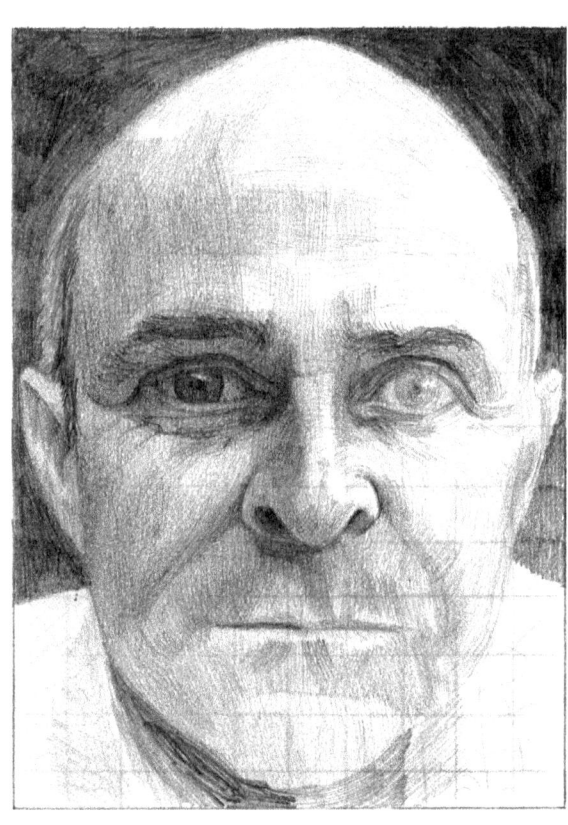

After establishing the range by noting the darkest values, begin to work in the mid range of values by comparing them to the set range.

Ask yourself if a shadow is darker or lighter than the value in the adjoining square. Is it as dark as the darkest dark? Is it lighter? How much lighter? Follow the system laid out in the tonal chapter (page 42) for developing a relative value scale in which to work. The rules from that chapter apply equally to the tonal range here.

Develop the full tonal range. The rules from the Drawing with Tone chapter (page 42) apply to the range here.

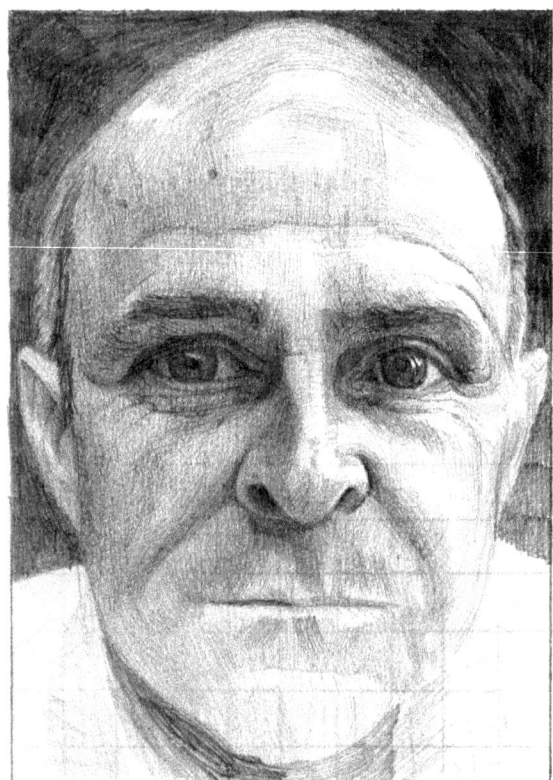

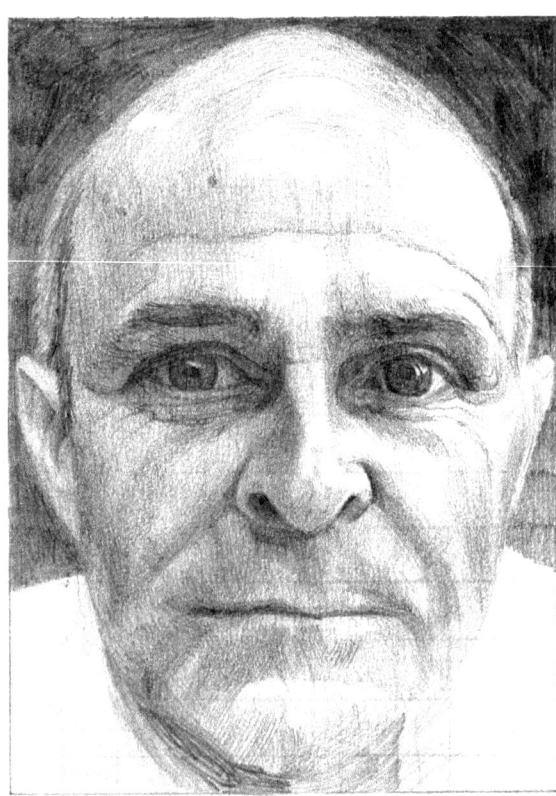

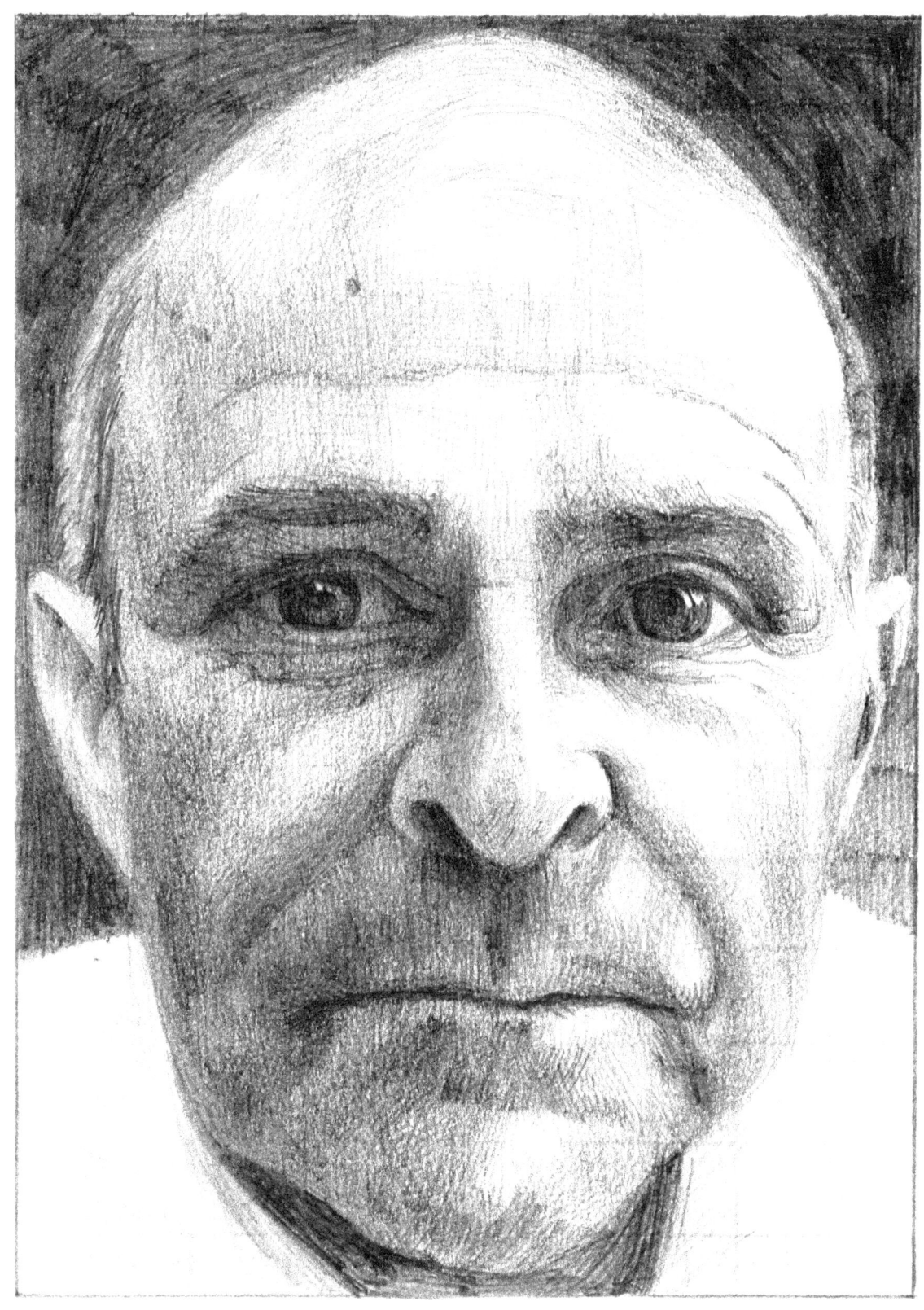

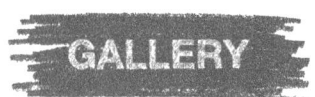

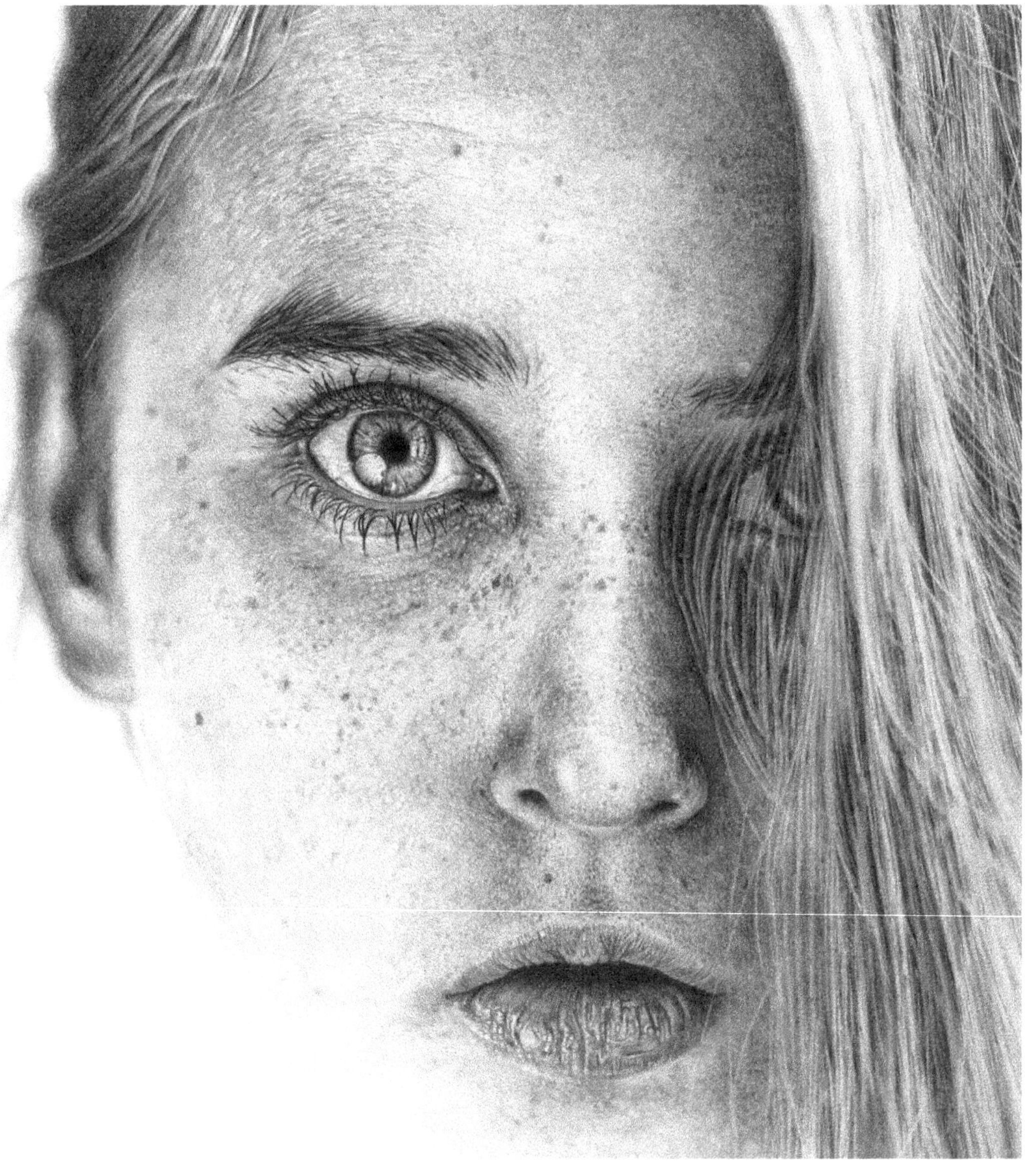

Monica Lee, *Alisa*,
pencil on paper.
Photo by Michelle Lee.

Monica Lee,
Fatoumata Diawara,
pencil on paper.
Photo by Flavia Schaub.

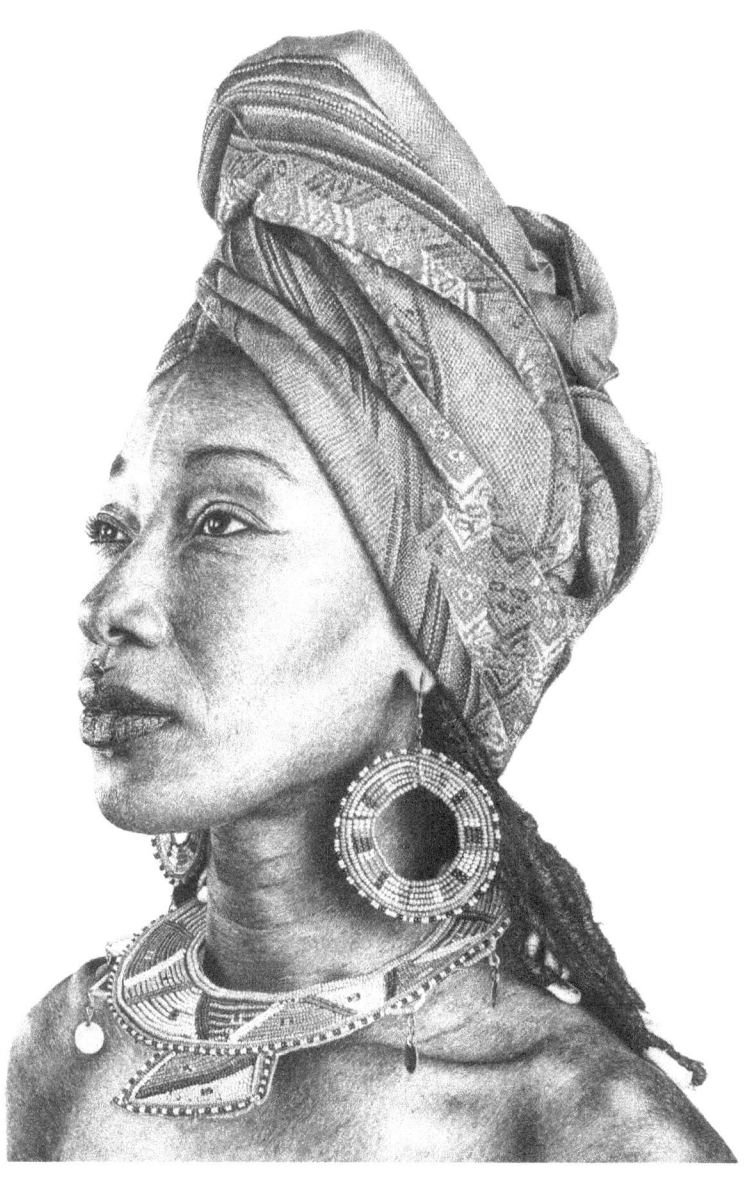

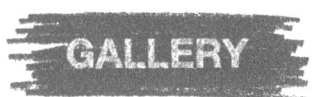

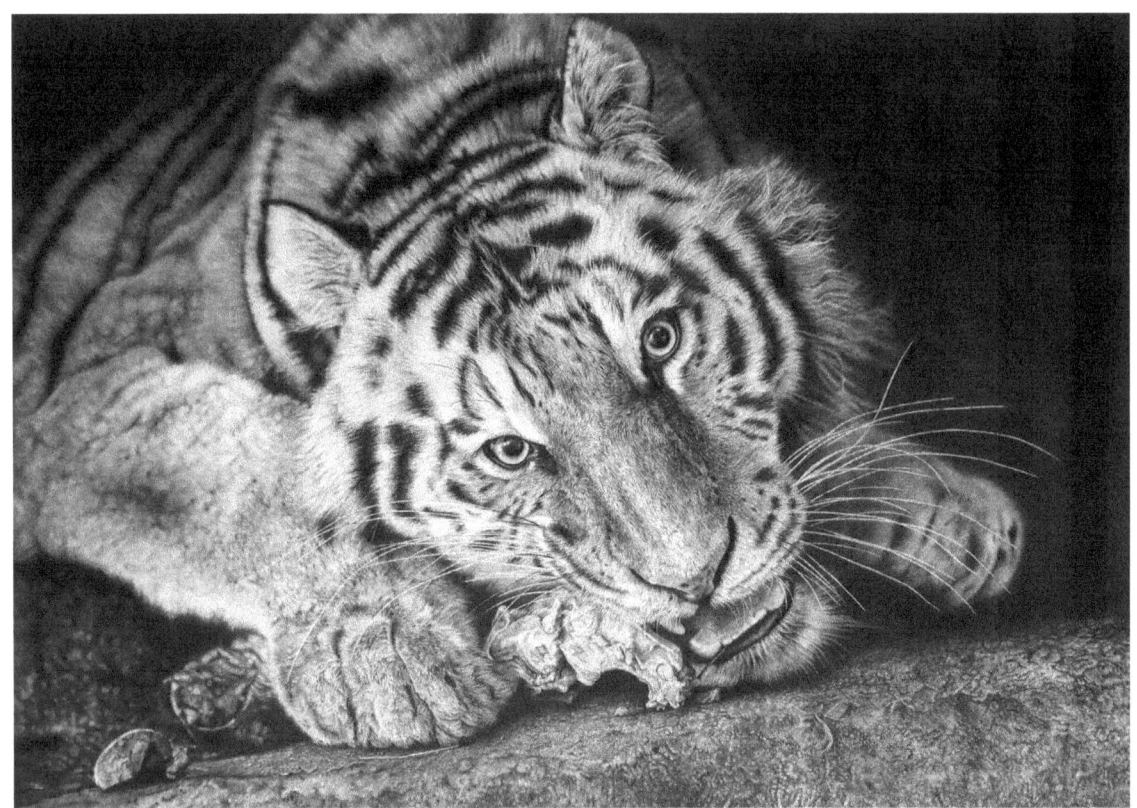

Monica Lee,
Tigress and Her Bone,
pencil on paper. Photo
by Emmanuel Keller.

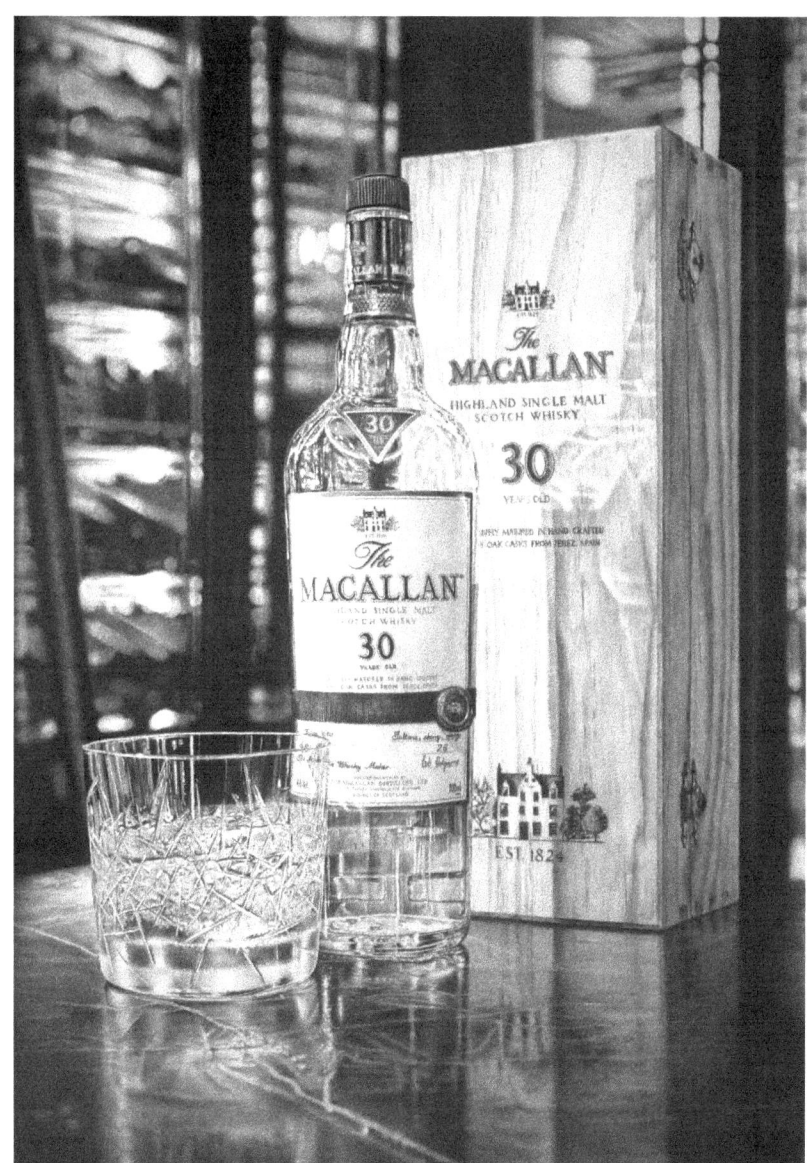

Monica Lee, *Macallan*,
pencil on paper.
Photo by Melvin Lee.

Color can be added to a pencil drawing with a variety of mediums: watercolor, gouache, ink, or colored pencil. When mixing color with graphite, first decide which is the most important ingredient: the pencil drawing or the color?

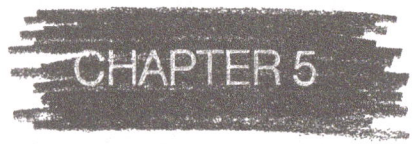

CHAPTER 5

ADDING COLOR

Is the purpose of the drawing to work out the composition of a piece in which all of the detail and rendering will be described through color? Or is the pencil the primary texture of the piece that is being lightly embellished by color? The two elements need to work together and not compete for the attention of the viewer—that could result in a murky image.

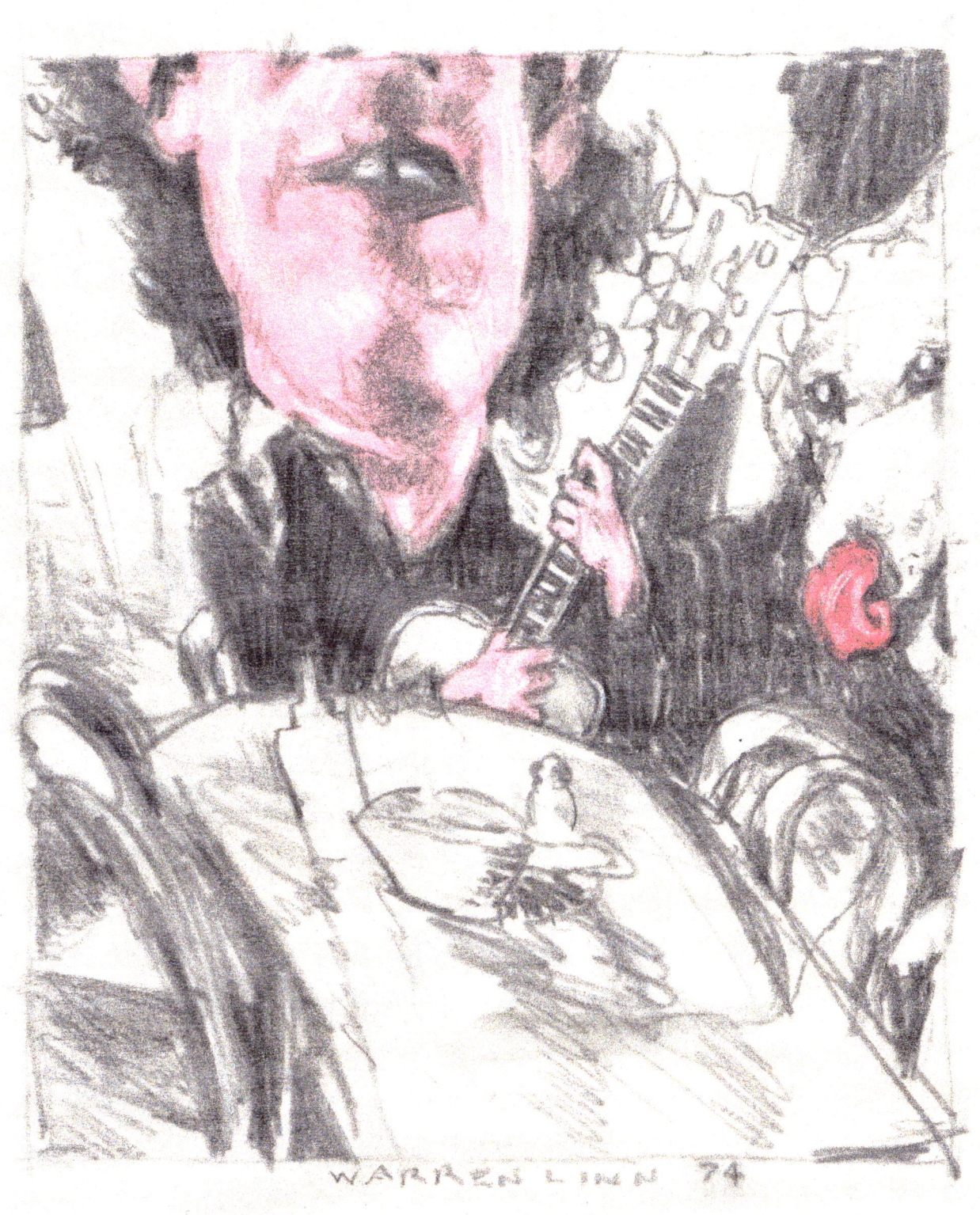

Warren Linn,
Chicago Mag '74,
pencil on paper

WET AND DRY

The smooth texture of graphite can make it tricky to mix it with other mediums. Graphite is a claylike mineral with a very smooth, slick texture. When you draw with it on paper, it creates a smooth sheen. Paper's fibrous texture makes it naturally absorbent, enabling it to hold wet media like watercolor and ink because the liquid and pigment or dye can soak into the fibers. Graphite seals the tooth of the paper, making it hard to layer liquid media on top.

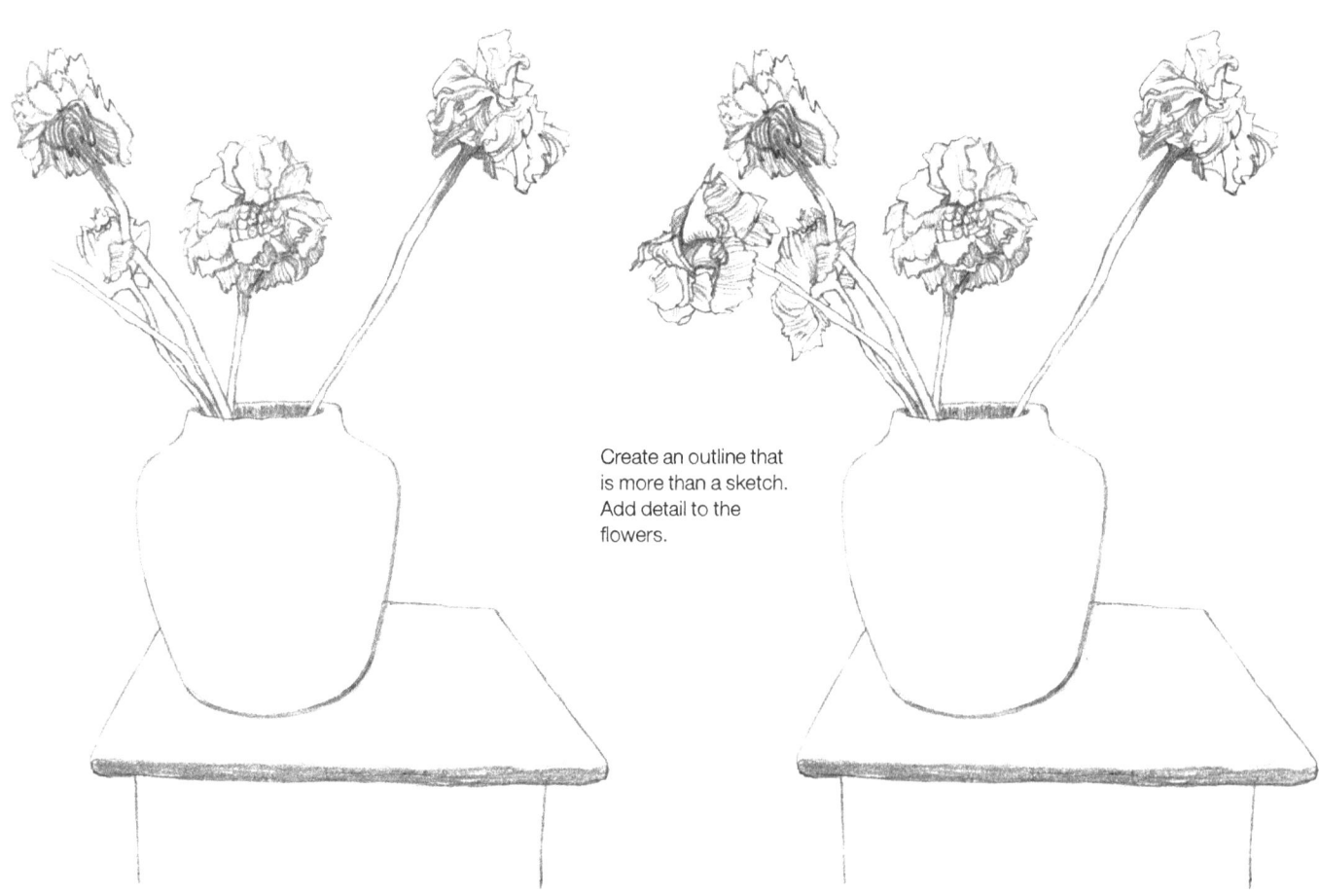

Create an outline that is more than a sketch. Add detail to the flowers.

If a page is covered with large areas of graphite and watercolor or ink is added on top, they will probably bead up and roll off. Graphite's first use was for lubrication on cannonballs, so that may help give you an idea of what graphite can do to the texture of paper. This does not prohibit the layering of paint, ink, or other media on graphite, but has the potential to complicate it.

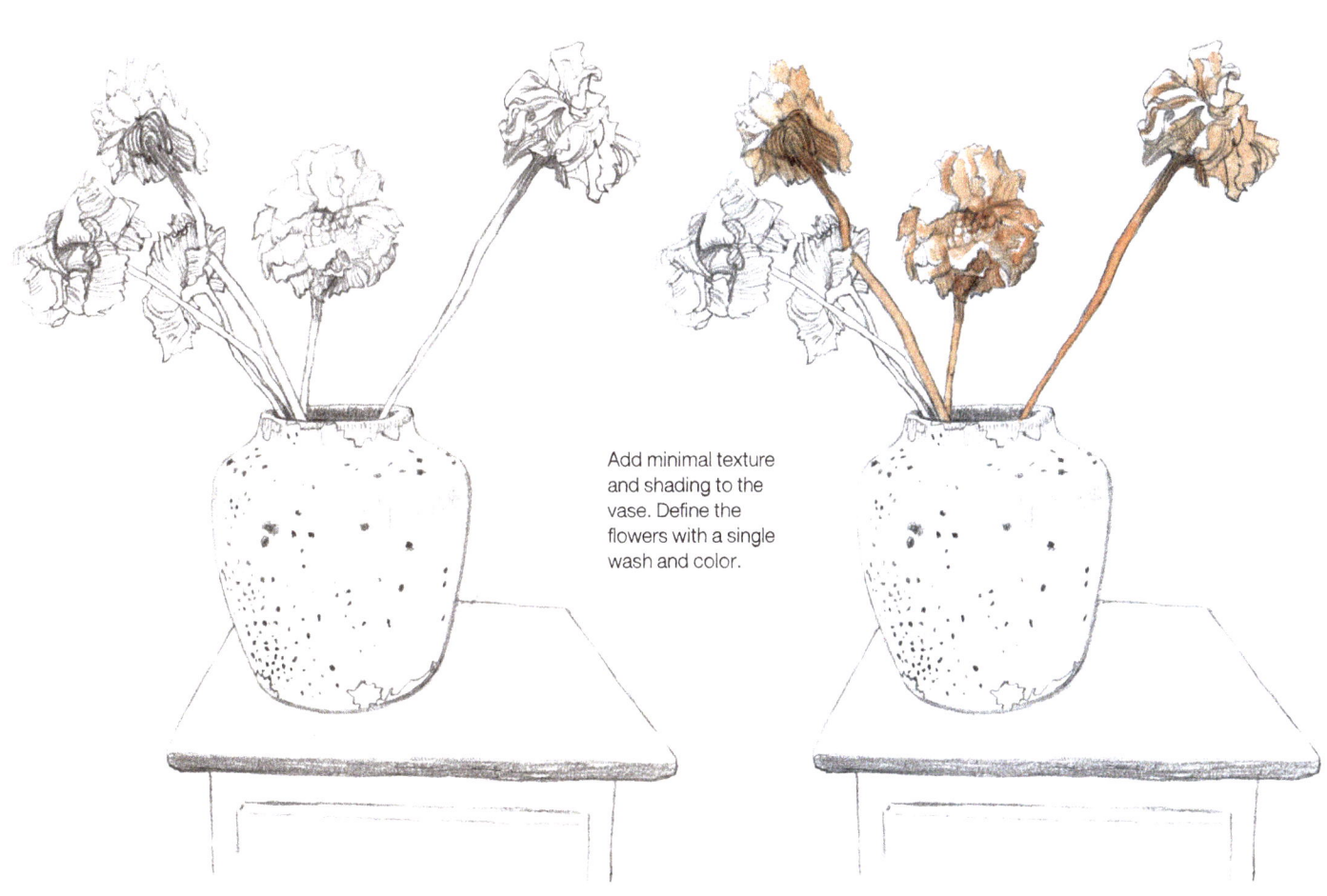

Add minimal texture and shading to the vase. Define the flowers with a single wash and color.

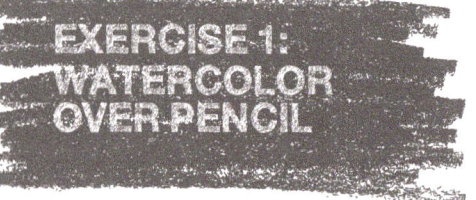

EXERCISE 1: WATERCOLOR OVER PENCIL

Probably the most common way of coloring a pencil drawing is with a watercolor wash. As long as the graphite is not too thick, watercolor will sit on top of it comfortably.

The important decision to be made before beginning is whether the drawing or the watercolor will be the emphasis. You need to decide how resolved the pencil drawing should be and how much room is left for the watercolor to resolve the image.

If the drawing resolves all of the shading and details, there may not be a lot of room to showcase the watercolor. Painting over a very detailed pencil drawing can result in an image that is murky, making neither the pencil nor the color look good.

Add a wash to the background. Define the stems of the flowers with a darker wash.

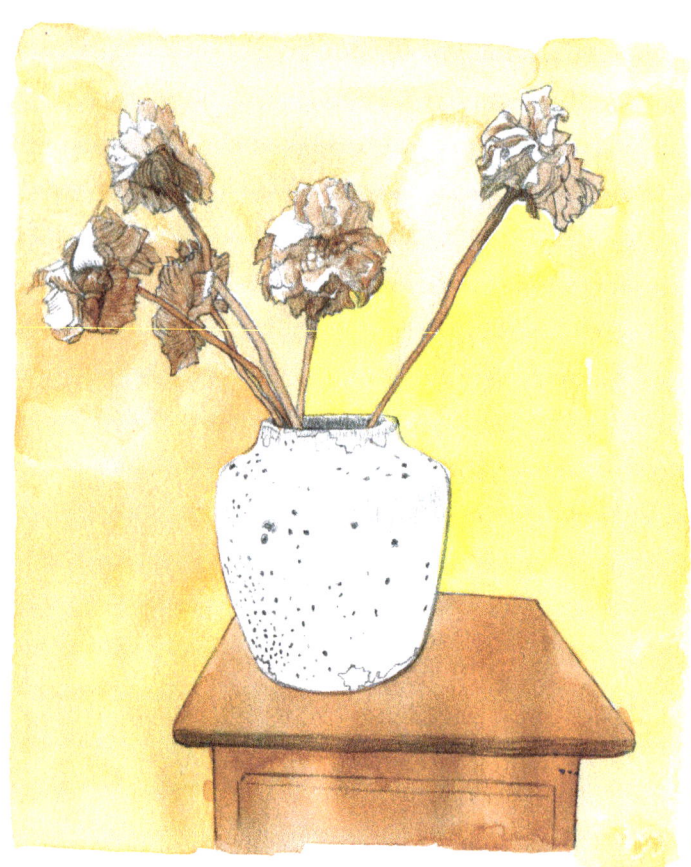

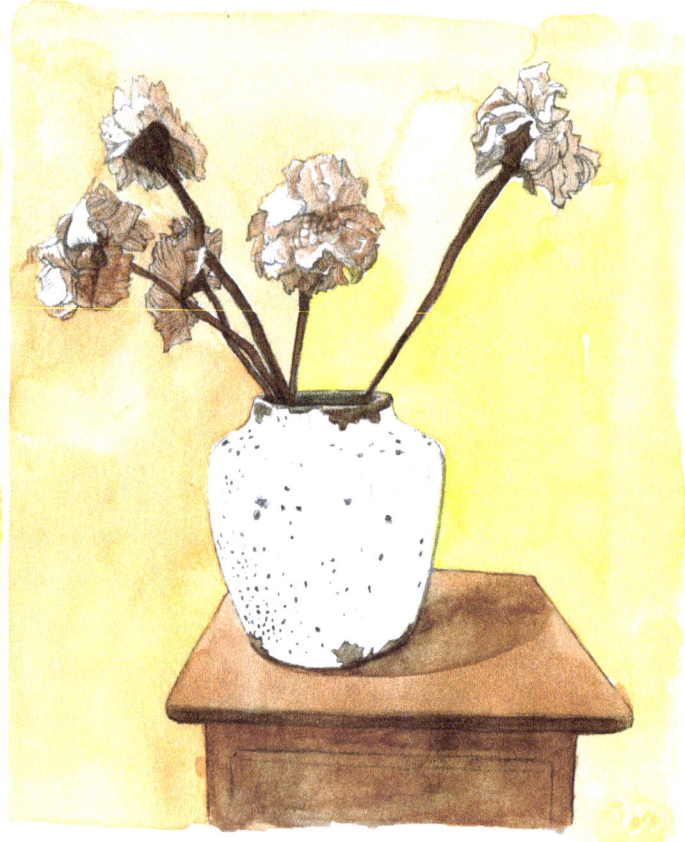

As an example, start with a drawing of a vase and flowers. First, create an outline. The vase will have the most color, so that is the part of the drawing left least resolved in pencil. However, the outline should be more than a sketch. Finish it by drawing boldly with a 2–4B pencil.

Give more graphite emphasis to the flowers. While you needed to add only minimal texture and shading to the vase, you can articulate the flowers more clearly with pencil line because of the complicated folds of the leaves.

Add color to the flowers with a brown wash, but only one wash and one color. You don't want to overwork an already detailed area. Leave the highlights of the flowers untouched by watercolor.

Add a yellow wash to the background to pop the highlights of the flowers.

Give the stems of the flowers another darker wash. Because the stems were left as outlines in the pencil drawing with no particular details, the darker wash will not cover up any pencilwork.

The washes added to the vase will have the most color and the most actual painting. Add a layer of blue as a flat wash and paint the chipped areas with a dark brown.

The final touch is a purple wash over the blue that works as a shadow and gives volume to the vase. Purple is a good choice because it is warmer and darker than the blue, so a light wash is enough to indicate the shadow. Add the wash loosely without overworking the painting, maintaining just a slight difference between the blue and the purple.

The underdrawn vase allows for the quality of the watercolor to really come forward and not compete with the drawing, resulting in a clear, simple final drawing.

The washes on the vase have the most color. Add a coat of blue and define the chipped areas with brown. Add shadows to the vase with purple.

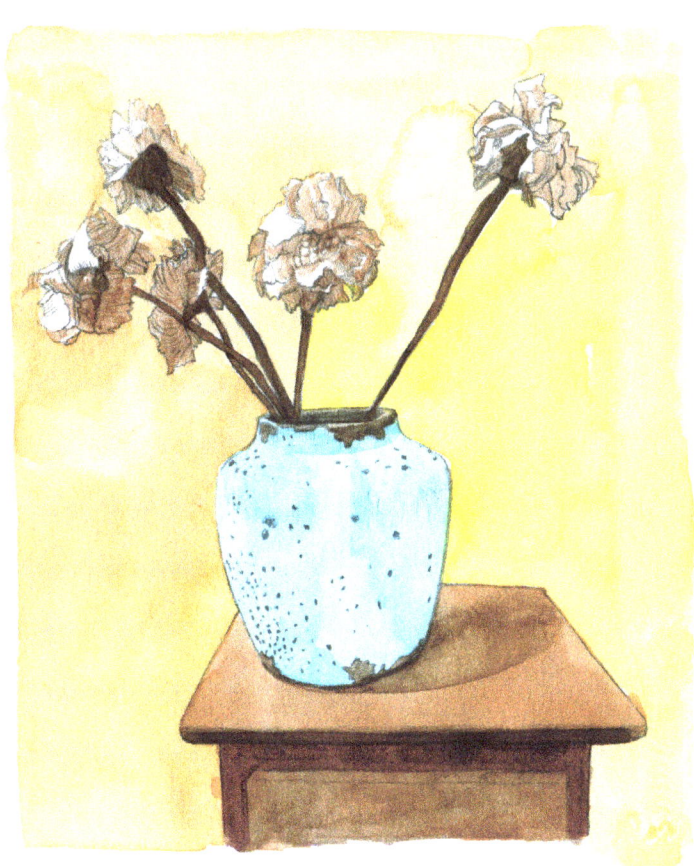
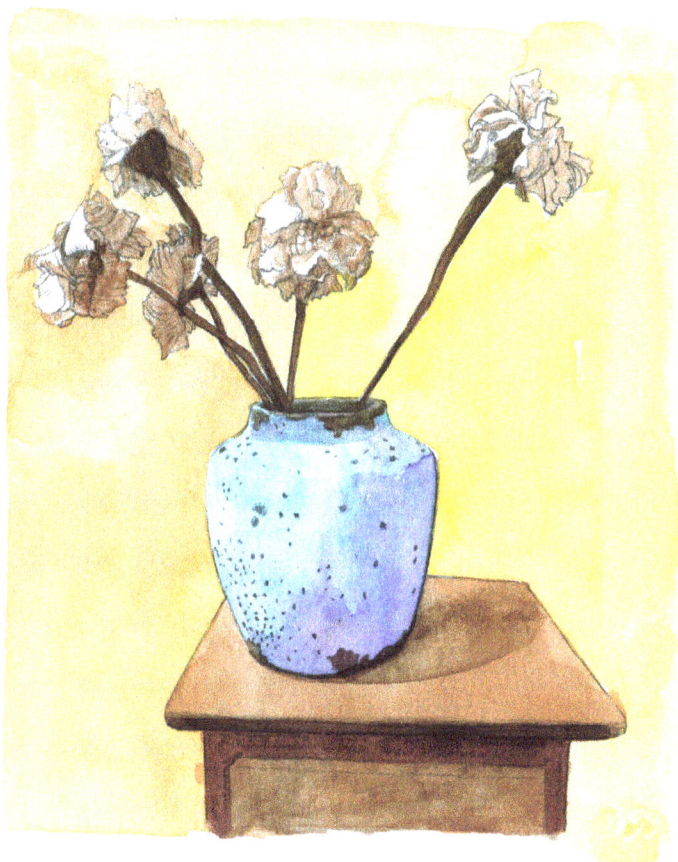

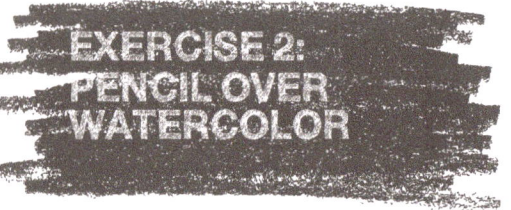
In the previous exercise, we added watercolor over pencil. But pencil can just as easily be added over watercolor to pull out details and sharpen areas.

Starting the drawing with pencil and adding watercolor means the drawing will be all in outline. Starting with watercolor means that the line can be used more selectively, and can allow for a looser, more unrestrained feeling in the rest of the image. Watercolor raises the tooth of the paper, giving it more texture, making it easy to draw on with graphite.

Start with a light pencil drawing that can be hidden by watercolor. The first wash should be very light.

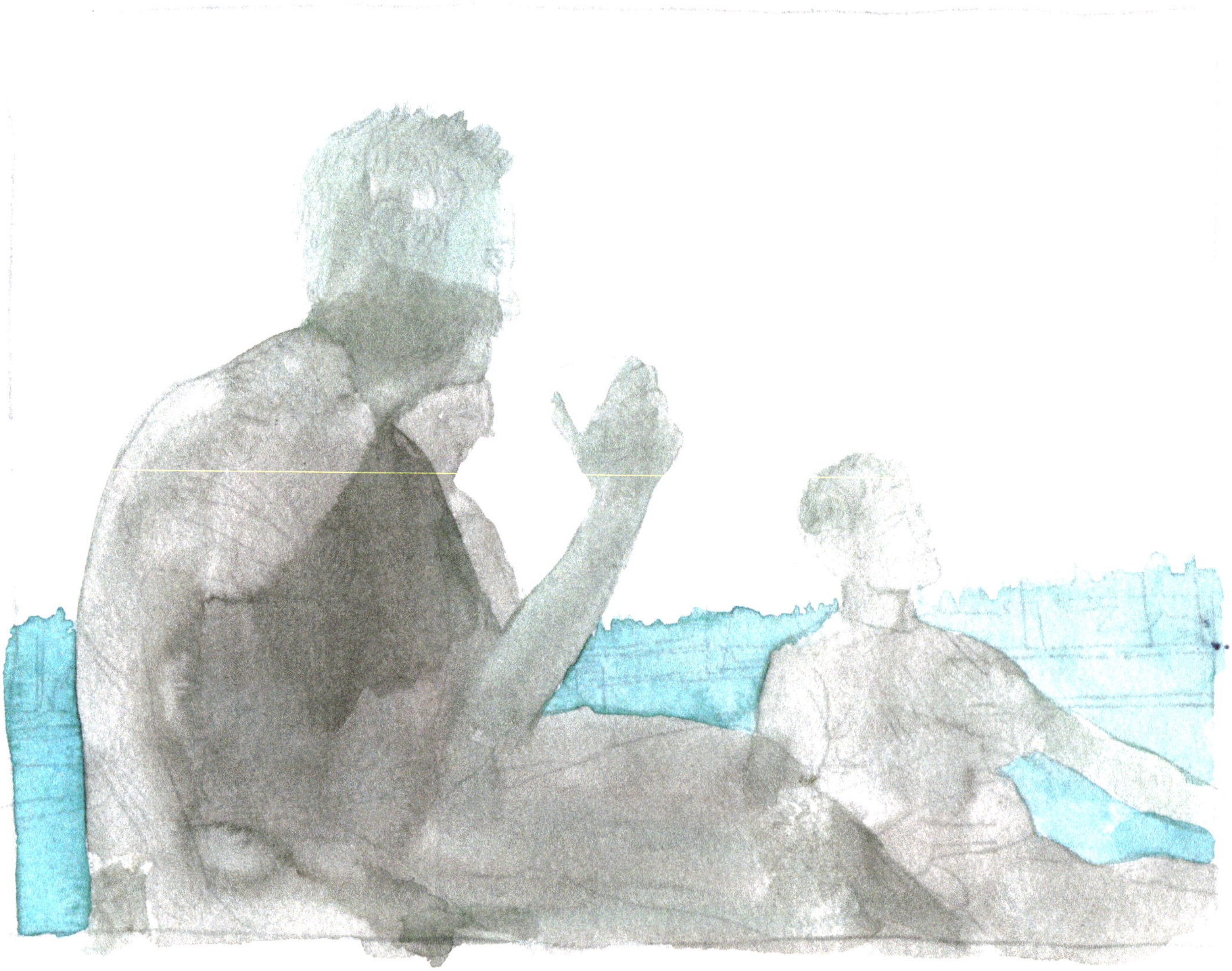

Start the drawing with a light pencil drawing. A light drawing will allow the watercolor to cover the line. Another reason to draw lightly is that once the pencil has been painted over with watercolor, or any wet media, it becomes very difficult to erase.

You don't have to do all the painting at once. In the first pass, paint in the main areas of color to give an overall sense of the shape and form of the subjects. The first wash should be light and the color should be mostly on the warmer side, especially if you intend to add more washes later. It's easy to cool down a warm wash but difficult to warm up a cool wash.

In the second pass, the washes can bring out some of the darker shapes. After you establish a clear sense of the composition with the large forms, use a dark pencil—2, 3, or 4B—and decide what details need to be described more sharply with line. In this example, the hair and beard are well served with line, along with the figure's eyes, mouth, and some of the folds in the shirt. Drawing everything in outline could flatten the space. Leaving the shirt, pants, and skyline as unoutlined shapes allows the watercolor room to breathe.

Some of the details in the background that may have been too delicate to handle with the brush can be defined in pencil. In this drawing, I've delineated the fence and architectural details of the buildings.

When the pencilwork is done, add watercolor to define the evening sky. Add shadows over the faces to heighten their silhouettes against the sunset and to finish off the image.

Washes bring out the darker shapes in the second pass.

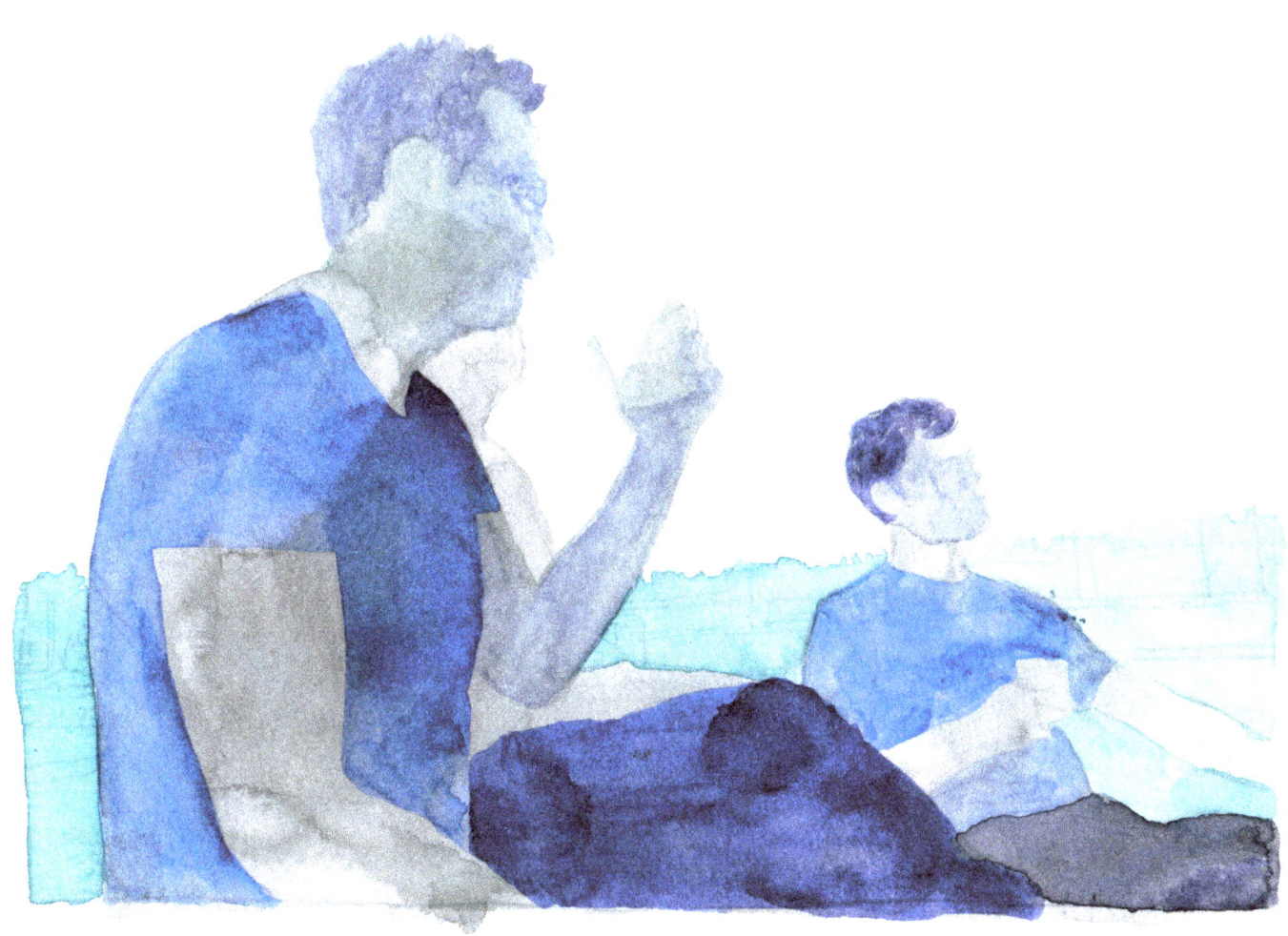

Use a dark pencil to
describe important
details.

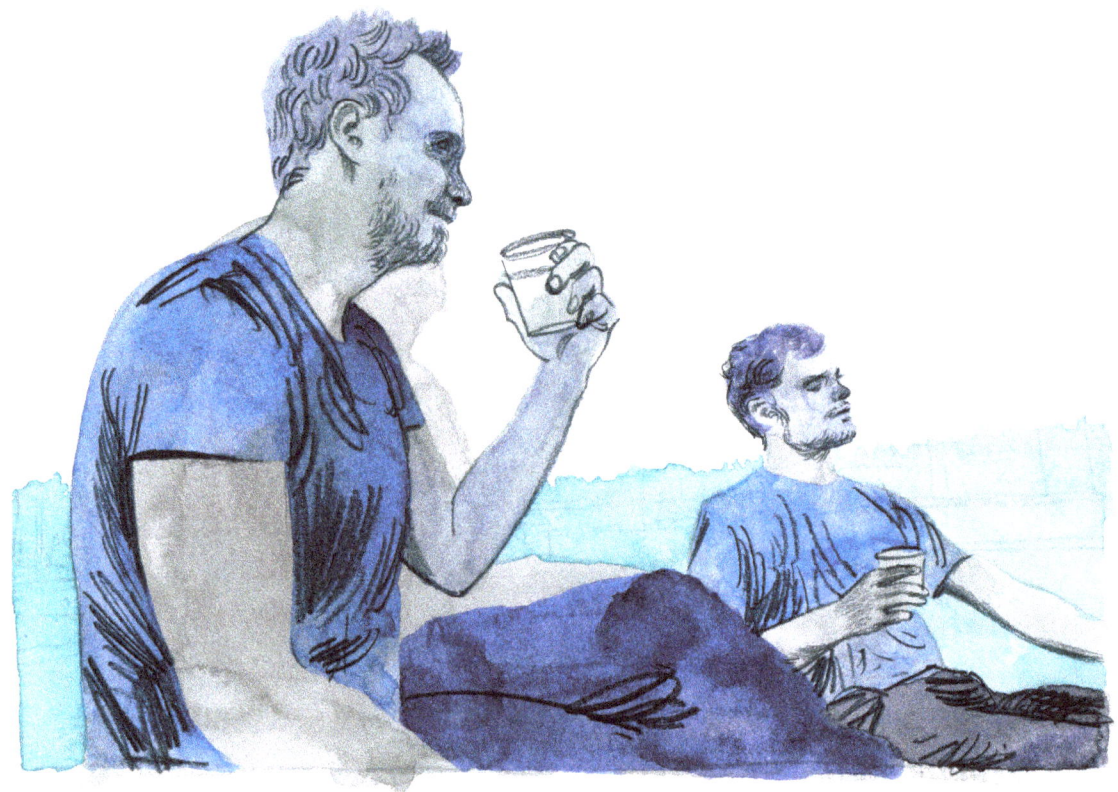

Gradually define the
background with
pencil line.

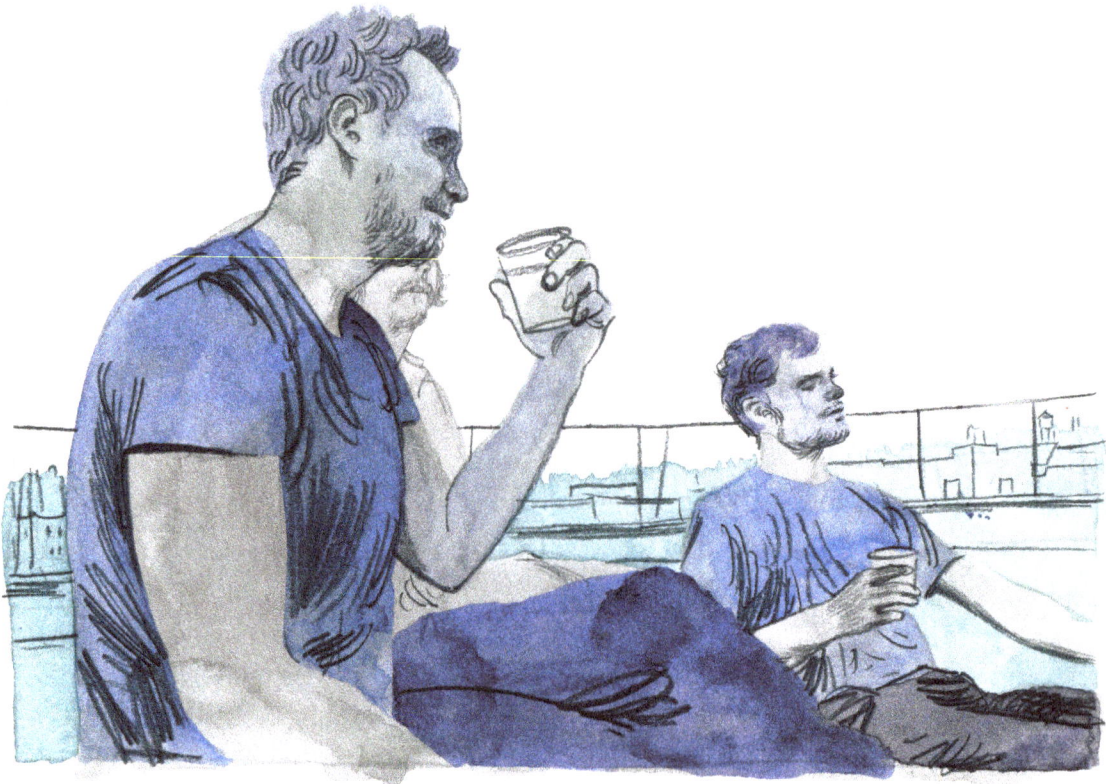

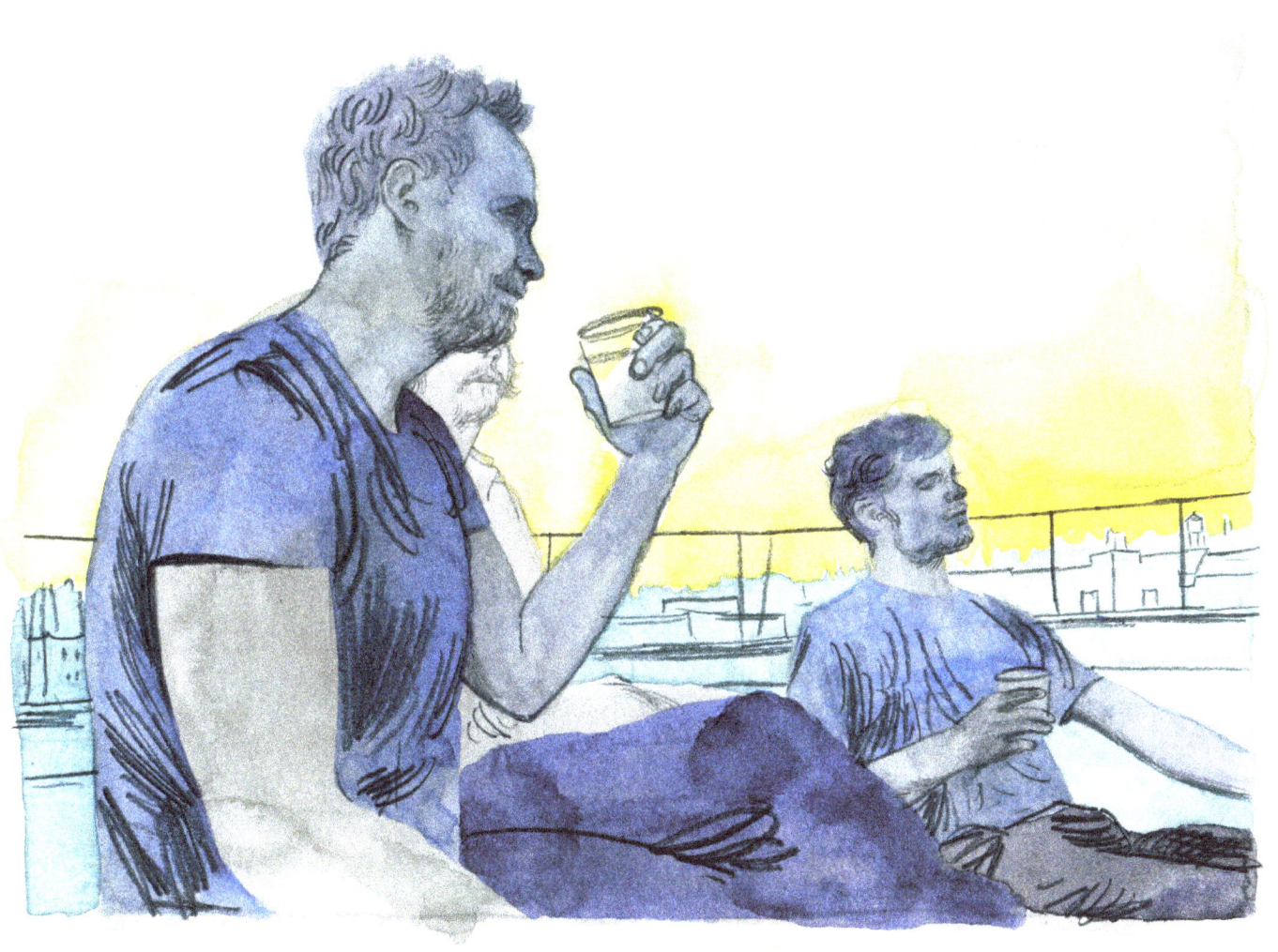

When the pencil line is complete, add watercolor to define the sky.

Colored pencil lines have a smooth waxy finish, similar to the finish of graphite. The two mix well, but they can also become very messy, which can be fun for experiments.

Begin with a minimal pencil outline. Use a light pencil that will disappear into the colored pencil.

When colored pencil is drawn on top of or combined with graphite, it smears and pushes the graphite around. The graphite causes the vibrancy of the color to gray out or neutralize. Depending on the desired effect, that can be a good or a bad thing.

In this exercise, we'll combine colored pencil and graphite pencil to create a spacial environment. You'll use pencil line to describe the figures in the foreground and colored pencil to draw the building in the background. The colored pencil describes the shapes and color of the building, but without outlines, so the building appears to recede farther back in space. The outlines of the figures emphasize their forms and bring them into the foreground.

Begin the drawing with a minimal outline of the entire composition. Use a light pencil line (2H) so that it will disappear when the color is drawn over it. Draw the figures first to separate them from the rest of the composition. I've used a 4B pencil to make the crowd significantly darker than the value of the building.

When you add the first color, the blue of the sky will define the shape of the roof and distinguish the form of the structure. Next, add the color of the main shapes, the orange walls, purple roof, and gold trim. The colored pencil should cover the light pencil sketch of the building well enough so that the lines don't need to be erased.

These colors are not exact, but they are approximate. We're using pure color as it comes from the pencil, without mixing, so the color is bold instead of blended and muted. There is nothing wrong with blending layers of pencil color, but the intention here is to have the colors be bold and bright, if exaggerated.

Next add the rest of the façade and then the smaller details of the windows. Working from large to small helps to ensure that the scale is accurate when you reach the smaller details. Finish up by penciling in a darker brown to give a slight shadow to the walls and the molding around the roof, creating a three-dimensional feel to the architecture.

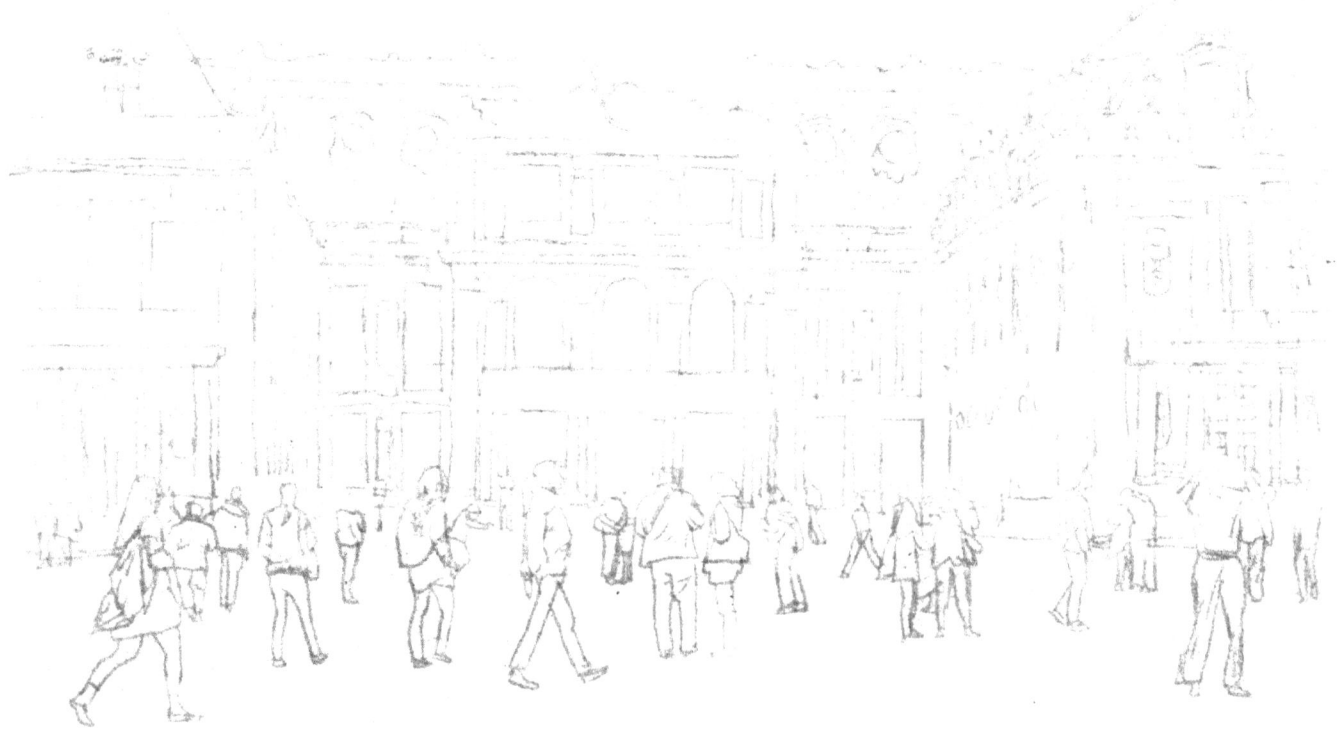

Use a softer,
darker pencil to
define the figures
in the foreground.

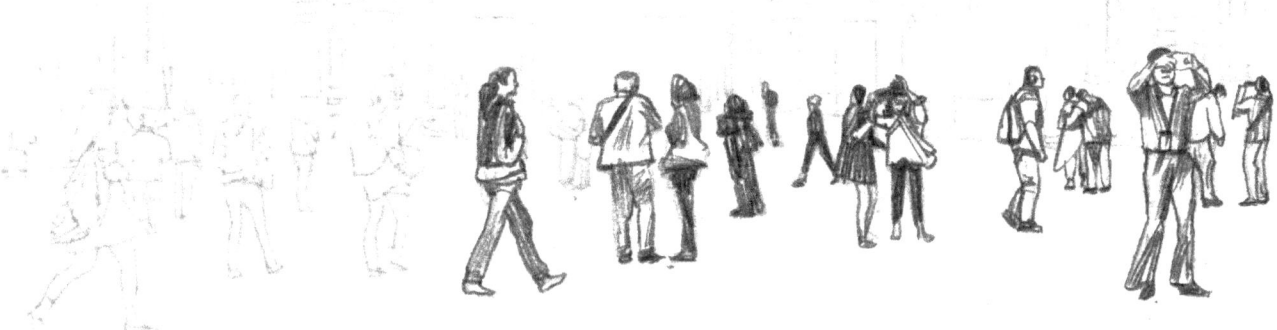

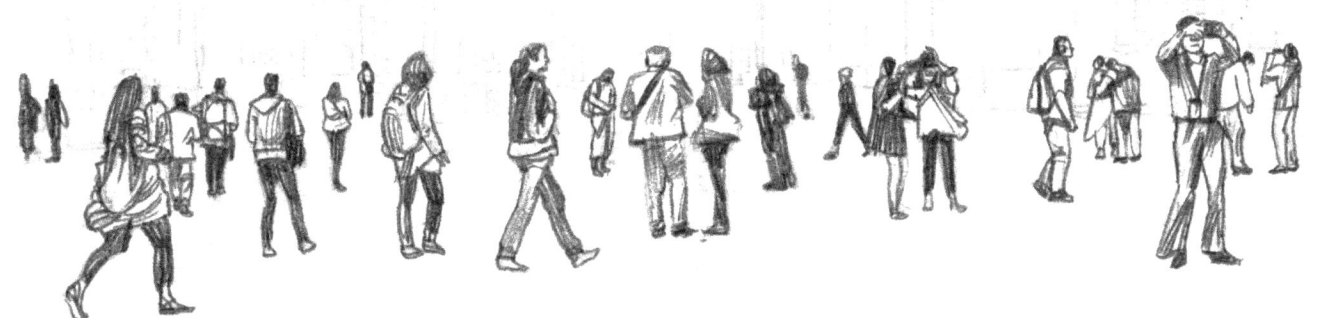

Color the sky to distinguish the shape of the building. Begin to define the main shapes of the building with color.

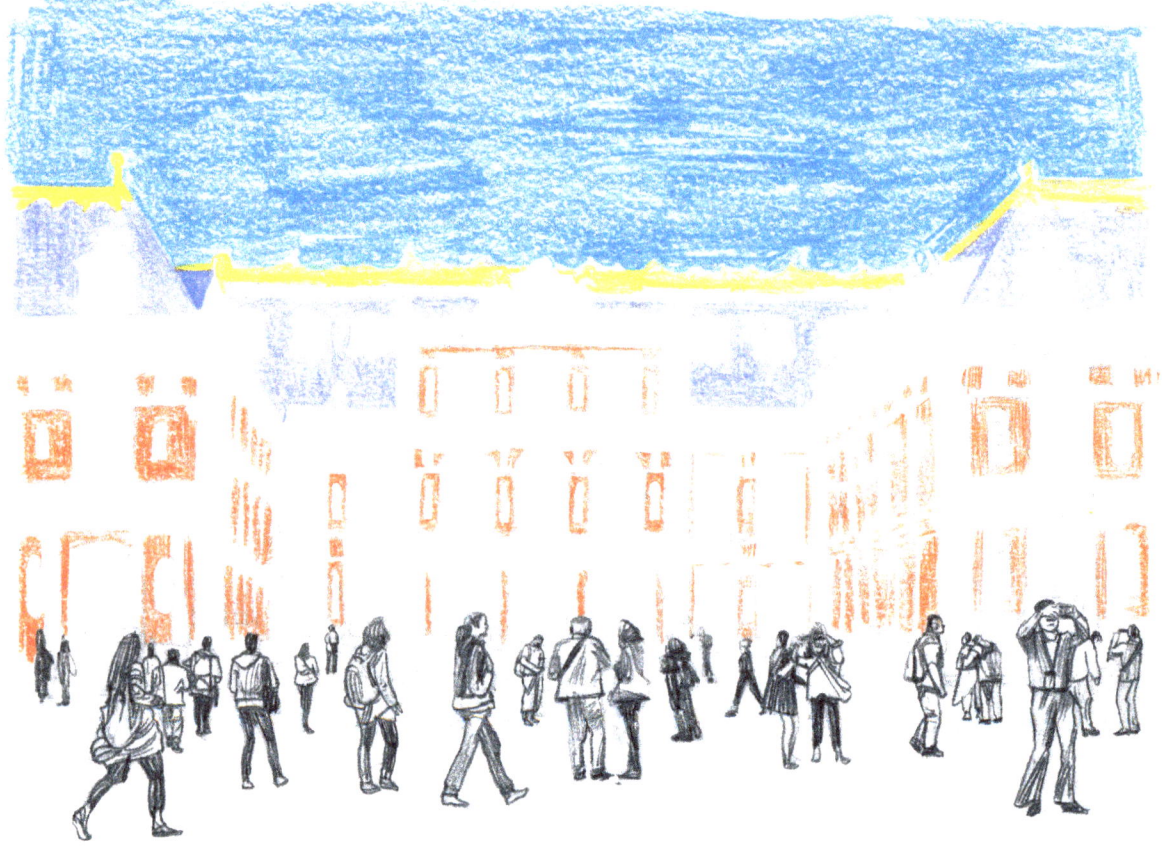

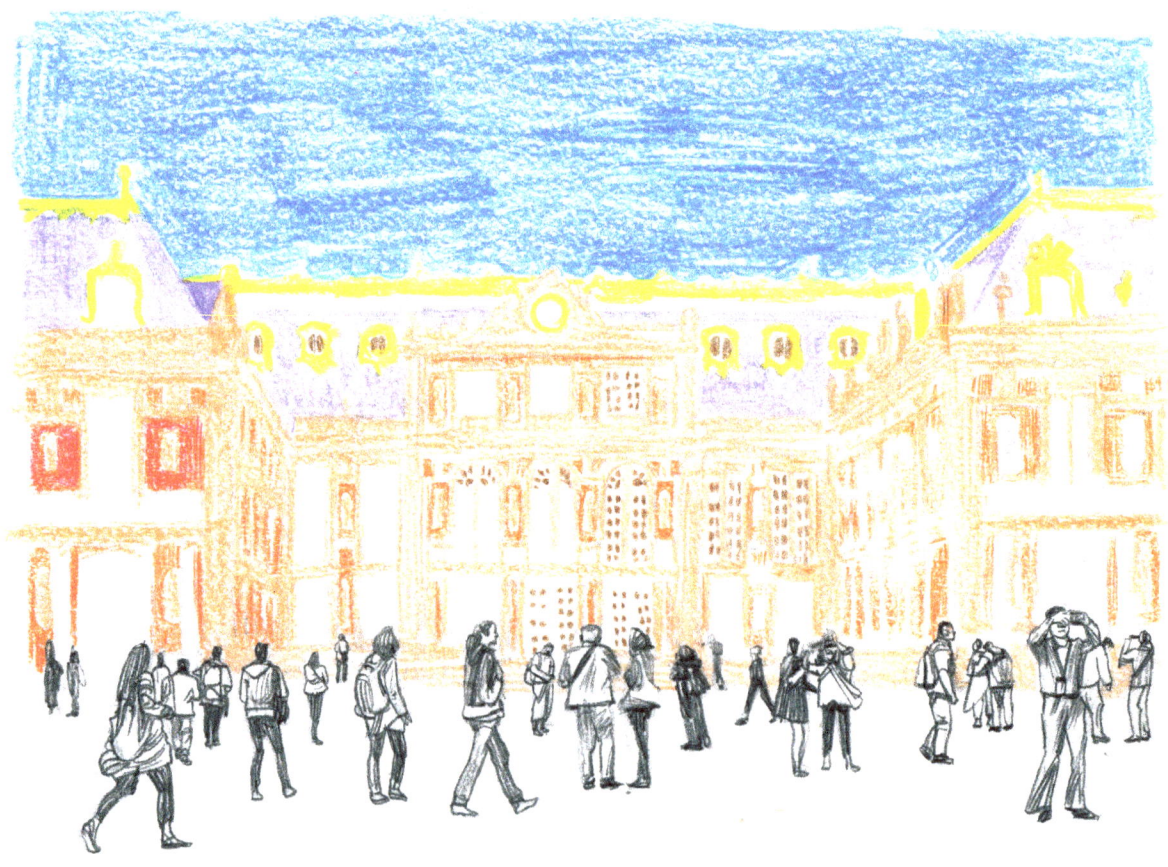

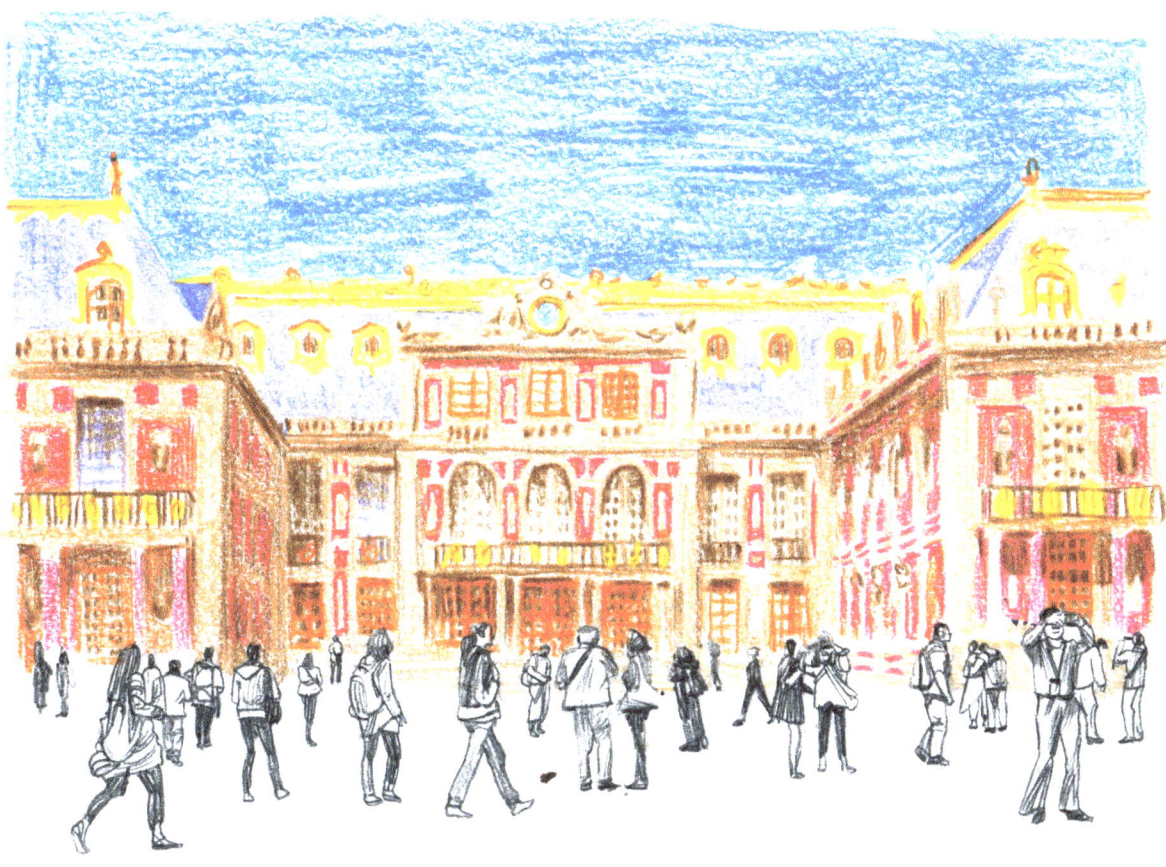

Work from large to small, adding color to the façade and the windows. Finally, add defining lines and shadows to create a three-dimensional feel.

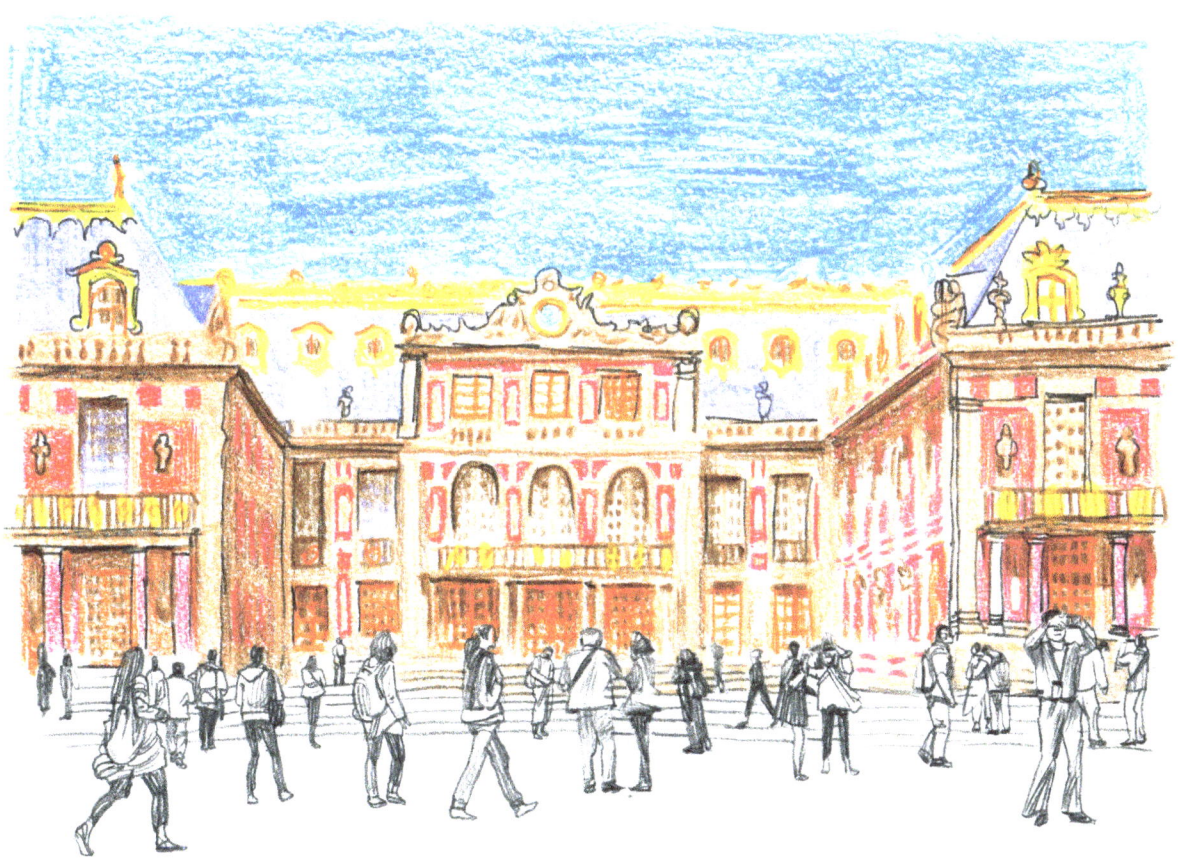

EXERCISE 4: PENCIL AND INK

Ink and pencil have very different textures on paper. Ink (in this case Higgins Waterproof Color Drawing Ink) dries with an almost acrylic finish. It's more transparent than acrylic, however, so in that way it is similar to watercolor. Ink sits on the surface of the paper rather than soaking in (unless a lot of ink is used).

It's difficult to draw over ink with pencil, but you can draw with ink on top of graphite, as long as the graphite has not been used too heavily. So ink and pencil can be layered.

Another way to approach using graphite and ink together is to weave them into the same composition by finishing part of the drawing with pencil, and another with ink (as in the example of the deer drawing).

Start with a basic, light sketch of the image (try a light pencil for this—2H or 3H). Choose the areas you want to finish in pencil and render them while leaving the rest of the drawing unfinished. In this example, the deer are rendered in pencil and the forest is left unfinished for the ink. However, parts of the deer are behind the trees and emerging from the forest. When the ink is added, it will include rendering trees in front of as well as behind the deer, so the deer and the forest will not feel as if they are separate drawings but, instead, are woven together into one drawing.

Use a range of pencils for the deer—F–2B will provide enough contrast to make the pencil stand out. When you complete the deer, you're ready to work in ink. Begin to draw the forest around the deer as well as drawing on their backs to create some interplay between the ink and graphite.

The styles of drawing at play in this example are unique to each of the two mediums. The deer drawn in pencil are more tonal and soft, and there is a wider range of value used to describe their form. In contrast, because ink is such a flat medium, the lines are bolder and the style of shading is more linear and flat. Combining the two styles spatially forces the viewer to interpret the space and the deer in the woods as a unified image.

Use a light pencil sketch for the areas that will be drawn over with ink.

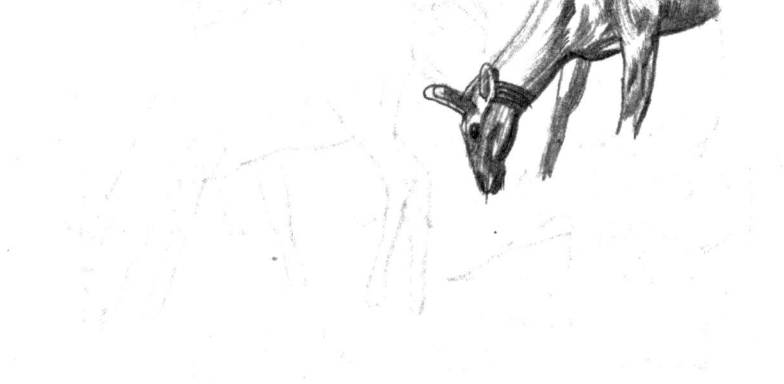

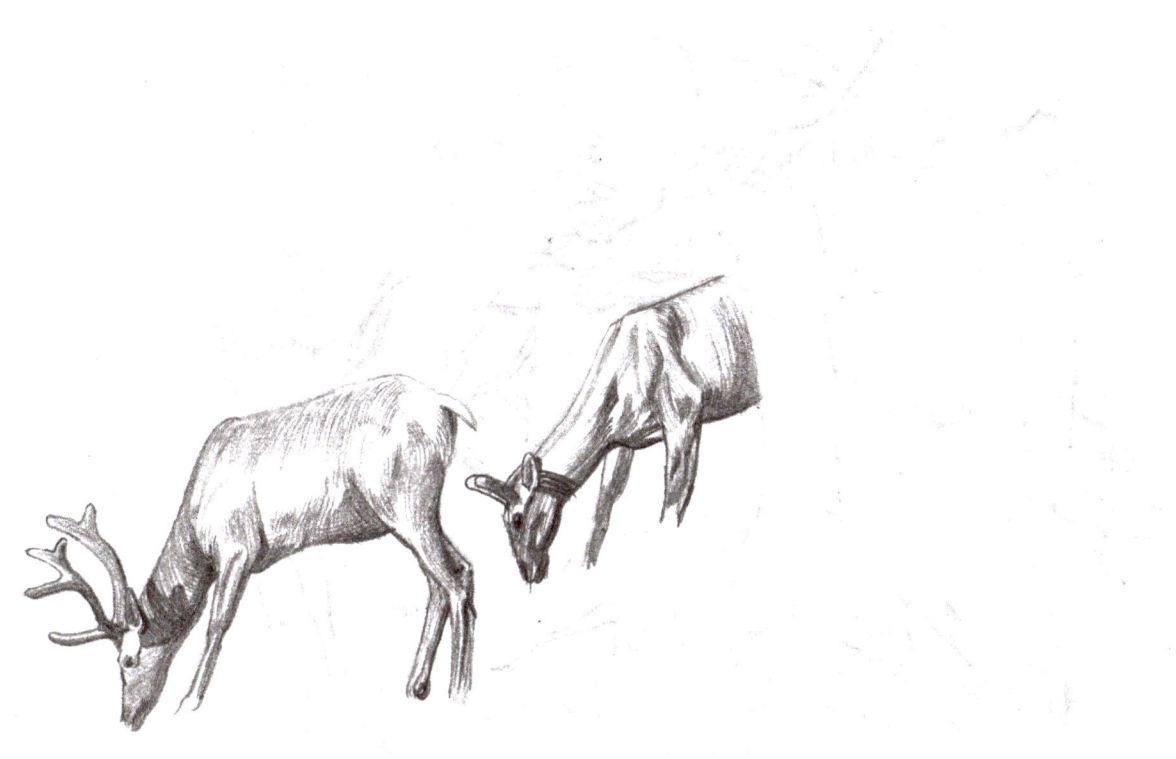

When you complete the deer in pencil, you're ready to fill in the background with ink.

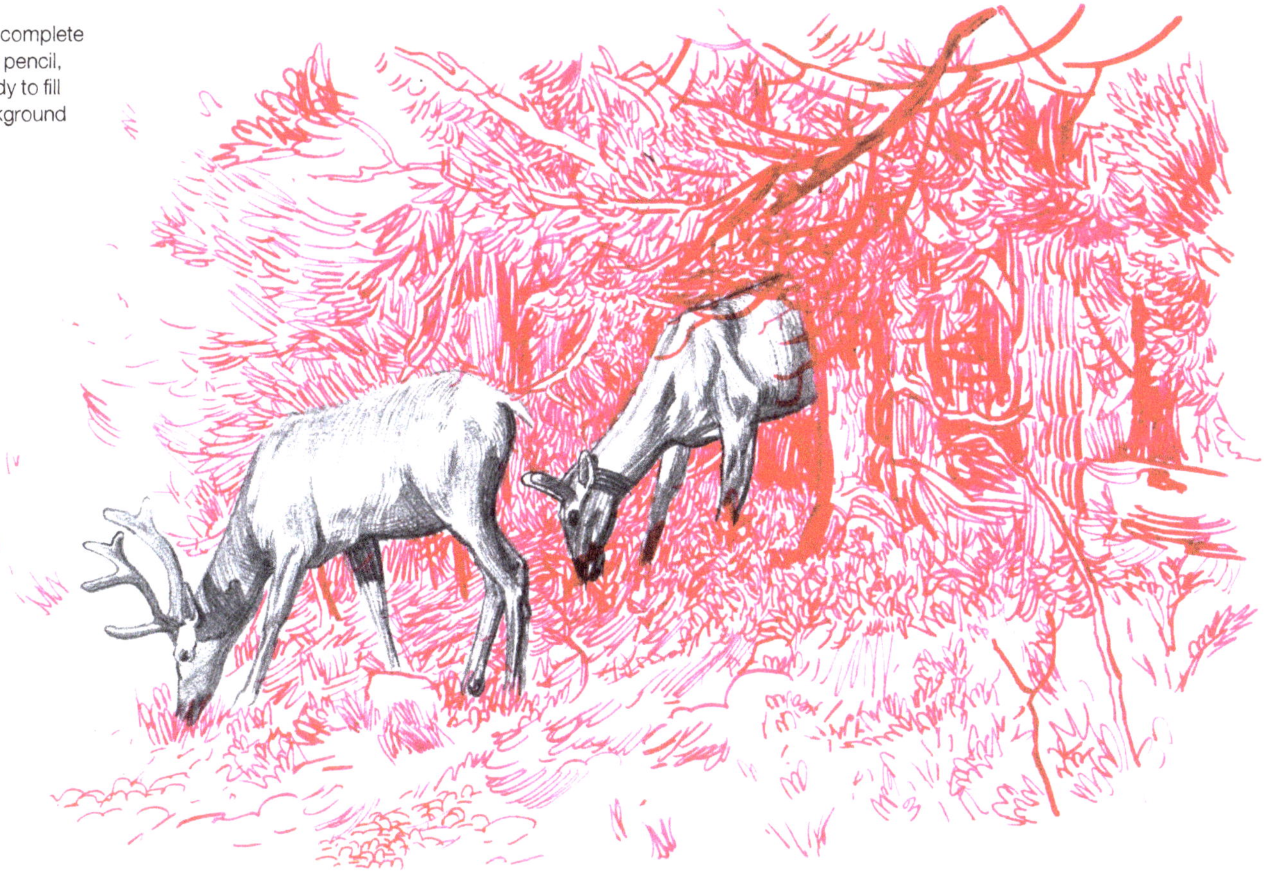

EXERCISE 5: PENCIL AND GOUACHE

Gouache is a lot heavier and more opaque then watercolor. It can be used in transparent washes much like watercolor, but it can also be built up in thick layers more like acrylic or oil paint. Both qualities can be used in a single image.

When using gouache with pencil, anticipate a much heavier painting than you'd get with watercolor. Gouache layers easily over pencil, and the reverse is also true: Pencil draws quite nicely over gouache. More interplay is possible between gouache and pencil than between pencil and watercolor, though when painting in gouache over pencil, much of the detail of the pencil will be lost.

Start by creating a drawing, but don't completely resolve the drawing; leave room for adding washes of gouache. Experiment with adding lighter and darker washes to get a sense of the thickness and transparency of the paint.

If areas of the pencil become obscured by the gouache, try to pull out the details with opaque (not watered down) gouache strokes. If an area feels like it's lost its definition and clarity, add pencil drawing (2B or darker) on top of the gouache to tighten the image again.

Begin with a light pencil sketch.

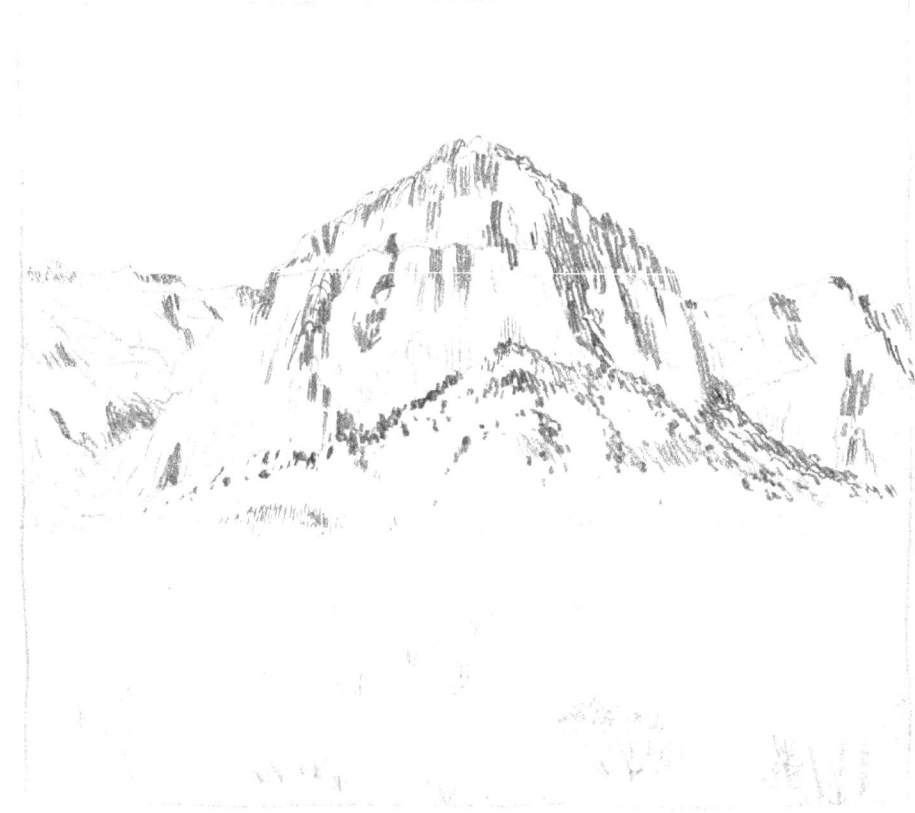

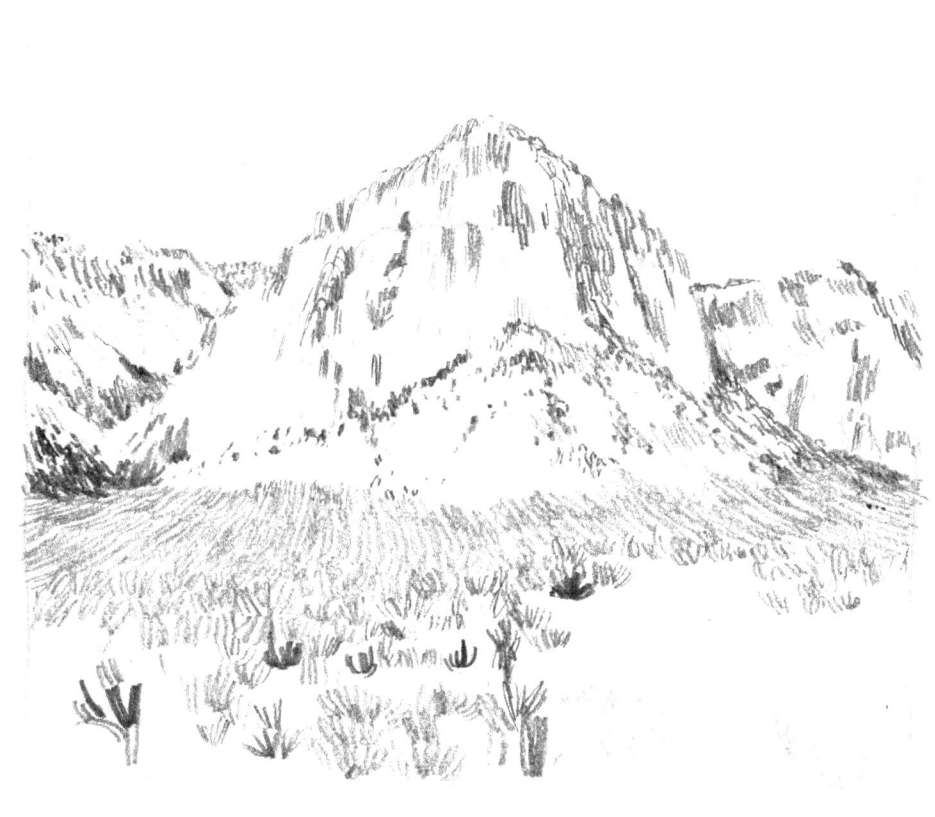

Add detail in line,
but don't completely
resolve the drawing.

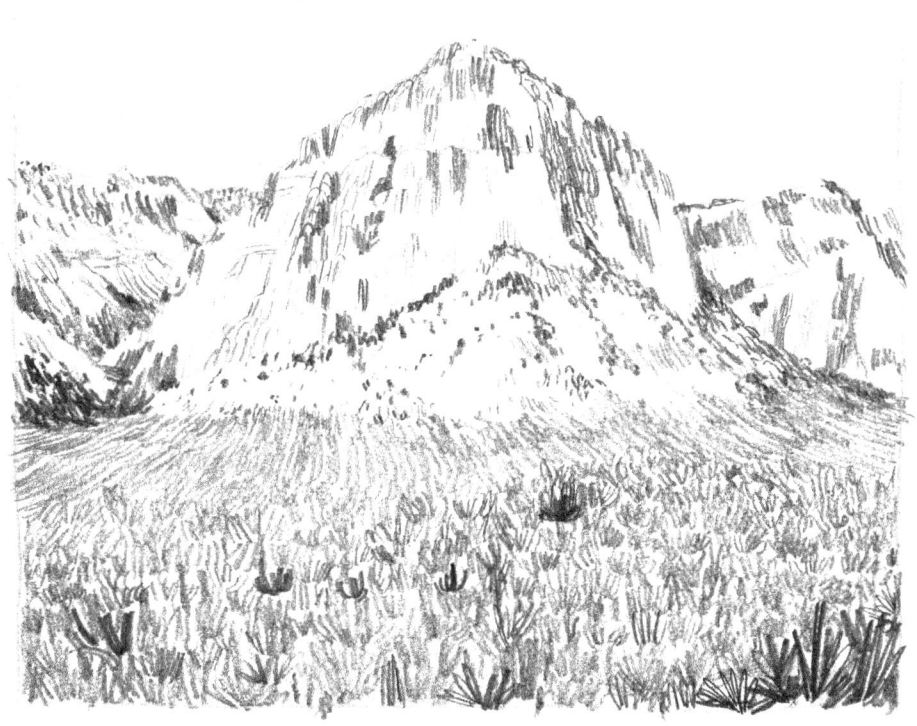

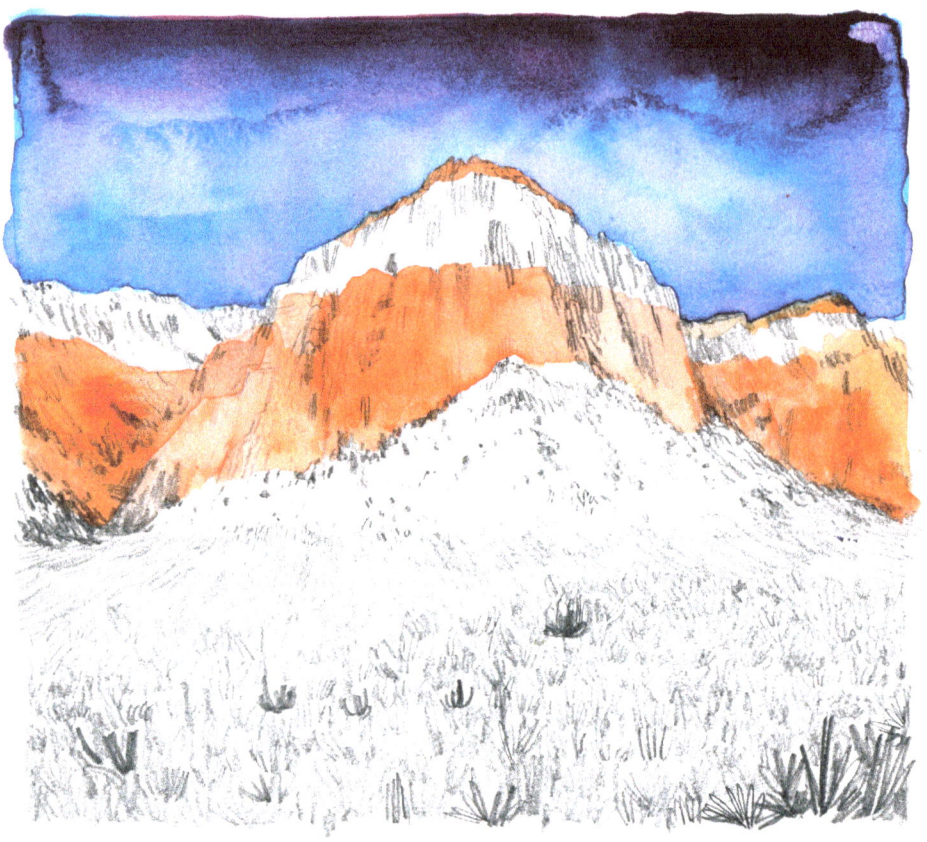

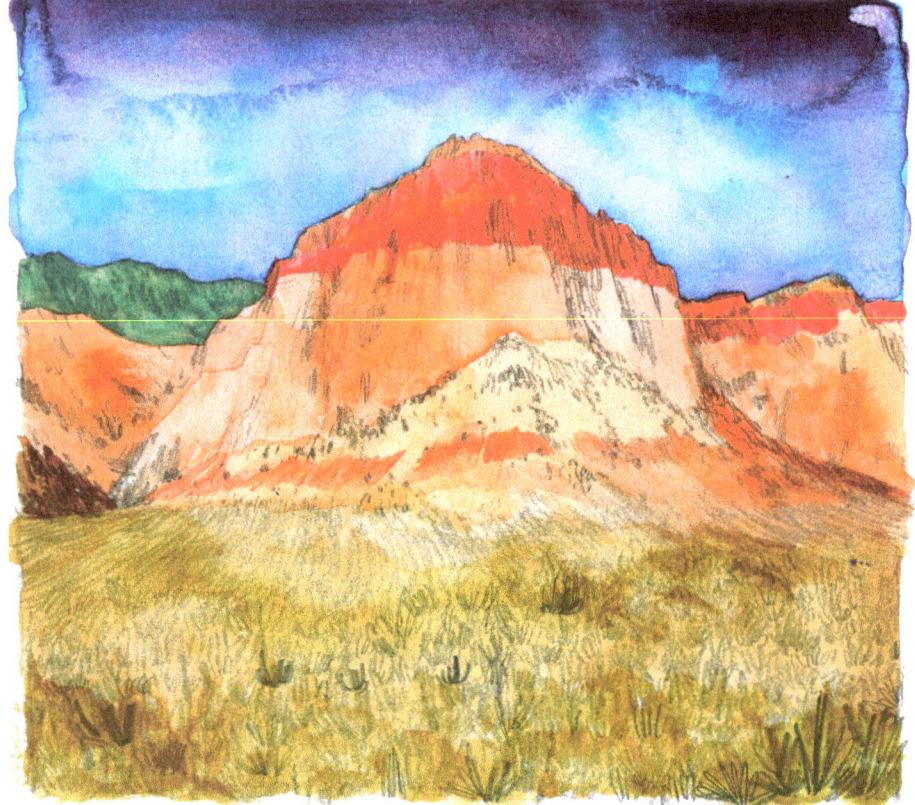

Begin adding light
washes of gouache.

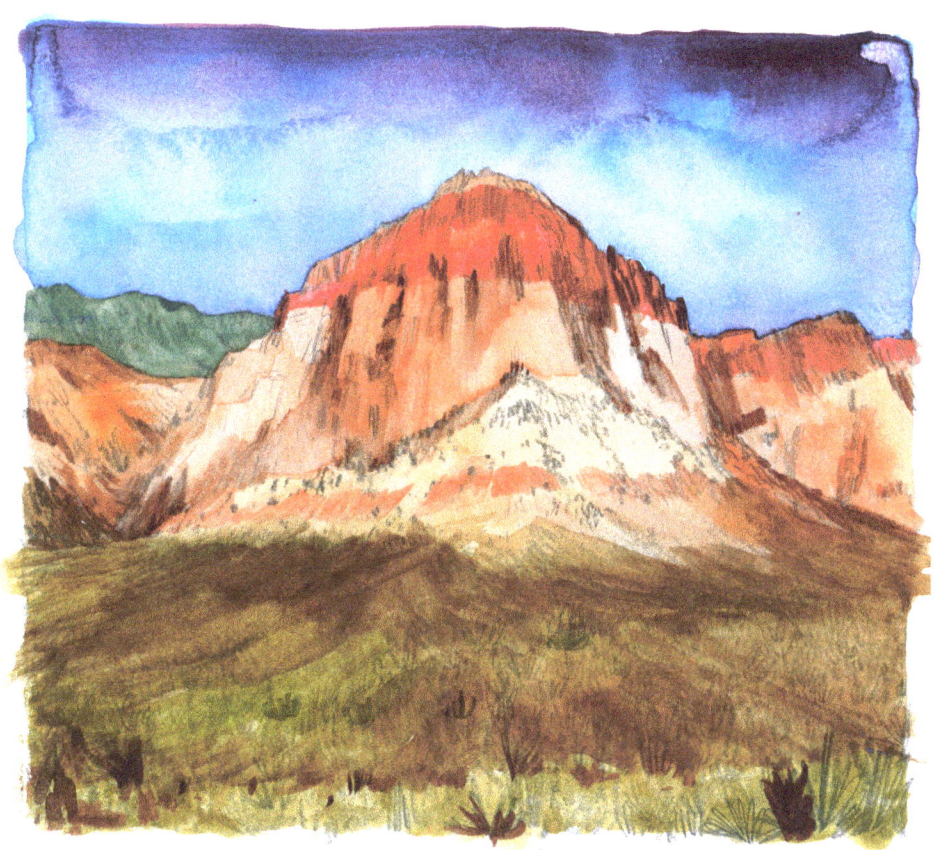

Experiment with
darker areas of
gouache to get a
sense of the thickness
and transparency of
the paint.

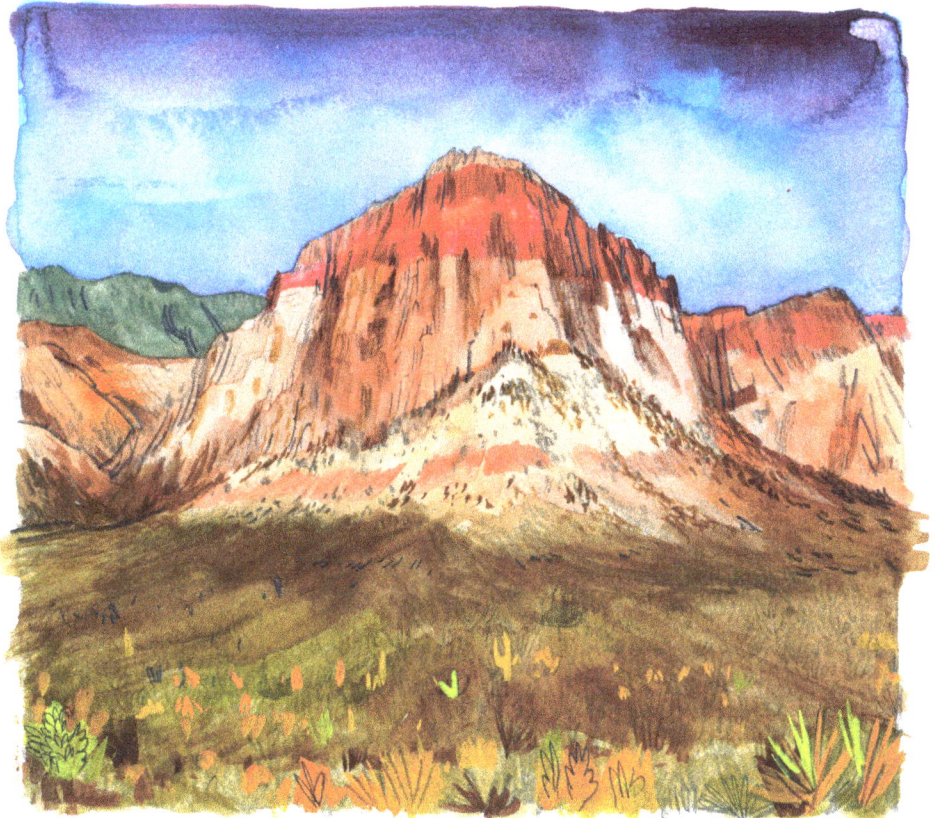

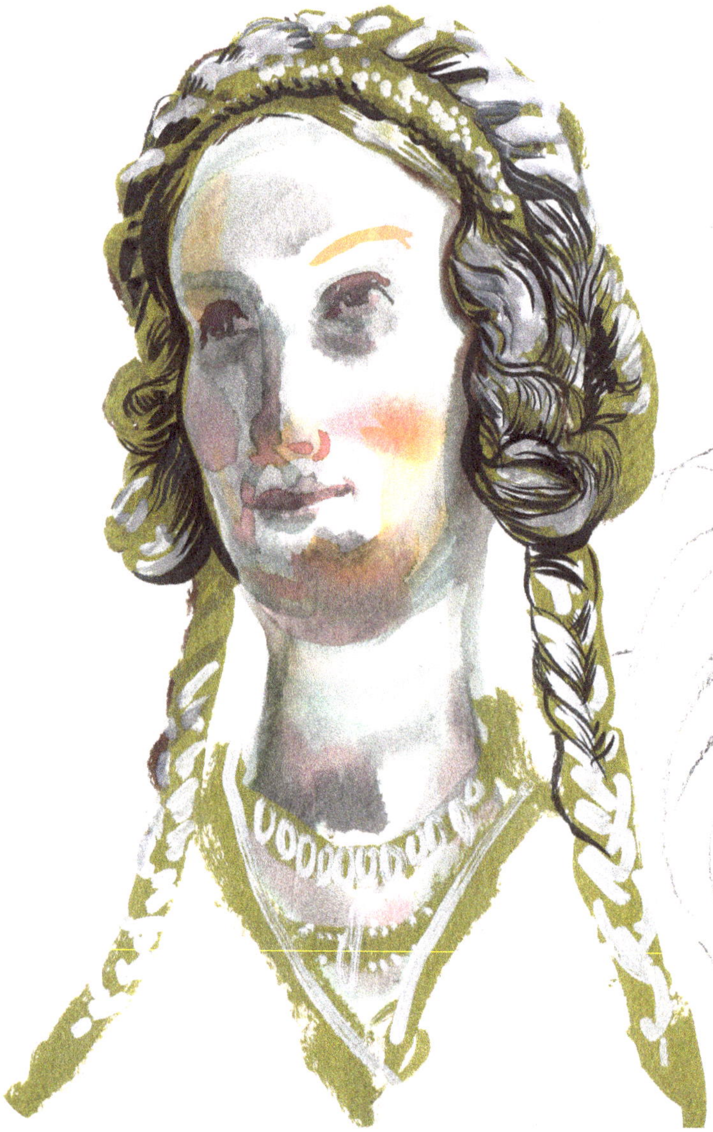

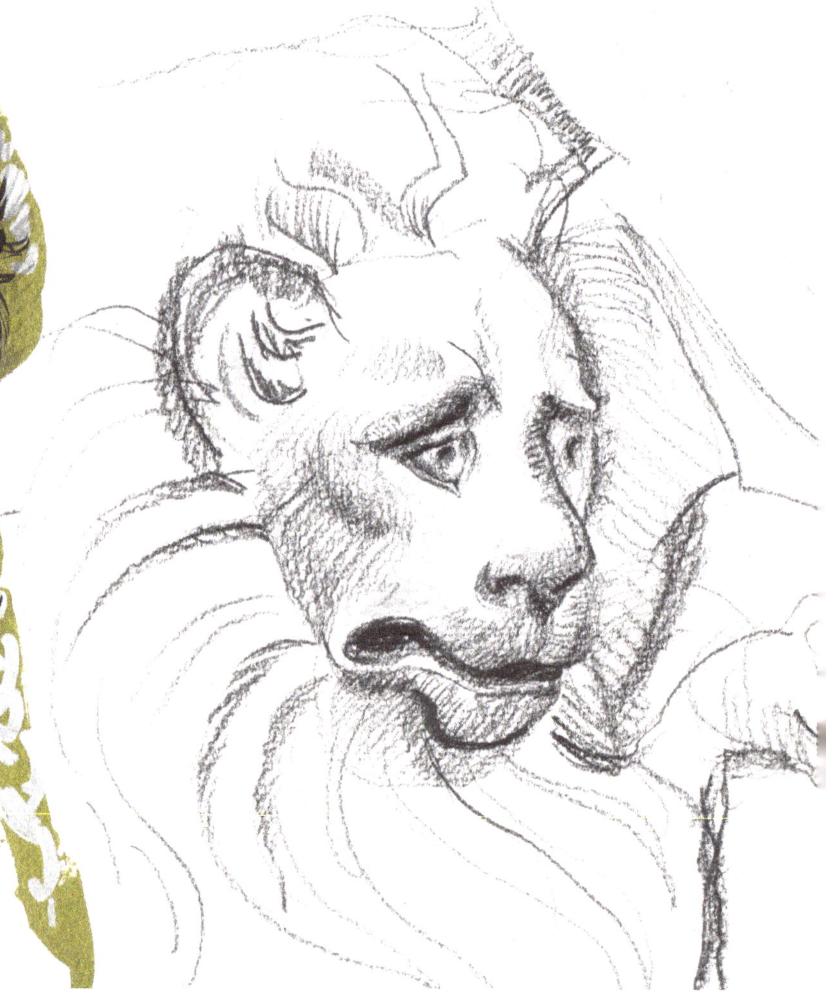

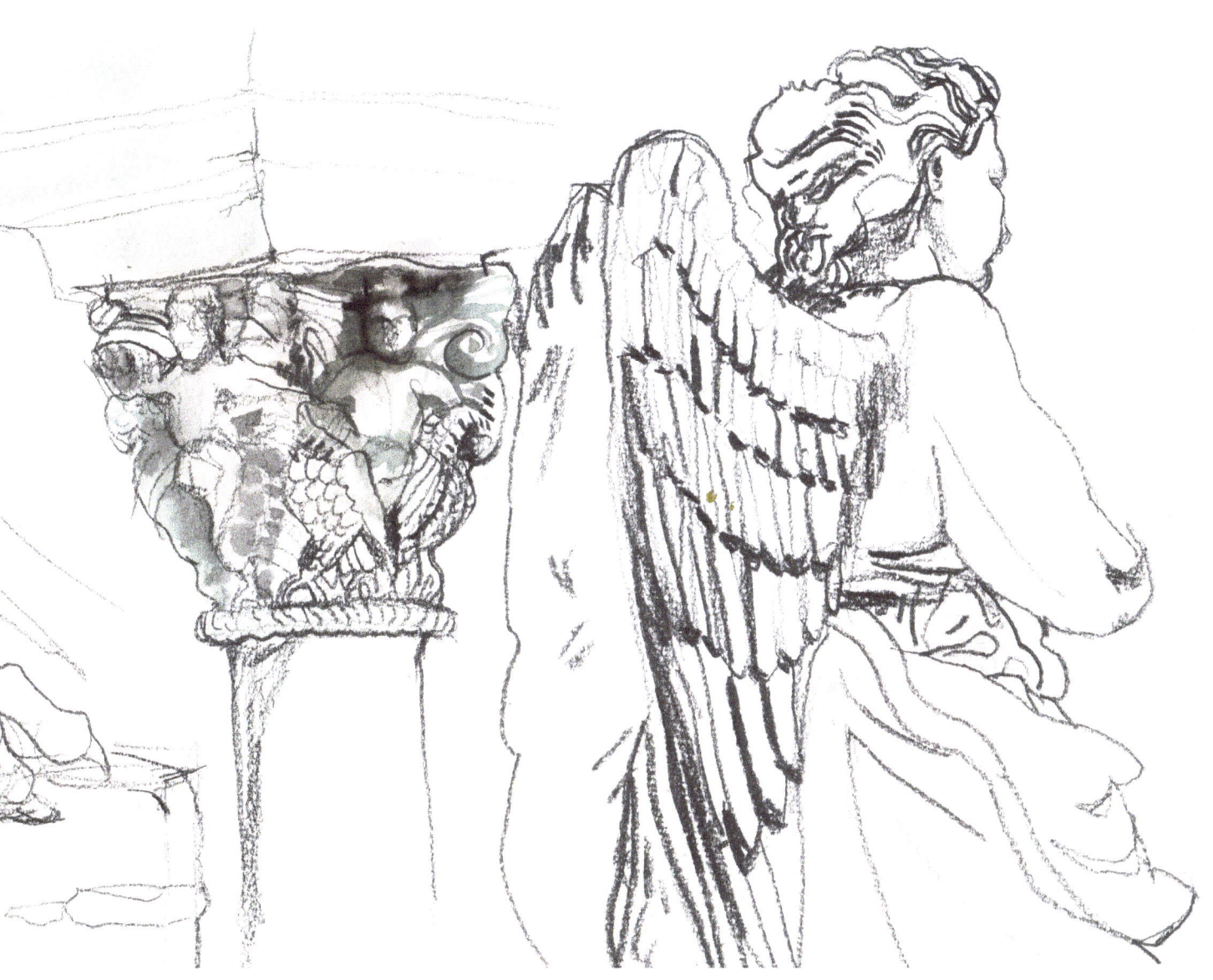

Carol Fabricatore,
Cloisters Sketchbook,
pencil, watercolor,
and gold brush ink

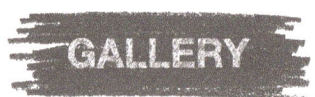

Ryan Peltier, *Transients 1*, pencil, colored pencil, gouache, and acrylic

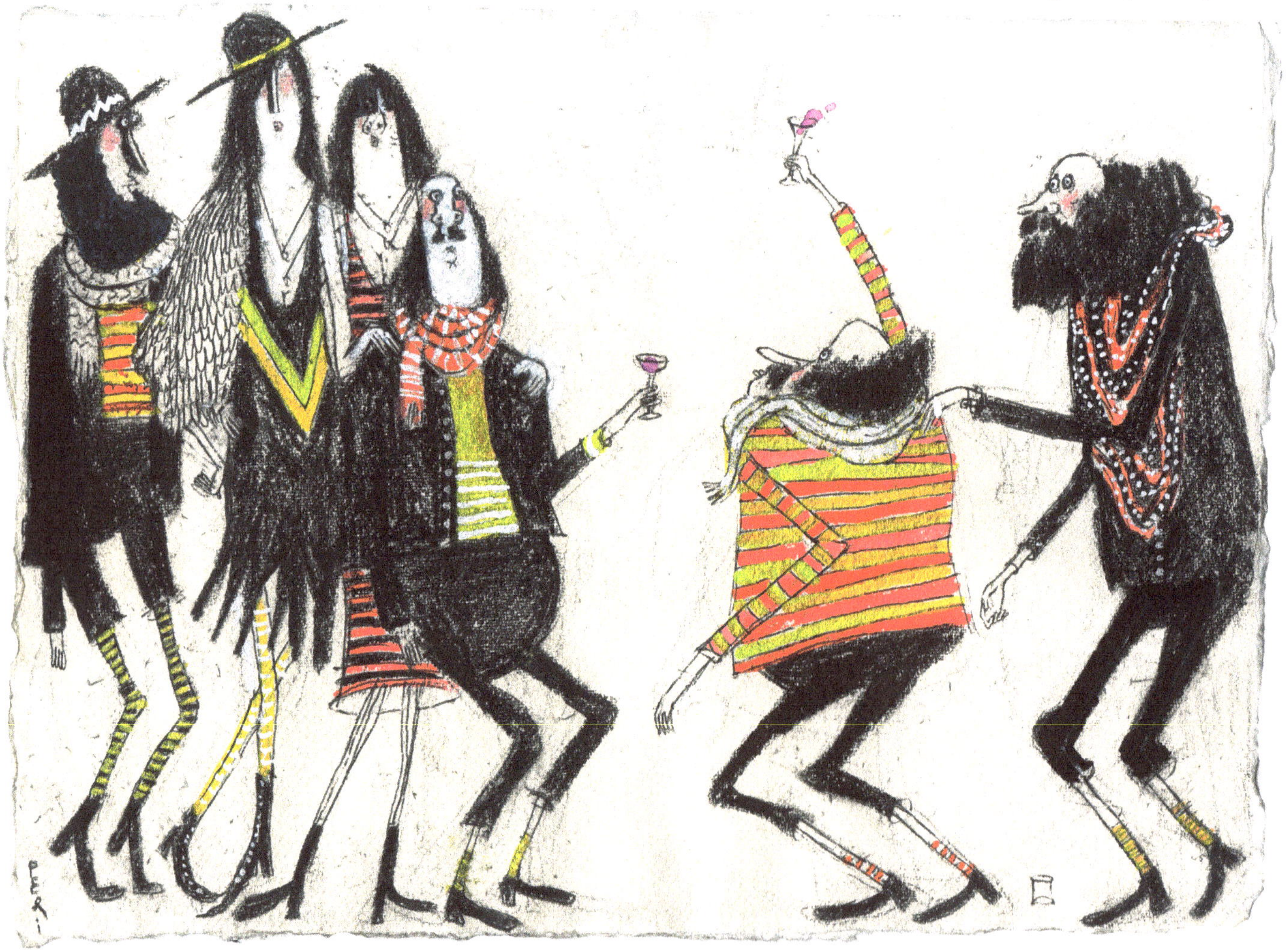

Ryan Peltier, *Transients 3*,
pencil, colored pencil,
gouache, and acrylic

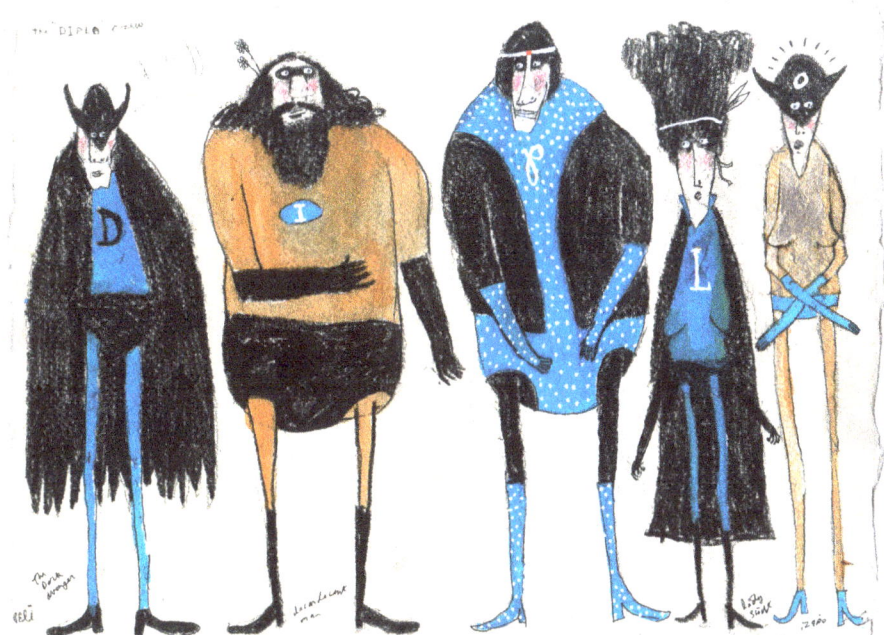

Ryan Peltier, *Transients 2*,
pencil, colored pencil,
gouache, and acrylic

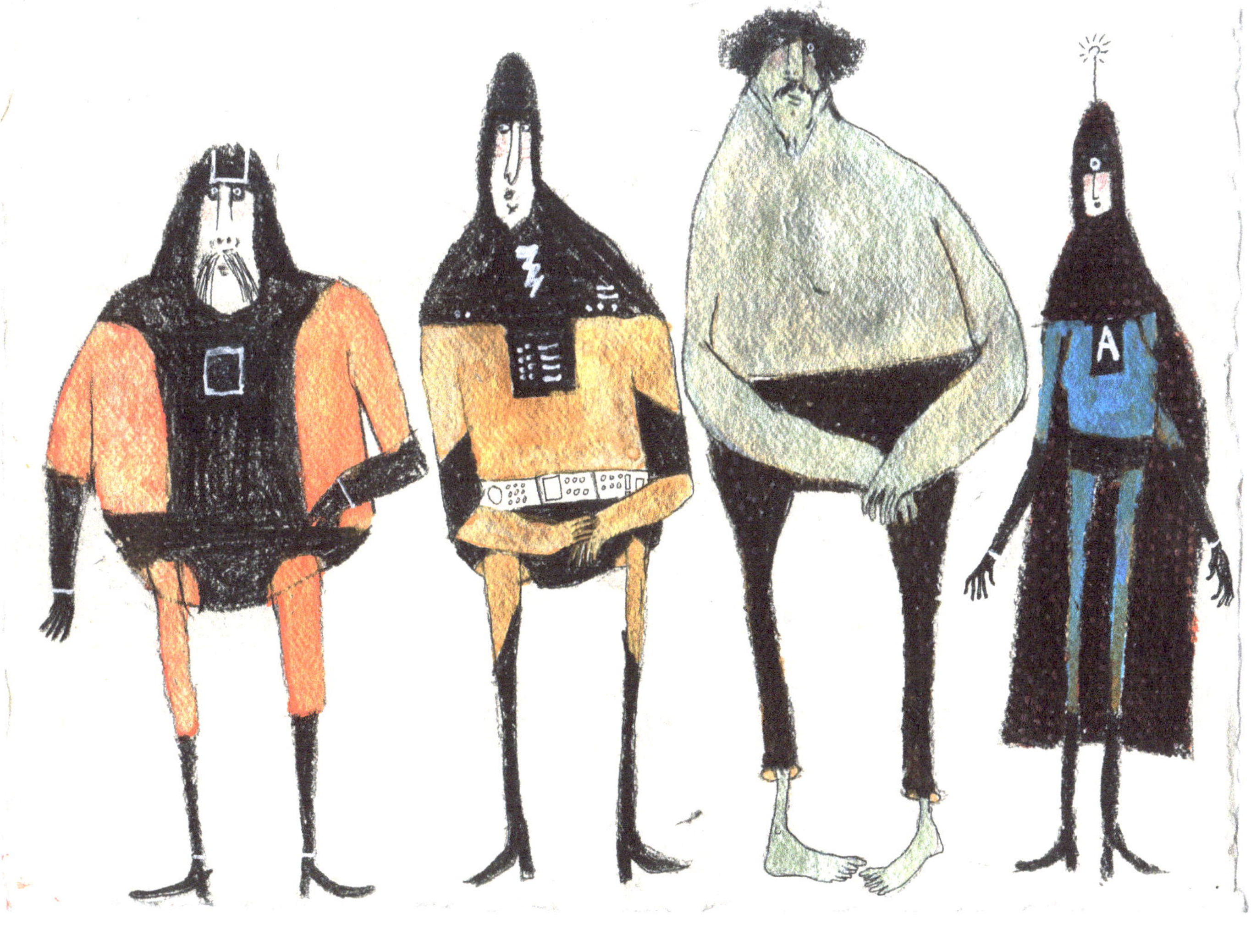

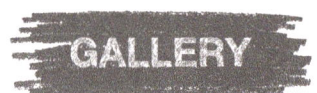

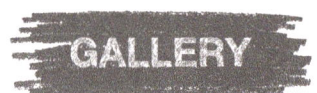

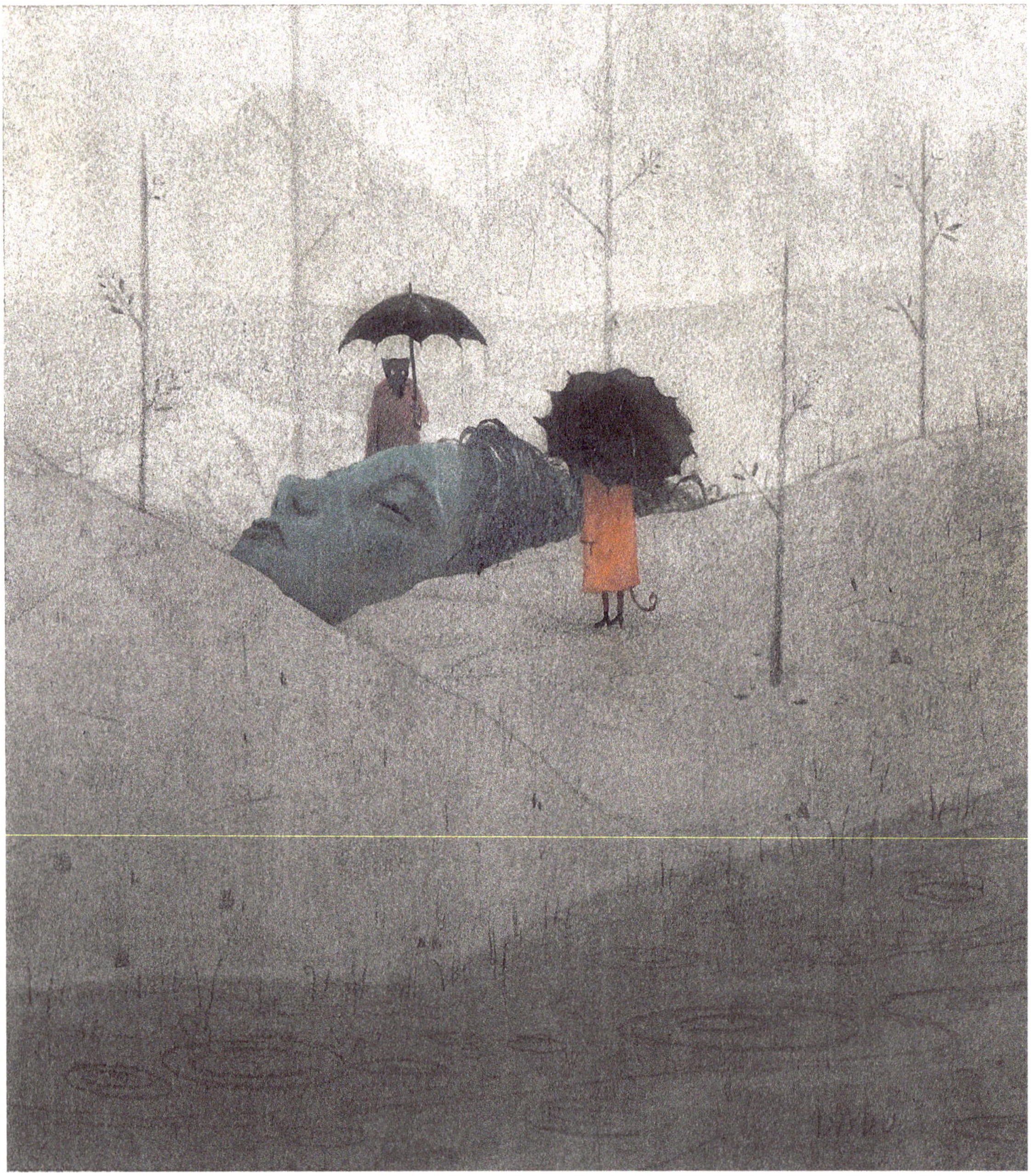

Dadu Shin,
Under the Weather,
pencil and gouache

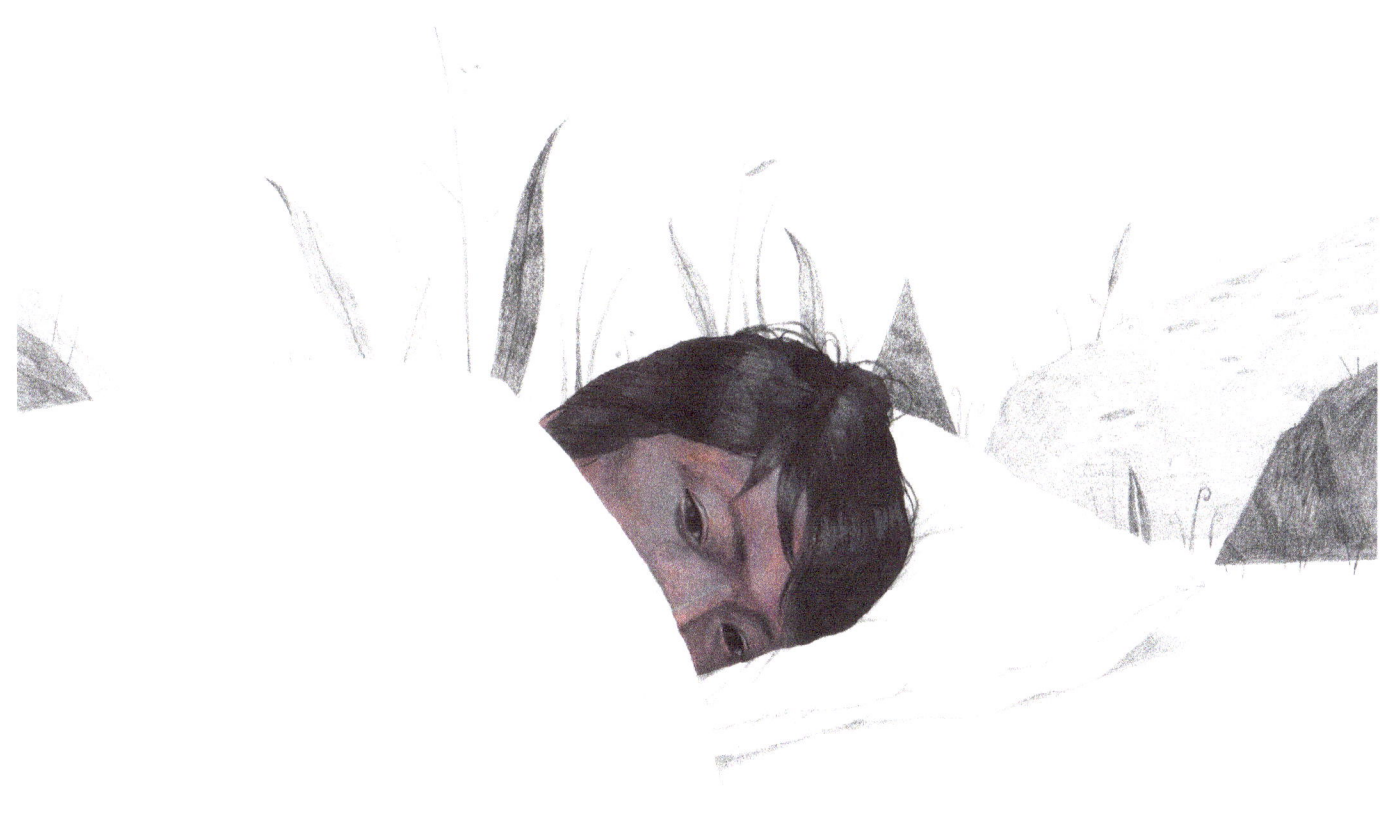

Dadu Shin, *False Memory*,
pencil and gouache

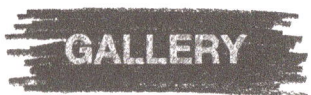

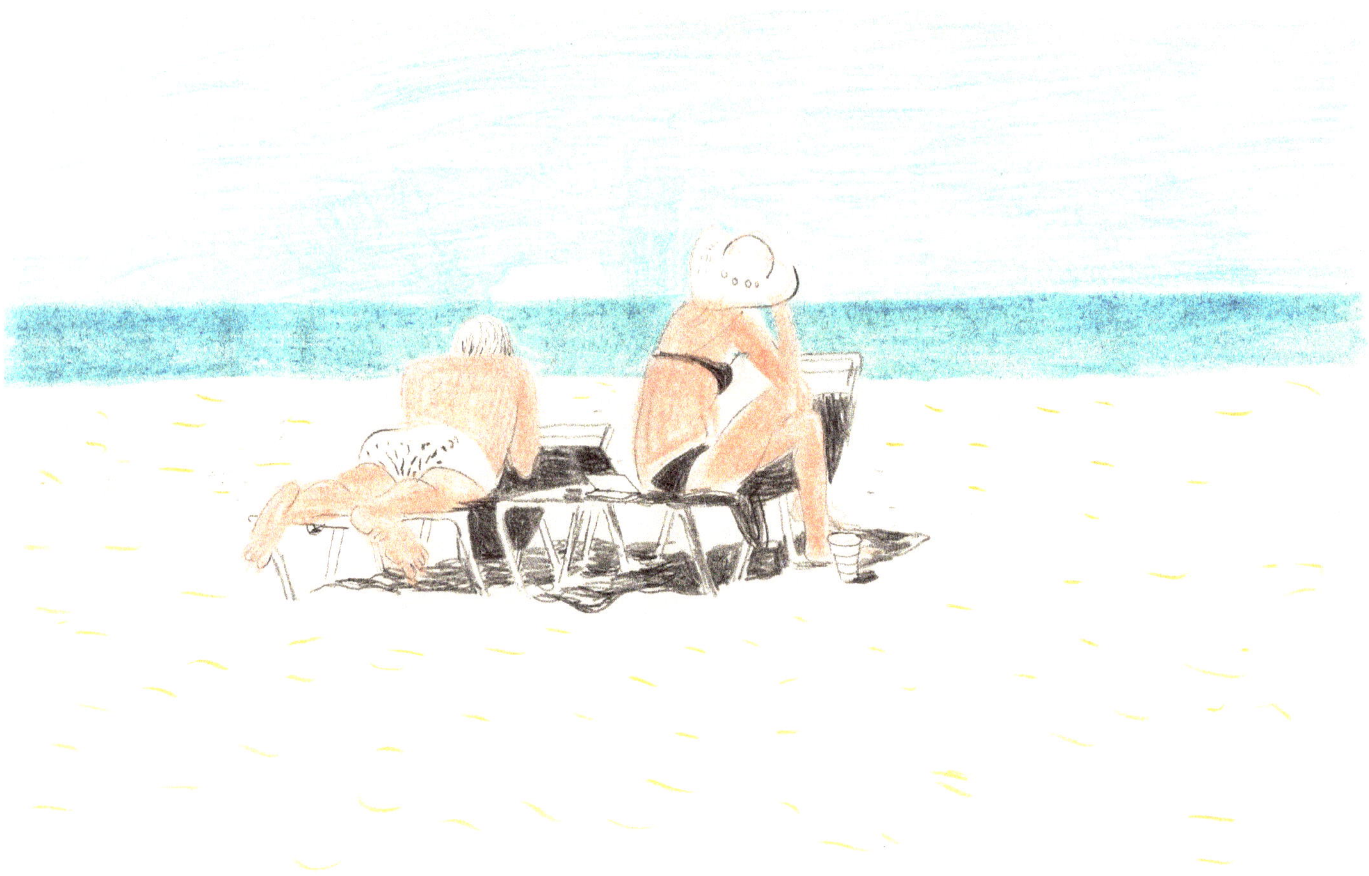

Peter Oumanski, *Aruba 2*,
pencil and colored pencil

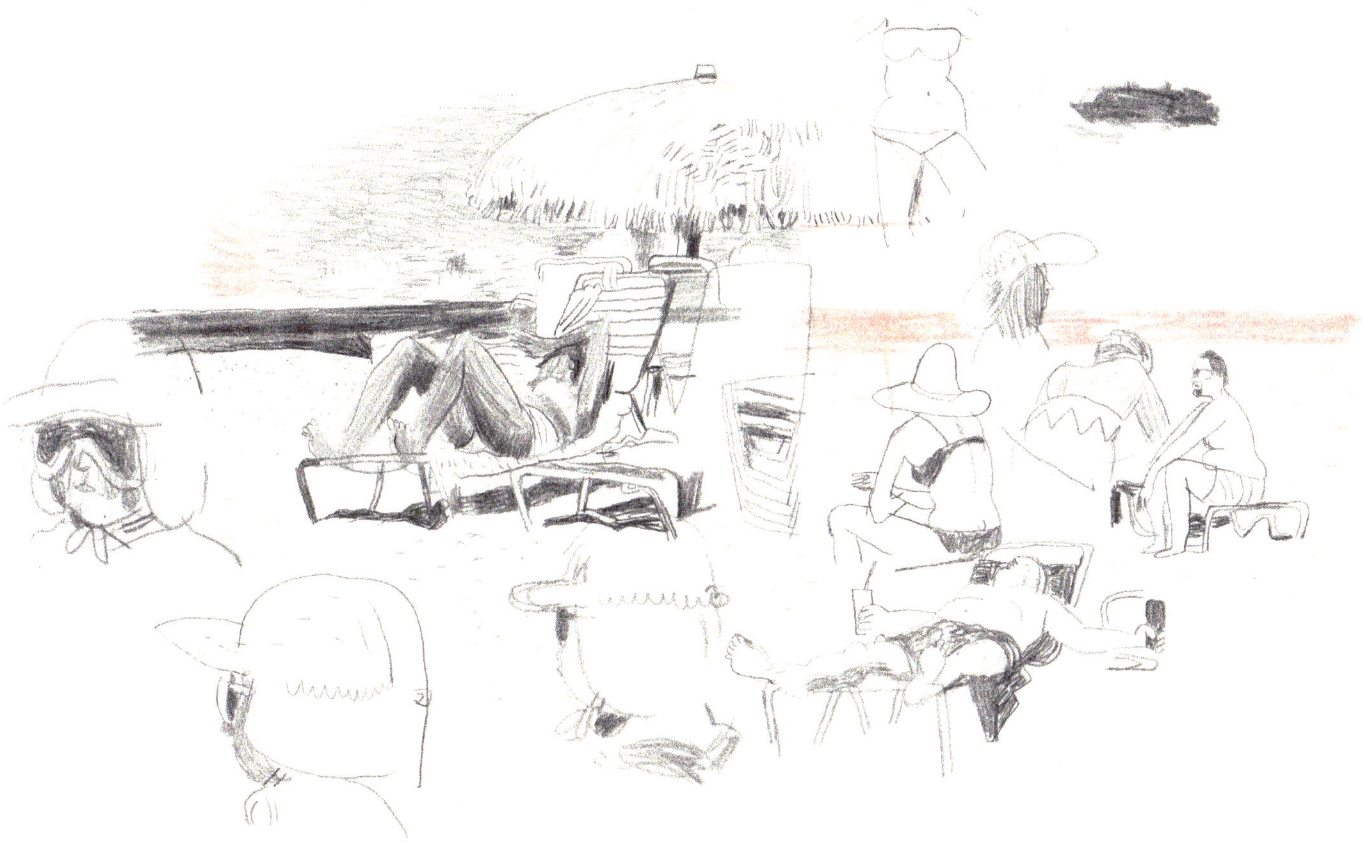

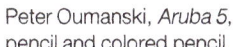

Peter Oumanski, *Aruba 3*,
pencil and colored pencil

Peter Oumanski, *Aruba 5*,
pencil and colored pencil

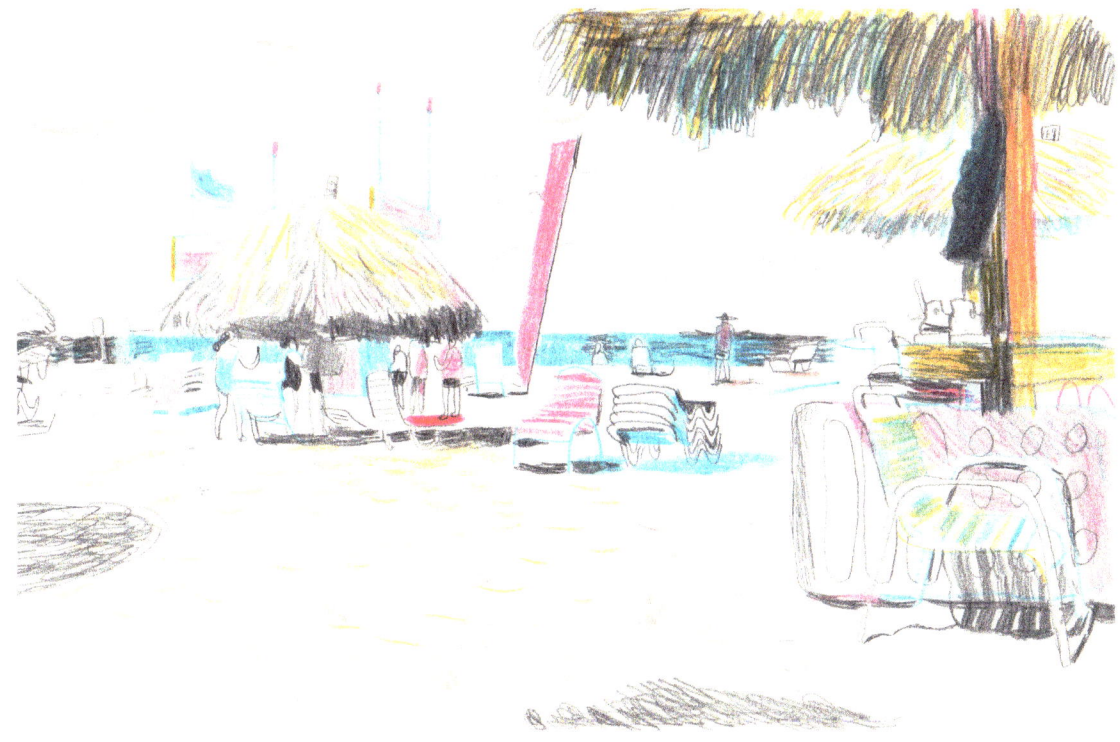

CONTRIBUTORS

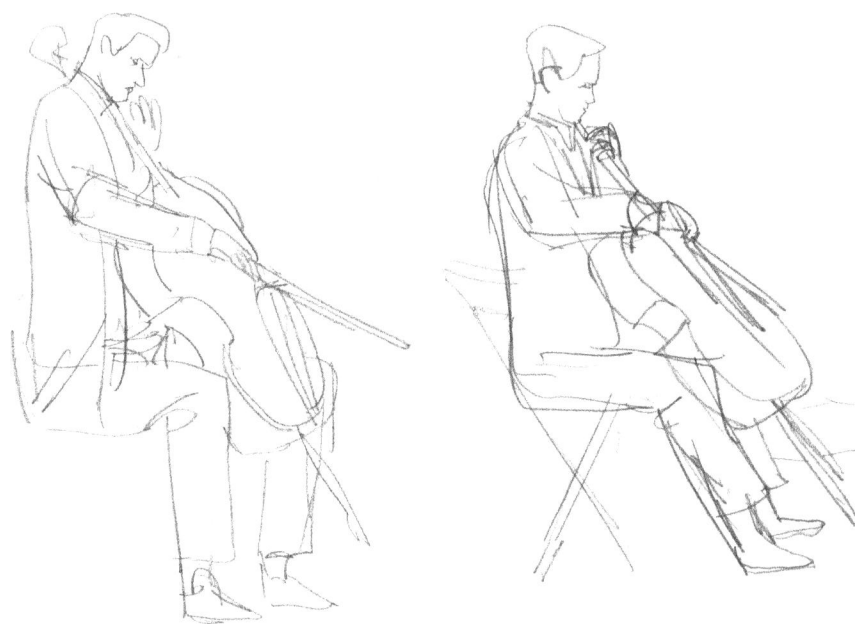

JUN CEN
9, 17, 38–41
WWW.CENJUN.COM

Jun was born in Guangzhou, China. He received an M.F.A. in illustration from the Maryland Institute College of Art in 2013 and currently lives and works in New York. Working both with drawing and animation, his work has been featured in a variety of publications including *The New York Times*, *The Washington Post*, and *The Boston Globe*. His work has been recognized by The Society of Illustrators, American Illustration, *3X3*, and others.

HENRIQUE DE FRANCA
58–59
WWW.HENRIQUEDEFRANCA.COM

Henrique's figure drawings explore the blankness of the paper and the possibilities of lines, shadows, and negative spaces, starting from random images that tell evasive, nostalgic narratives and creating a dialogue about the limits between urban and rural in contemporary Brazil, with shades of the recent past.

CAROL FABRICATORE
4, 37, 130–132
WWW.CAROLFABRICATORE.COM

Carol lives and works in New York City. She graduated from, and now teaches at, the School of Visual Arts. Her work focuses mainly on drawings done from life and has been featured in numerous books, magazines, and newspapers.

BENOIT GUILLAUME
4–5, 86–87
WWW.BENOITGUILLAUME.ORG

Benoit is an illustrator working out of Marseille, France. His work focuses primarily on drawing and largely documents urban life in locations including Paris, Montreal, Algiers, India, Vietnam, Laos, and Cambodia. His work has appeared in books, comics, magazines, and newspapers internationally.

AMAYA GURPIDE
64–65
WWW.AMAYAGURPIDE.COM

Amaya's work is centered around the figure. She was born and raised in Spain and was educated at the School of Arts of Pamplona. She later relocated to New York, studying at the Art Students League and Grand Central Academy. She later returned to Spain where she focused on the development of a more personal style of in her work; during this time, she taught out of her studio and at ESDIP (Escuela Superior de Dibujo Profesional). Amaya eventually returned to the U.S. She lives and works in Jersey City and is an instructor at the U.S. branch of the Florence Academy of Art

MONICA LEE
93, 106–109
WWW.INSTAGRAM.COM/ZEPHYRXAVIER

Monica grew up in Kuala Lumpur, Malaysia. She is currently based in Malaysia, where she attended the One Academy and received a diploma in 3-D animation, before working as a digital-imaging artist for an advertising photography studio for twelve years. She started drawing again in 2013.

WARREN LINN
4, 90–91, 111
WWW.WARRENLINN.COM

Warren has worked as an illustrator for over forty years, winning numerous awards and exhibiting his work internationally. Originally from Chicago, he now lives and works in Baltimore and is a professor at the Maryland Institute College of Art.

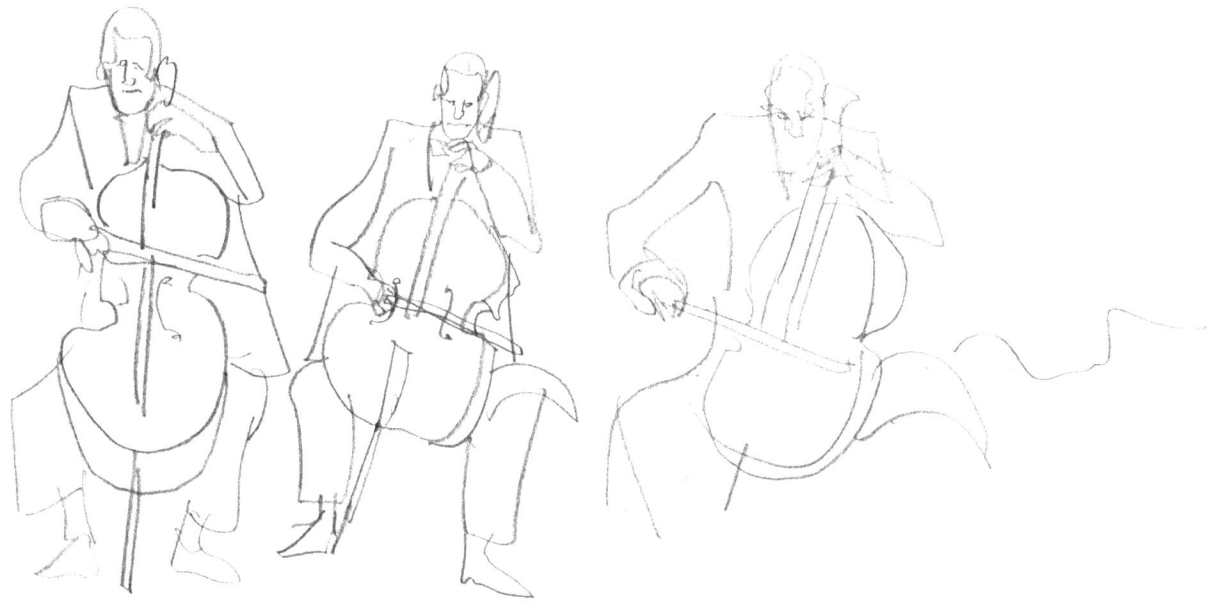

PETER OUMANSKI
136–137
WWW.PETEROUMANSKI.COM

Born in St. Petersburg, Russia, Peter studied at the School of Visual Arts. His illustration clients include *Maxim, Fast Company, Billboard, Los Angeles Times, New Jersey Monthly*, and MTV. Peter lives in New Jersey with his wife, Marina.

ISAAC PELEPKO
11, 43, 56–57
WWW.ISAACPELEPKO.COM

Isaac studied at the Pennsylvania College of Art and Design and later at Grand Central Academy, the Art Students League, and New York Academy of Art, where he received his M.F.A. His work is primarily focused on the figure. He has exhibited in galleries in Paris France, New York City, and throughout the eastern United states. He lives and works in New York.

RYAN PELTIER
5, 132–133
WWW.RPELI.COM

Ryan is an artist and illustrator based in Minneapolis, Minnesota. He teaches at colleges around Minneapolis and Saint Paul and makes illustrations for clients such as *The New York Times, Esquire, The New Yorker, The Stanford Business Review*, and *Plansponsor*. His work has been recognized by Adobe, American Illustration, *3X3, Print* magazine, and the Society of Illustrators of Los Angeles.

ANAND RADHAKRISHNAN
67, 88–89
WWW.BEHANCE.NET/ANANDRK
ANANDRK.TUMBLR.COM

Anand is a freelance illustrator working in Mumbai, India. He graduated with a B.F.A. from Sir JJ Institute of Applied Art in and later studied illustration at The Art Department. His work is focused on drawing and painting, but he is passionate about storytelling in any medium. Anand is currently working on several projects including comics, book covers, and personal stories.

DADU SHIN
134–135
WWW.DADUSHIN.COM

Dadu was born and raised in Massachusetts. After attending the Rhode Island School of Design (RISD), he moved to New York City and now works as a freelance illustrator. He has worked for such clients as *The Boston Globe, The New York Times*, and *Plansponsor*.

DEANNA STAFFO
13, 34–36
WWW.DEANNASTAFFO.COM

Deanna is an illustrator from Baltimore, Maryland, where she is an instructor at the Maryland Institute College of Art. Her work has been featured in numerous magazines and books including *A Circle in the Fire and Other Stories, The Progressive, L.A. Weekly, Runner's World*, and many others.

AARON WIESENFELD
60–63
WWW.ARONWIESENFELD.COM

Aron's artwork has been the subject of eight solo exhibitions in the U.S. and Europe since 2006. Among the many publications his work has appeared in are *Hi-Fructose, Art in America, American Art Collector*, and *The Huffington Post*. His work has been in a number museum shows, including the Long Beach Museum of Art, Bakersfield Museum of Art, and the Museum Casa Dell'Architettura in Italy. His paintings have been used on covers of eight books of poetry, including *The Other Sky*, a collaborative project with acclaimed American poet Bruce Bond. In 2014, a large monograph of his work titled *The Well* was published by IDW Press.

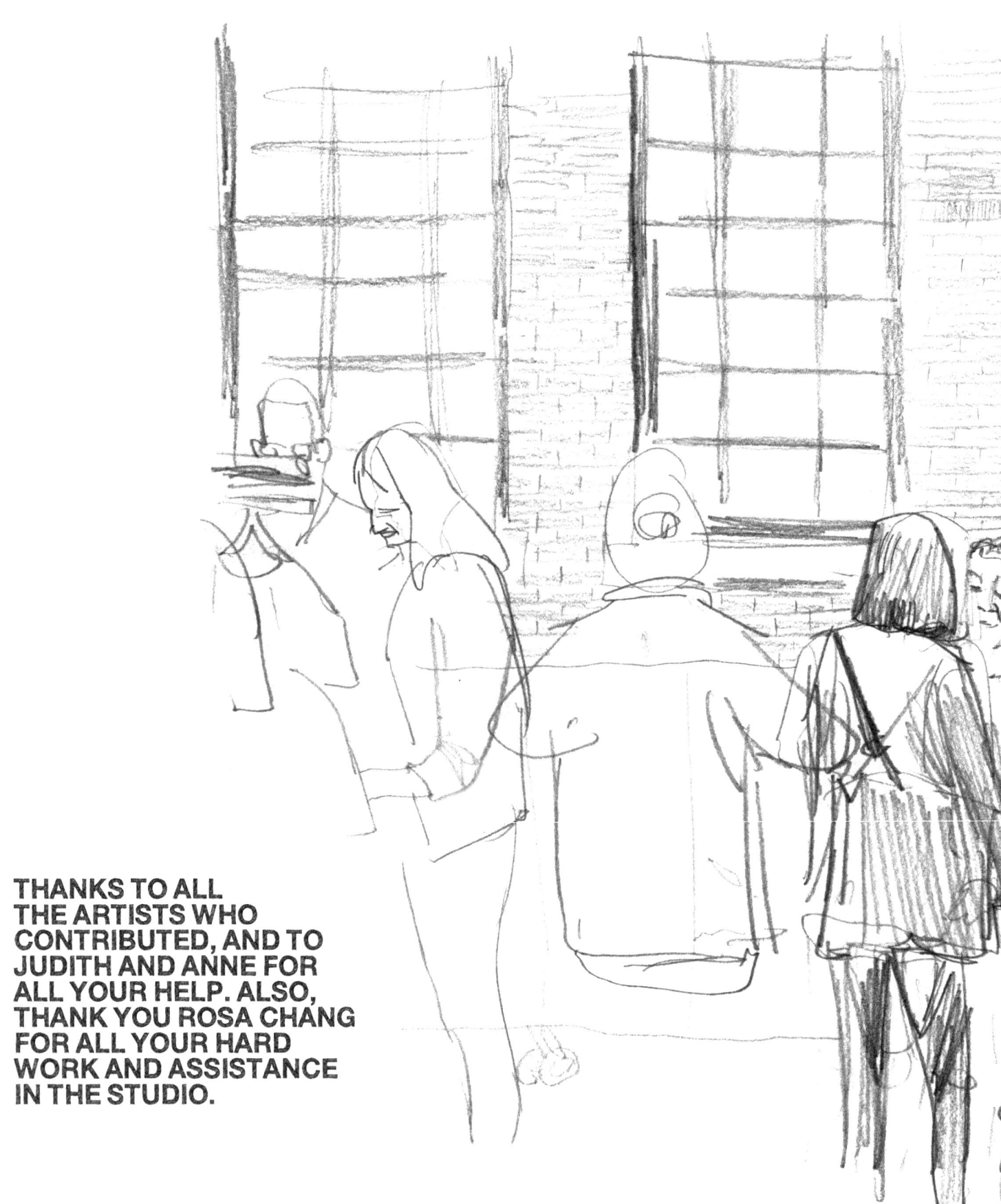

THANKS TO ALL
THE ARTISTS WHO
CONTRIBUTED, AND TO
JUDITH AND ANNE FOR
ALL YOUR HELP. ALSO,
THANK YOU ROSA CHANG
FOR ALL YOUR HARD
WORK AND ASSISTANCE
IN THE STUDIO.

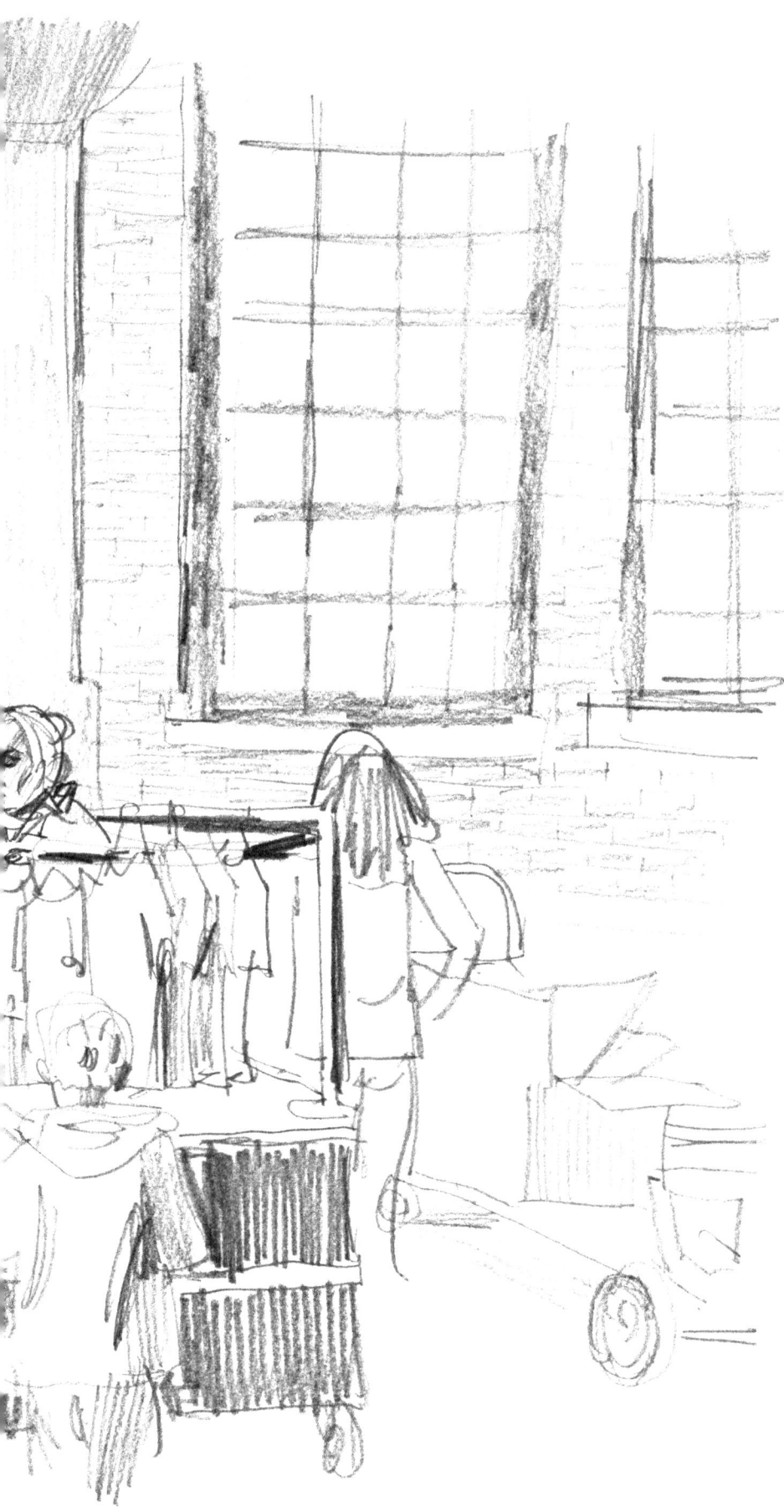

ABOUT THE AUTHOR

Matt Rota is an artist living and working in Brooklyn, New York, and is an instructor at the School of Visual Arts and the Maryland Institute College of Art. His clients include *The New York Times*, *The New Yorker*, *New Republic*, *Los Angeles Times*, *Fast Company*, *McSweeny's*, *Foreign Policy* magazine, *Smithsonian* magazine, *The Washington Post*, *The Boston Globe*, Chronicle Books, Medium, Pro Publica, The Center for Investigative Research, *Columbia Journalism Review*, *GQ Italia*, *Vice*, and more. He's received awards and recognition from the Society of Illustrators, Communication Arts, *3X3* magazine, *Spectrum*, *American Illustration*, and *Lürzer's International Archive*. His drawings have been displayed at galleries in New York, Paris, and Los Angeles.

His first book, *The Art of Ballpoint*, is available from Rockport Publishers.

INDEX

www.ingramcontent.com/pod-product-compliance
Lightning Source LLC
Chambersburg PA
CBHW041923180526
45172CB00014B/1369